Reaching Men

Strategies for Preventing Sexist Attitudes, Behaviors, and Violence

Endorsed by the Indiana Coalition Against Domestic Violence

Rus Ervin Funk

Reaching Men: Strategies for Preventing Sexist Attitudes, Behaviors, and Violence

Published by JIST Life, an imprint of JIST Publishing, Inc.
8902 Otis Avenue
Indianapolis, IN 46216-1033
Phone: 1-800-648-JIST Fax: 1-800-JIST-FAX E-mail: info@jist.com

Visit our Web site at **www.kidsrights.com** for information on JIST, a support center that offers links to information to help in t he important work of healing families, book chapters, and ordering instructions for our many products!

Quantity discounts are available for JIST books. Have future editions of JIST books automatically delivered to you on publication through our convenient standing order program. Please call our Sales Department at 1-800-648-5478 for a free catalog and more information.

Acquisitions Editor: Barb Terry
Development Editor: Jill Mazurczyk
Interior Designer: designLab
Page Layout Coordinator: Toi Davis
Cover Designer: Trudy Coler
Proofreader: Linda Seifert
Indexer: Tina Trettin

Printed in the United States of America
11 10 09 08 07 06 9 8 7 6 5 4 3 2 1

Library of Congress Cataloging-in-Publication Data

Funk, Rus Ervin.
Reaching men : strategies for preventing sexist attitudes, behaviors, and violence / Rus Ervin Funk.
p. cm.
"Endorsed by the Indiana Coalition Against Domestic Violence."
Includes bibliographical references and index.
ISBN-13: 978-1-55864-177-8 (alk. paper)
ISBN-10: 1-55864-177-7 (alk. paper)
1. Wife abuse--Prevention. 2. Sex crimes--Prevention. 3. Abusive men--Counseling of. 4. Group counseling. 5. Social work with men. 6. Sexism--Prevention. I. Title.
HV6626.F86 2006
362.82'927--dc22

2006008091

ISBN-13: 978-1-55864-177-8
ISBN-10: 1-55864-177-7

ABOUT THIS BOOK

All men know and love people who have been victimized by other men. Most men know and love men who have perpetrated abuse against a woman or a man. Although men perpetrate most forms of violence and abuse, there is nothing inherently violent, abusive, or wrong with men. Few men are involved in the efforts to end sexual violence, domestic violence, and other forms of sexism, yet men are often in the audiences of presentations on these topics.

This book provides the solid foundation you need to reach men and empower them to be allies in the movement against sexism, sexual assault, and domestic violence. Based on his more than 20 years experience as a man working with men to end sexism and violence, Rus Ervin Funk provides clear, concise, and practical information about how to effectively reach men in a way that engages them in the conversation and motivates them to take further action.

This manual

- Addresses the specific challenges that educating men presents
- Summarizes the key issues you will want to address in educating men
- Provides presentation strategies, outlines, and exercises that have proven to be effective with men's groups
- Outlines the history of the women's and men's movements against sexism, sexual abuse, and domestic violence

Do not begin an initiative to educate men until you have read *Reaching Men.* The information it contains will not only save you hours of research, but it will also help you avoid the frustrations and dead-ends that often occur when educating men.

Acknowledgements

There were many people involved in this project who deserve my deepest appreciation. This manual would not have been finished and would not be nearly as complete or as strong without their support, encouragement, and critical feedback throughout the writing process. Thank you!

First of all, I want to acknowledge the women with whom I have worked throughout my journey and, in particular, the women who first got me into the movement. You continue to inspire me, and I am more grateful than words can express for your patience in teaching me.

Second, I want to thank the men who helped raise my consciousness about the roles of men in working to end men's violence. You provided models of men taking responsible action to address gender-based violence and working to create solutions. The vision of gay, bisexual, and heterosexual men working together, and European American men and men of color working in partnership with women to create gender justice is a magnificent vision, and in all of you I've seen and experienced the real-life glimpses. I am indebted to you. Thank you!

I also want to thank Laura Lederer, the Kentucky Association of Sexual Assault Programs (particularly Eileen Rectenwald), Ross Wantland, and Jeff Cullen for permission to use their work in this manual.

Thanks to the men who were the first guinea pigs of the first training. Your enthusiastic participation in that first training and your critical feedback since (and your ongoing involvement in Mobilizing to End violeNce) has been a great gift. Thanks to Nick Reese, Saeed Ali, Michael Radmacher, Michael McQuerry, Ryan McKinley, and Jose Neil Denis.

The women who took the risk and supported the first training of men in Louisville where the foundation of this manual was developed: Rebecca Derhohannasian of Planned Parenthood, Sharon Larue of the University of Louisville PEACC program, and Darlene Thomas of the Center for Women and Families. The training would have never happened without your efforts (especially Sharon Larue's), and I appreciate the faith you showed in me and in men to develop this project.

My sincere thanks to the people who read various sections and versions of this manual and offered me wonderful and thoughtful feedback. You are all so very busy, and I very much appreciate the time that you took to help me make this manual as strong as it is: Rebecca Whisnant, Lois Herman, Vednita Carter, Gayle Thomas, Yvonne Haller, Melissa Farley, Eileen Rectenwald, Craig Norberg-Bohm, Rita Smith, and Sally Laskey. Dr. Carol Mattingly provided critical feedback in the final stages of the writing of this manual, and I greatly appreciate her efforts. I thank you all very much!

My colleagues at the Center for Women and Families who provided a great deal of support for this project and some wonderful editorial comments and feedback: Wendy Helterbran, Meryl Thornton, Karen Davis, Corissa Phillips, and Carrie Hunter, thank you. Lena Crabtree deserves special mention for the ways that she went out of her way to support me and this project.

To Laura Berry and the rest of the staff of the Indiana Coalition Against Domestic Violence who were instrumental in the publishing of this manual, and whose enthusiastic support and excitement about bringing this to fruition has been quite impressive, thank you!

The staff of JIST Publishing has been incredible to work with. I have rarely had the opportunity to work with a publisher who took more care, or was more respectful and enthusiastic. In particular, I want to thank Barb Terry and Jill Mazurczyk for amazingly gentle yet scrupulous editing, Trudy Coler for her work on the cover (which was decidedly NOT an easy task), and Acacia Martinez for promotional support. Thanks y'all!

On a more personal note, Maureen Burke, Jon Cohen, Nigel Pizzini, Cesar Alvarado, and most especially Amy Mudd continued to provide sources of inspiration and support to me in my life and as I wrote the various versions of this manual.

In Memory of those who have been killed

In Honor of those who have survived

In Gratitude of those who work the front lines

In Commitment to end sexist violence

Dedication

Dedicated to the memory of Jon Cohen and his tireless efforts for gender, racial, and sexual justice.

CONTENTS

Introduction

Educating men about sexism and violence can be a daunting task. Men will challenge, disagree, confront, disengage, tune-out, and dismiss. At times, men overtly try to push educators' buttons just to see how they will respond or to try to generate a particular reaction. Educators often confront questions about how to approach men, how-to questions such as

- How to phrase the issues so that men can (and will) hear the message?
- How to respond to men's defensiveness?
- How to convey the messages without inciting men's anger?

Educators largely have no real training or information about how to effectively reach men. This means that most educators are left to their own devices in terms of answering these questions and figuring out how to educate men.

Having men sit politely in a room and listen to a presentation is decidedly *not* the goal. Creating a space in which men can choose to move *is* the goal. But men, like any audience, are unlikely to make any movement as long as they are comfortable. The topics covered in this manual are inherently uncomfortable. For men, who have often had less experience in talking about these issues than women, this discomfort, and their reactions to this discomfort, are a part of the dynamics and difficulties educators face when educating men.

This manual describes some of the theory and provides some practical ideas for talking to men about issues that men rarely discuss—rape, sexual assault, sexual harassment, domestic violence, dating abuse, stalking, pornography, and prostitution. Although women make up the majority of people who are victimized by these crimes and men are the majority of perpetrators, both women and men are victimized, and both women and men can be perpetrators.

That being said, the forms of violence and abuse discussed in this manual are clearly gendered. That is, they tend to target a certain segment of society (women) and be perpetrated by another (men). These forms of violence are also gendered because they are used to maintain a particular system of power and control—sexism. For that reason, the forms of violence are referred throughout this manual as sexist violence. Using the term *sexist violence* acknowledges that both women and men are victimized, and at the same time acknowledges the gendered nature of these forms of violence and abuse.

In society at large, and for men in particular, these topics are understood and defined as women's issues, and, as such, are generally not something that men discuss. When men do talk about these issues, it is generally in a defensive manner ("not all men are bad..."), or one in which they sympathize with the women or men who have been victimized ("those poor victims" or "if that were me, I'd kill somebody"). Neither of these responses, men's defensiveness nor men's sympathy, is an appropriate response to women or men who have been victimized. Nor has either proven effective as a tactic for moving men to become more actively involved in the efforts to respond to and combat sexist violence. This manual is designed to do just that, namely, to provide the theory and tools to educate men about sexism and violence in a way that motivates them to take action.

In recent years, increasing attention has been given to how to effectively talk with and organize men to become more proactively involved. These efforts to educate and organize men are still rather limited in scope and quite sporadic in nature. Most of the educational efforts to address sexism and violence, in general, continue to be generated by rape crisis centers, battered women's shelters, sexual harassment programs, and agencies working on issues of prostitution and pornography. As such, and because the resources to support educational efforts are extremely limited, most of these efforts focus on educating women. When programs do attempt to educate men, it is usually within the perspective of and organized around targeting women—as if men are simply part of the audience that educators are talking to.

Furthermore, few educators are aware of the differences in talking with men about these issues, nor are those educators taught the skills to effectively reach men. Although some materials in print specifically address talking with men, most target men as educators (i.e., men talking with men about sexual violence), and none of them incorporate the full range of sexist violence.

Finally, this recent trend towards educating men has attempted to describe rape, domestic violence, sexual harassment, and the rest as if they are gender-neutral crimes that do not have a foundation in sexism. It is as if educators and/or the programs for which most educators work believe (erroneously) that men do not (or cannot) already understand that most of this violence is gendered.

The Purpose of This Book

The purpose of this manual is to offer tools on *how* to talk with men about sexist violence. The tools it describes have a theoretical foundation, and so this manual provides an overview of the theories that are important in developing educational programs for men. The majority of the readers are likely to be women, and this manual is written with that in mind, but written so that both male and female educators, activists, and advocates will find practical information for thinking about and planning to effectively work with men.

Although this manual focuses on formal educational programs, much of what is offered here can be easily applied to informal settings as well (e.g., when sitting with male friends after dinner, at a bar or ball game, discussing the latest music video, and so on). Educators and activists have opportunities to educate men beyond formal settings. Most, it seems safe to assume, have male friends, family members, or "hang out" with men in settings other than formal presentations. The information and skills offered in this manual can be transferred to these informal settings as well.

Education, in and of itself, may not be effective in changing the cultural norms to end sexist violence. Education alone is not particularly effective in changing attitudes or encouraging male involvement. Education is *one* tool, or more accurately, one series of tools, that can be used to create the social change and the individual motivation needed to end sexist violence. The goal of educating men is to mobilize and organize men to take action against sexist violence. Education is simply a crucial first step.

From this perspective, education is understood as a form of political activism. "Education is power," and therefore, the act of educating can be understood as a form of empowerment. (See Paulo Freire, *Pedagogy of the Oppressed* (1970) and *Education for Critical Consciousness* (1973); bell hooks, *Teaching to Transgress: Education as the Practice of Freedom* (1994); and Henry A. Giroux, *Pedagogy and the Politics of Hope: Theory, Culture, and Schooling* (1997). Education is a process to help raise men's awareness about the issues and nuances of sexist violence and place individual acts of violence and abuse in a larger socio-cultural context. Placing incidents of sexism and violence in such a larger context more accurately defines the abuse and provides many more avenues for men's engagement.

Education can also be used to foster and develop men's critical consciousness not only about sexist violence but also about masculinity, sexuality, and issues of race, class, and "difference." This critical consciousness can be the foundation for increasing the chances that men will choose to act proactively to respond to sexism and violence, and, ultimately, to work to stop men's violence.

Understood in this way, the point of educating is not only to raise consciousness or awareness but also to change society. Educational efforts can be seen as training opportunities for men, namely training men to better support their loved ones (female or male) who are victimized, and training men to become engaged in the efforts to end sexism and violence. By including specific and concrete examples of men's relationships with and responses to sexist violence, educators better position these as issues that also affect men, thereby increasing men's ownership of them and, thus, the desire to work to stop them.

It is by men coming to personally own the problem (and the solutions) that they become engaged to take personal action. Ultimately, men taking the initiative (not the leadership) to confront other men's attitudes and behaviors will result in the kind of change in attitudes necessary to end sexism and violence. The ideas that educators develop need to be grounded in a sound theory, which is the educational part of the work.

It seems quite clear that, by and large, men *are* willing to be involved in the efforts to combat sexism and violence. This may seem counterintuitive. After all, men often do not listen to the women in their lives when they are asked not to hit, or not to touch in certain ways. In addition, the experience of most educators seems to contradict the suggestion that men are willing to be involved. By and large, men seem hesitant to hear the message that men *can* be pro-feminist, and tend to respond with extreme defensiveness, denial, and minimizing when confronted with these issues, especially if offered from an overtly feminist perspective.

At the same time, however, men *are* involved in and have been since the initial efforts to address and end various forms of sexism and violence. Men *do* understand that when other men act in violent and abusive ways, it not only harms the women assaulted, but it also hurts women in general, and ultimately it hurts men. Men understand that when they act in sexist, violent, or abusive ways, they lose a layer of their own humanity, for in order to treat someone else as less than human, people must dissociate from their connections with that person and from their own humanity.

Most men actually do recognize the connections between various forms of sexism and violence and know that sexist violence is, in fact, *men's* violence. They know that most rapists are male, that most batterers are male, that most people who use and buy pornography are male. This is no big secret. Labeling it as men's violence is only giving voice to what men already know. Labeling it accurately also provides men an open invitation to get involved and become part of the solution. Offering men a way to be part of the solution and to take a more active and progressive effort in redefining their relationships with each other and with women offers men an invitation to their own liberation.

The Organization of This Book

This manual begins with an exploration of the assumptions that educators have about educating men, followed by a brief overview of education theory and an in-depth discussion about how to educate men. From there, the manual turns to an overview of the various forms of gender-based violence mentioned earlier. This overview will likely feel frustratingly incomplete. It is meant as an overview, and readers are encouraged to explore the additional resources that are provided to develop their knowledge and understanding of sexism, violence, education, and the other topics address here.

It is important to understand where we have come from, so there is a brief historical overview of the feminist movement to address violence with particular attention to how educational efforts fit within these political movements. There is also an overview of the men's pro-feminist movement. Next, the manual examines the sociopolitical context of sexism and violence, clarifying how the different forms of sexist violence are connected, and explores the importance of working against sexism and violence.

Men have an enormous ability (as yet, largely untapped) to respond to sexism and violence, both individually and collectively. Focusing on men's *abilities* to respond is an effective tool in overcoming their sense of being blamed, accused of guilt, or shamed for sexist violence. This discussion also lays the foundation for a deeper discussion of what men can do.

When exploring men's response-ability, one must address concretely how every man's attitudes and behaviors are shaped by living in a sexist society. By discussing the continuum of sexism, both educators and activists can explore with men how "everyday" actions are related to other forms of violence. In this way, the door is further opened to address how men can take action. By taking action against "everyday" expressions of sexism, men become more involved in the movement to end the violence that is generated by sexism.

This discussion then leads to an exploration of some of the ways that men have and do take the initiative to end men's violence. It is difficult to do this work without hope or role models. By showing that other men are taking action and being effective, educators and advocates offer men a way to generate new ideas and new energy.

This manual concludes with a brief discussion of self- (and other) care. Working to end sexism and violence is extremely difficult and draining. Working with men in the movement to end men's violence can be as tedious and frustrating as it can be rewarding and inspiring. In order to keep giving beyond a few weeks, educators and activists need to think seriously about themselves and how to nurture themselves and each other in this work. For men in particular, this is a crucial step. Seeing men nurturing themselves and other men is contrary to what most of them are taught about what it means to "be a man." Teaching men to be nurturing can be some of the most important work in the effort to end sexism and men's violence—and abuse that stems from sexism.

People engaged in this effort are periodically called man-haters. Quite the opposite is true. Educating men and taking action against men's violence is one of the greatest ways to honor men and an expression of love for women, children, and the planet. By finding ways for men to connect with each other on a deeper level, as well as with women and children, you are giving men an opportunity to find a more full and complete sense of their own humanity.

The appendices offer a toolbox of additional materials. In them, you will find additional sample outlines, exercises, additional readings and the bibliography.

The Language Used in This Book

How one uses language is critical. Language, and how it is used, not only describes one's view of reality, but it also shapes one's view of reality. The terms *gender-based violence, sexist violence,* and *men's violence* are used interchangeably in this manual. This language is used because the forms of violence discussed are understood as being based upon institutions of sexism.

As mentioned earlier, these forms of violence are gendered. They are perpetrated by men against women. While it is true that some women also perpetrate some of these forms of violence (almost always against other women) and that men are also victimized (almost always by other men), the overwhelming majority of all these forms of violence are perpetrated by men against women. In addition, the dynamics of these forms of violence derive from and maintain systems of sexism, systems that consider women and femininity as less than men and masculinity.

The common terms used to describe the people involved with men's violence are *perpetrator* and *victim*. For many reasons, this terminology is problematic.

For women or men who are victimized, the label *victim* suggests that they are damaged or broken as a result of the experience. To counter this message and to reject the pathologizing (making something into an illness that is not necessarily so) of the experience of being victimized, the feminist anti-violence movement has preferred the term *survivor,* which better reflects the reality of women and men who have been victimized It acknowledges and emphasizes the strength, resiliency, and internal resources that people who are victimized have but often don't acknowledge. *Survivor* also acknowledges that some people do not survive. Sexist violence does sometimes result in the murder of women, children, and men. Many people who have been victimized find the term *survivor* a much more comforting and empowering term.

That being said, the label *survivor* is also problematic. It is still a label, and it suggests an identity or role. Being victimized, even if when it is prolonged victimization, is an experience (or series of experiences). Having the experience of being victimized is not a role and certainly not an identity. In this manual, I use "people who were victimized." There is more to the person than the experience of being victimized, and it is important to hold onto and magnify their personhood.

Similarly, the term *perpetrator*, or *rapist, abuser, batterer, pornographer,* and so on is problematic. First, although we know the vast majority of people who perpetrate these crimes are men, all these terms are gender-neutral, suggesting that perpetrating sexist violence is a gender-neutral activity.

Secondly, the term *perpetrator* (or any of the similar terms) strips the men who abuse of their humanity. Just as there is more to people who are victimized than their experiences of being victimized, there is more to men who abuse than their abusiveness.

Therefore, I refer to them as "men who perpetrate" (men who rape, men who batter, men who prostitute women, men who harass, men who use pornography, and so on). Not only does this require a recognition of their humanity (thus making it easier to connect and reach out), but it also acts as a reminder that the abusiveness is a behavior based on a choice for which *people* are accountable. Labeling men who perpetrate violence as rapists or batterers colludes with the process of not holding them accountable because they become monsters, not human beings who make active choices to harm other people.

Admittedly, such thoughtful or deliberate humanization of perpetrators is a challenge. It is far easier to think of men who do these things as "monsters." It can also be a real challenge to retain men's humanity when faced with the extreme forms of inhumanity that some men display towards others. Attempting to do this may be particularly challenging for educators who have been victimized in their own past. It is a challenge that I encourage you to consider, even if you ultimately choose to disregard it.

Finally, the manual frequently refers to the terms *ally* or *allies* (a notion that will be developed further in the chapters that follow). The whole purpose of this manual is to encourage more men to act as allies for women in ending sexism and violence. An *ally* is a person (in this case, a man) who is not from a particular group but acts in that group's best interest.

In several chapters of the book, you will find sections entitled "A Note About Language." Those sections clarify any misconceptions about words associated with that particular topic.

PART I
Introduction to Educating Men

These first three chapters provide the key information and some primary resources for programs or educators who are considering educating men about sexism and violence. Admittedly, there is a lot of information packed in—and it may seem beyond the scope of your current resources to consider all of the questions and issues addressed in these chapters in the process of planning a process to educate men. That being said, the information offered here is not terribly different than what people should be considering whenever they're planning an educational effort with any group—male or female, young or old.

Before even beginning to think about educating, it is important to think about who is educating. Chapter 1 starts by listing some of the key qualities that should be sought in identifying people who may be able to educate men. All of these qualities are important, although it would be asking too much to expect any educator to have **all** of these qualities. In addition, all of the qualities listed are qualities that can be developed.

We all have assumptions about the audiences being targeted for educational programs. Without acknowledging those assumptions and doing the work to challenge these assumptions, educators are likely to act them out in ways that undermine their effectiveness. As such, particularly when educating men, it is important for educators to examine the assumptions they do have and explore where those assumptions came from. Chapter 1 provides a means to begin examining these assumptions.

While it is important to identify and challenge preconceived assumptions about educating men, there are some assumptions that seem important to hold on to—that men **do** care, that men are not innately violent or sexist, and that men can be a part of the solution, among others. Educators who challenge themselves about the assumptions they have about men, and particular groups of men, and who strive to behave act according to the assumptions outlined in Chapter 1, prove to be more effective educators in terms of educating men.

All good work is based on solid theory. Educating men is good work, and the best efforts to educate men are based on the most solid educational theory. Chapter 1 concludes with an examination of educational theories. The liberatory educational theory and praxis discussed in Chapter 1 provide an excellent theoretical foundation to begin building efforts to educate men. These theories, developed largely through the work of Paulo Freire, bell hooks, and Henry Giroux, lay the foundation for effective educational programs with men.

In Chapter 2, the focus shifts to determining the goals for an educational program with men. In order to be most effective, educators and the programs for which they work need to clearly identify the goals they have for educating men in general, and their goals for educating men at each presentation. By clarifying the goals that educators have, they can recognize when they may have an overwhelming list of goals that they want to accomplish (which would result in an ineffective educational effort), as well as design an educational program or campaign that is specific to the goals in mind (thus increasing their effectiveness).

Chapter 2 also includes a discussion about differences in providing educational programs for men in mixed-gender or gender-specific settings. As is described in the chapter, determining the kind of format to use is based largely on the goals that educators have. Regardless of whether or not advocates educate men in mixed-gender or gender-specific settings, it is important that educators consciously and strategically think about why they're educating in one setting over another, and how it will best achieve their goals. If educators are not given the option, then they still need to specifically plan the educational goals and activities for the audience.

In Chapter 3, we begin looking at how to use the theory discussed in Chapter 1, and the goals discussed in Chapter 2, to begin developing educational programs for men. This chapter focuses primarily on developing educational programs for the men that will be in the audience. Chapter 3 discusses the differences that men of different class, ethnic, and sexual backgrounds have in relation to sexism, privilege, and violence. As a result, effectively educating men requires taking these other factors into account. Men are not a monolithic group, and educational efforts need to develop educational programs that are designed with specific groups of men in mind.

Similarly, men are different in their attitudes about sexism. In order to be effective, educators need to do a quick assessment of the men who are participating in an educational program and provide a tone and activities that attempt to accept men from where they are coming from (as opposed to where an educator may want them to be) and challenge them to take one step. Educators are not going to make all men become pro-feminist activists against sexism and violence based on one presentation. Challenging men to critically examine the ways that they support sexist attitudes, behavior, and violence can begin a process whereby men become more active.

CHAPTER 1

Laying the Foundation

Sexism and violence are complicated, challenging, and often overwhelming topics that are interconnected in ways that continue to challenge our ability to explain them. Trying to find ways to communicate this morass effectively with men just adds another series of challenges and difficulties. This chapter begins the communication process by laying the foundation for how to talk with men about sexism and violence in ways that they can connect with and that engage them in the conversation.

This foundation begins by identifying the characteristics of effective educators. All educators have certain assumptions about educating men. Because of this, a part of the foundation of any effort to educate men requires that educators (and the agencies or programs for which they work) examine the assumptions that they do have. This chapter offers ways for educators to examine their assumptions and offers some proposed working assumptions for effectively educating men. Finally, this chapter will define the key terms used in this manual and provide an overview of educational theory. Because any good practice is grounded in solid theory, this overview provides an opportunity for educators to examine these theories and challenges them to begin developing their personal theories for practice.

Identifying Effective Educators

In examining the process of educating men about sexism and violence, it is necessary to begin by identifying key qualities an educator needs in order to be effective. Regardless of how well the educator uses the skills offered in this manual, it is unlikely they will be effective if they lack certain qualities. Educators must be

- Knowledgeable, thoughtful, and passionate
- Flexible and adaptable
- Self-aware
- Aware of and attentive to their emotions
- Honest and authentic
- Comfortable with chaos

- Able to handle confrontation
- Organized
- Positive and hopeful
- Able to actively listen
- Nonjudgmental

The following sections take a quick look at each of these characteristics. They are offered as ideals: No educator has all of them. In addition, these are qualities that can be developed in educators as they grow. These are offered to provide a sense of the kinds of traits that one can personally develop, as well as traits that a director or supervisor can look for in hiring educators.

Educators Must Be Knowledgeable, Thoughtful, and Passionate

Educators need to be *knowledgeable, thoughtful*, and, of course, *passionate.* Educators need to be knowledgeable of the topics that they're educating about and present themselves as experts on the topic at hand. If educators don't feel that level of confidence or competence, they should take the time they need in order to be so comfortable with the content that they can present with expertise.

Not only should educators be knowledgeable, but they also should be thoughtful. They should present each point as though they are considering differing opinions, not dictatorially. It can be a challenging balancing act between being knowledgeable and being thoughtful. With as much as is known about sexism and the various forms of violence that spring from sexism, there is still so much that is not known. Educators offer a perspective—one that is (or should be) grounded in knowledge. That being said, other perspectives can also be of value. The best educators find ways to present the knowledge they have while simultaneously being open to different perspectives. Educators also need to be informed about the issues that they are presenting and the local ways that the issues are manifest (such as the local resources, the ways that different audiences are affected by the issues, and so on).

Educators should be passionate: People in general, and men are no exception, respond better to people who care about what they talk about than they do to "talking heads," people who are just talking. So it is important to look for people who can demonstrate that they care about the topics.

Educators Must Be Flexible and Adaptable

Educators should be *flexible* and *adaptable.* They should be able to gauge an audience and shift their style (without losing focus) based on the shifting needs of the audience. While it is obviously important that educators prepare ahead of time and know what it is that they are going to present, they need to engage with the audience and respond to its interests and concerns. Educators need to continuously be aware of their audience, noticing when the people may be getting bored or overwhelmed, and subtly adjusting the program to maintain the audience's attention and engagement in the conversation.

Educators Must Be Self-Aware

Educators, of course, must be *self-aware;* they need to know themselves. Educators need to know which topics are more difficult for them to present, which audiences may prove more challenging for them, and how they handle stress and confrontation.

Most educators are drawn to this kind of work for very personal and particular reasons. They have been victimized themselves or are close to someone who has been. A part of knowing oneself includes knowing where one is in their healing process. For many people, educating others is a means to try to resolve feelings they have about sexism, being victimized, or knowing or loving someone who was victimized. While becoming an educator can be, and often is, a powerful step to take during the healing process, the goal of educating is not to do one's personal healing: Educators are there to educate the participants. Educators need to be aware of where they are in their own healing process in order to assess whether they are educating because of a desire to educate others or as a way to meet some other need.

Educators Must Be Aware of and Attentive to Their Emotions

Educators must be *aware of* and *attentive to* their anger, pain, and other feelings regarding sexism and sexist violence. Educators do this work for a reason. For many, it is because they have been personally affected by the forms of abuse they are discussing. That is a very real strength and often makes for the best educators. However, it is important to not allow the anger, pain, or passion to overwhelm the audience. Educators must use the anger as a motivator or the passion to emphasize certain points. Educators need to be in control of their emotions, not the other way around.

THE ROLE OF SELF-DISCLOSING

There can be, and often is, a strong temptation for educators to disclose personal experiences regarding sexism and violence—particularly with male audiences. Self-disclosing can be a transformative experience for people who attend presentations. That being said, educators should consider any personal disclosure carefully—both in terms of their own needs as well as how such a disclosure will benefit the educational experience of the audience. Before considering any kind of disclosure in terms of how it may benefit the participants, educators should consider what they gain from disclosing (what kind of response do they want from the audience, and what do they want from the experience of disclosing) as well as what they fear from disclosing. Deciding to disclose should come from a place of

(continued)

(continued)

strength, and educators should be prepared for any possible response. There are times when self-disclosure can backfire. In addition, any disclosure can detract the audience from the purposes of the conversation. The audience may respond to the disclosure as an invitation to ask more details and for more personal information—information that the educator may not be prepared to share. Educators need to decide ahead of time how much they are willing to and comfortable in sharing and strategically use disclosure to reinforce certain points within the broader presentation.

Educators Must Be Honest and Authentic

Educators should be *honest* and *authentic.* It may be tempting to embellish some statistics or stories in order to make them sound more dramatic or to make a stronger point, but educators must never indulge in this temptation. Similarly, educators need to be *authentic* with audiences. They must be genuine with the feelings and thoughts that arise while doing the presentation, but not let these feelings or thoughts derail the program.

Educators Must Be Comfortable with Chaos

In educating men (especially younger men, such as high school- and college-aged men), educators should be *comfortable with some degree of semi-organized chaos.* Sexism and violence are extremely emotionally-charged topics. It is unlikely that men have had any experience in talking in depth about these topics. Because of these factors, the men may act out their discomfort by laughing (which can be understood as a way of relieving feelings of tension, embarrassment, and discomfort) or by talking amongst themselves. It is helpful to allow room for this kind of acting out without allowing it to distract from the main points or the goals of the presentation.

Educators Must Be Able to Handle Confrontation

Educators also need to be able to *handle confrontation.* Men not only are likely to challenge the points that educators make, but also will often confront the educators. Educators should be able to turn these confrontations into educational opportunities.

Educators Must Be Organized

Educators need to be *organized.* They need to be able to organize their thoughts and present themselves in an organized manner. Educators also need to be able to respond to questions or concerns as they come up during presentations but be able to return to and reinforce the main points of the presentation. In addition, educators need to be organized enough to keep track of their schedules and follow through with outreach efforts.

Educators Must Be Positive and Hopeful

Educators should be *positive* and *hopeful.* Although issues of sexism and violence are difficult, painful, and often considered "downer" topics, educators should be able to present the information in a positive manner that does not diminish the seriousness of these issues. Although sexist violence is horrible, the majority of people who are victimized *do* heal and *are* able to move forward. It is possible to hold onto the hopefulness that these realities represent without diminishing the pain and horror that the person who was victimized went through. In order to effectively reach audiences, educators need to be able to convey their messages and the points positively.

Educators Must Be Able to Actively Listen

Educators should be *able to actively listen,* the ability to listen and to hear what audiences are truly asking. This is particularly true for men who often will ask questions that have two levels of meaning attached. Educators should be able to respond to the surface question as well as the deeper question that lies beneath.

Educators Must Be Nonjudgmental

Educators must *be nonjudgmental;* they must be able to listen without making judgments. This will be a challenge, but in order for men to feel comfortable in saying what they need to say or asking the questions that need to be asked, they need to know that they will not be judged. This doesn't mean that educators should not challenge men's comments or statements. One point of educating is, in fact, to challenge statements or comments that indicate attitudes that are sexist or encourage abusiveness. Challenging someone's statements and judging a person are two different responses. Audiences can distinguish the difference. Educators need to be able to do the same.

Assumptions About Working with Men

Those who consider educating men about sexism and violence need to begin by clarifying their assumptions of what it means to work with men. Every educator has assumptions about any group she or he educates. This is particularly true with the more intense work of educating to mobilize or organizing people to take action. When considering educating men, it is essential to explore the preconceived ideas one may have about what the experience will be like. Educators must be conscious and clear about their assumptions, for these assumptions will come out in the design of the program and in the ways the educational programs are offered.

Before reading further, take a moment to consider your assumptions about working with men. Ask yourself the following questions, and then quickly write down your answers before you have the time to think too long.

DOING YOUR WORK: ***Recognizing Your Assumptions***

What do *you think* men think about rape, domestic violence, and pornography?

Why do you think men have not become more involved in the movement to end violence against women?

What do you think men think about women who work on these issues?

What do you think men think about men who work on these issues?

What do you think men think about feminists and feminism?

How do you expect men to respond to you?

How do you expect men to respond to your presentation?

Look at what you have written and notice the assumptions that you make about men vis-à-vis violence against women that are imbedded in these responses.

How will this impact the educational work that you do with men?

How do you think these assumptions influence your educational efforts?

Next consider working with different groups of men (fraternity brothers, athletes, judges, lawyers, Jews, men who are physically challenged, African Americans, Latinos, Asians, homosexuals, and so on). Examine how the answers to these questions change when you think about different groups of men. Any changes that do arise suggest attitudes or beliefs that may reflect biases (positive and/or negative). Those biases may become barriers when you are educating that group of men.

All educators have biases. The sooner an educator is able to acknowledge these biases, the better able they will be at educating effectively. The point is not to suggest that educators can't have assumptions. Rather, the point is to examine these assumptions and explore the ways that educating while maintaining these assumptions may create yet more barriers to effectively reaching men.

The educator who walks into a room full of men while carrying an array of unacknowledged or unrecognized assumptions is creating additional barriers to the process. There are enough inherent challenges in effectively educating men without bringing in additional difficulties such as unstated assumptions or biases.

CASE STUDY

For example, Jerry (not his real name) is an educator who has worked for many years educating about rape and child sexual abuse. He has had numerous experiences with trying to educate judges and has found that they tend to be largely dismissive of him and his perspective. When preparing for an educational program for judges, he finds himself more anxious about working with that group than with other groups of men. He realizes that he is becoming angry that he has to try to educate these judges who "aren't going to listen to him anyway."

If Jerry proceeds with a presentation without examining these assumptions and at least being aware that they exist, he will likely walk into the presentation with an attitude that the judges will notice and react to. Thus, they will not only react to what Jerry has to say, but also to the bias that he brings with him. Jerry will increase his effectiveness by recognizing his bias and preconceptions about judges. He can then do whatever he has to do in order to put those biases and preconceptions aside and go into the presentation prepared to educate.

Just as each educator has personal assumptions about working with men, this manual is based upon several assumptions about men and working with men. These assumptions guide the work of this manual and the work that flows from this manual. These assumptions include the following:

- Everyone has experienced various forms of violence and abuse.
- Everyone has the right to be free from violence, abuse, and threats.
- The problem of violence is both a social and a justice issue, as much as it is a personal one.
- Men who perpetrate sexist violence are more than the violence they perpetrate (i.e., men are more than "rapists," "batterers," or "pornographers").
- Male violence is a choice.
- Men are *not* the problem.
- Men are *not* naturally or innately sexist, violent, or abusive.
- Men do care.
- All people have an unlimited and inherent capacity to feel empathy for others.
- Men can handle their anger and other strong feelings that may be triggered as a result of talking about sexism and sexist violence.
- All of us benefit by working to end violence and abuse, and by challenging sexism.

- Men can work effectively alongside women and become strong allies in the work to promote social justice and human rights.

While reading these assumptions, educators need to consider the meanings behind them. They must consider what it may mean for them to begin adopting these assumptions. The way one educates changes as a result of adopting these assumptions.

While most of these assumptions are self-evident and require no explanation, the assumption that "men can handle their anger…" deserves some special attention. Sexism and violence are inherently vile, disgusting, and enraging topics. People (men included) *should* get upset when discussing them. The horror and pain inherent in these forms of violence demand an emotional response. There is a tendency amongst educators to find ways to educate men without making them upset. Educators would be better served by *expecting* men to be upset. Being upset (angry, sad, shocked, outraged, and so on) by the occurrence and impact of gender-based violence is a natural and very human response, one that should, in fact, be encouraged. Men may become upset for a number of reasons, not the least of which is that they know and love someone who has been abused, and/or they recognize some of their own behaviors as abusive. Getting upset may, for some men, be the catalyst to change or to become more involved in stopping sexism and violence.

This is not to say that educators should try to get an emotional reaction from men. But the job of educators is to educate, and one means to effectively educate men is to allow male audience members to grapple with the emotions that arise as a result of the content of the educational program. This is also not to say that educators should dismiss men or their feelings. Respectfully acknowledging the feelings that men express without allowing those feelings or their expression to sidetrack educators from the points of the presentation is the balancing act required.

It is also true that men will commonly direct their anger (and other emotions) towards the educator. After all, it is the educators' "fault" that men are being forced to confront this horrendous topic. Trusting men to be able to handle their own emotions not only enables educators to stay focused on the points of the program, but also conveys a message of respect and dignity for the men who are present. The feelings that men have as a result of attending a presentation are *their* feelings. They have a right to feel whatever they feel, and they can handle the feelings that arise for them.

There does appear to be an inherent paradox in the assumptions listed above, namely that *sexist violence is men's violence,* yet *men are not the problem.* All the forms of sexism and violence mentioned here are perpetrated overwhelmingly by men. On one hand, the reality of sexist violence is that it is men's responsibility (regardless of whether individual men perpetrate specific acts of violence), while on the other hand the assumption is that men are not the problem.

DOING YOUR WORK: *Working Within the Paradox*

Before continuing with the reading, sit for a moment with this apparent paradox that men are responsible but they are not the problem. For now, just notice it, and notice any reactions. While continuing to read the manual, come back to this paradox periodically and explore how your reactions to it may change.

This intersection—between understanding men's violence as men's responsibility and recognizing that men are not the problem—is where the work of educating really is, for it does no good to blame men for sexist violence, nor does it do any good to "soften the blow" by denying that this is, in fact, men's violence. Doing "both-and"—defining sexist violence as men's violence *and* refusing to blame men—is the heart of working to educate, mobilize, and organize men. The preceding reflexive exercise is meant to encourage educators to think and feel about this paradox and come to terms with it—or at least to some level of comfort. As people read this manual and increase their comfort and confidence in providing educational programs for men, it is not uncommon to find that the comfort level with this paradox changes. It is worth continuing to explore this apparent paradox throughout one's career as an educator.

Defining Key Terms

"Abuse is anytime one attempts to impose his will on another."

MAHATMA GHANDI

Any program should clearly define the terms it uses, and this manual is no different. This section provides definitions of the terms used in this book and some suggestions of how to use these definitions when working with men. These definitions are not meant as definitive definitions. Rather, defining these terms provides a starting point. It is not necessary to agree with these definitions. What *is* necessary for the purposes of the manual and exercises that flow from the manual is a common understanding of both the terms used and the forms of violence and abuse that are being discussed. These definitions, then, offer that common understanding.

These definitions are also designed to challenge readers to think about how they define sexism and these forms of violence. It is not uncommon for people to begin working and educating from unexamined definitions. The definitions offered here provide a way to begin considering how one uses terms and to clarify what they mean when they use those terms.

It is equally important to define the key terms when educating any population about an issue. This is particularly important when educating and mobilizing men around sexism and violence. Because of the complexity of the issues and the tendency of many men to become defensive, definitions can become key in grounding the conversation and keeping the presenter focused. Again, it is not necessary that men agree with the definitions offered. However, in order to have any conversation, there needs to be some starting point in establishing the vocabulary used. Definitions offer a foundation from which to start the conversation.

Educators need to define what is meant by "sexist" or "gender-based" violence as well as the specific forms such as rape, sexual assault, domestic violence, dating abuse, stalking, pornography, or prostitution. Men have rarely had the opportunity to talk in any way about sexist violence. As a result, men tend to have very rudimentary understandings about these issues, and their understandings are likely largely based on myths, misperceptions, and falsehoods. Unless educators begin by defining the terms, they may find themselves educating about one understanding of the issues, while members of the audience are hearing the presentation based on a very different understanding. This miscommunication may result in a very difficult and ultimately unsuccessful and unsatisfying educational experience for both the educator and the audience.

It is also important to offer definitions on two levels. First and the easiest (although by no means easy) are the cognitive definitions. These definitions provide the language and the literal meanings. These definitions are also the safest, as they are not as emotion-laden as the other kind of definitions.

The second level of definitions consists of the emotive or affective definitions. Men's violence is more than an intellectual experience; it is also emotionally packed. People experience very real and often raw feelings that run deep and strong about each form of sexist violence. Men need to go deeper than the intellectual level if they are going to have true, meaningful, and ultimately transformative conversations about men's violence. It is the responsibility of educators to take men to this deeper level.

All the forms of violence and abuse described in this manual fall under the umbrella of what is referred to as "sexist" or "gender-based" violence. While it is true that women do, occasionally, perpetrate these forms of violence against men, it is extremely rare. It is rather similar to "man bites dog." While this does occur, it is so rare that it isn't beneficial to focus on humans who bite dogs. Similarly, the educators' focus is better spent on where the bulk of the problem is: *Men's* violence against women and other men. Sexist violence *is* gendered (a point which is developed more thoroughly later), and educators must not lose this focus. There is a tendency to shy away from this message for two reasons:

1. Men are also victimized.
2. Men act defensively when educators say unequivocally what is known, that sexist violence does not go both ways.

Shying away from this focus does not benefit the movement nor does it generate effective solutions. Backing away from the message that sexist violence is gendered only reinforces men's power and privilege and ultimately inhibits men from becoming more involved. It is not the job of educators to make audiences (including male audiences) comfortable. These topics are inherently uncomfortable. Rather than trying to make the topics easier to discuss, the job of educators is to provide an environment in which people can talk openly and honestly about topics that are uncomfortable. Creating an environment where people can talk honestly about the problem means being honest that rape, domestic violence, stalking, harassment, pornography, and prostitution are *not* problems of women victimizing men.

Although women's violence may be an issue that is worthy of discussion, it is beyond the scope of this manual. This manual is about talking with men about the issues of sexist violence. Therefore, the focus remains on men's violence and abusiveness, because that is the part that men can most legitimately take responsibility for and, therefore, do something about. Men are not responsible for women's violence. To the extent that it occurs, it is women's behavior and one that women need to deal with. What men can accept responsibility for, individually and collectively, is their own behavior and, of course, the attitudes that lie beneath the behavior.

The definitions offered in this book are not legal definitions. Each jurisdiction has its own legal definitions of these behaviors that define them as crimes. From an advocate/activist perspective, legal definitions are often too narrow to address the harm or the full spectrum of behaviors that are abusive or violent. The definitions offered below are based on a feminist or victim-centered perspective. It is important for educators to have at least some understanding of the legal definitions in their state(s) in addition to these definitions because how each of these behaviors become criminal behavior differs from state to state. Each of these forms of violence is covered in more detail in later sections of this manual.

- **Consent** includes several important components. Both persons must
    - Share an understanding of what they are consenting to.
    - Share a cultural knowledge about the meaning of what they are consenting to.
    - Offer consent freely, without force, coercion, or manipulation.
    - Be fully mentally capable of offering consent.
    - Offer consent with the full knowledge that they can change their mind and that this change will be respected.
- **Dating abuse** is similar to domestic violence but occurs between dating couples. As such, it may not include the same expressions of power and control as domestic violence.
- **Domestic violence** is a pattern of behaviors using a variety of tactics in order to maintain power and control within a relationship. It may include physical or sexual violence, but often includes other behaviors, such as verbal abuse, coercion, intimidation, threats, isolation, extreme controlling behavior, and so on.

- **Femicide** is the final extension of sexist violence. This is the killing of women because they are women.
- **Gender harassment** generally includes more subtle forms of harassment and has the intent and effect of reminding women that they are women, and that they "don't belong." This behavior includes expecting the women of a meeting to clean up after the meeting or serve the coffee. It also includes using sexist language during a meeting.
- **Partner abuse** describes abuse between intimate partners. This includes both same-sex and heterosexual couples, and encompasses verbal abuse, threats, harm to animals, destruction of property, and physical and sexual violence. Partner abuse and domestic violence are synonymous terms, although state laws vary in their recognition of and protections for same-sex couples.
- **Pornography** is any sexualized depiction of women that shows them in a subordinate (to men) position or any depiction of sexualized harm.
- **Rape** is forced penetration. A man (or group of men) puts his penis, finger, or some other object into the mouth, anus, or vagina of another person. Legally, many jurisdictions define rape as vaginal penetration and/or penetration by a penis.
- **Sexism,** as best defined by D.C. Adams, "is a system of combined male controls: physical, psychological, derogatory beliefs about women, and institutional polices and regulations, that discriminate against women" (Adams, 1984).
- **Sexual abuse** is sexual victimization (in any form) against children. Sexual abuse can include nonphysical contact (watching a child undress, forcing a child to watch an adult masturbate, using sexualized language, and so on) as well as all forms of sexual violence that have been described earlier.
- **Sexual assault** is an umbrella term often used to describe forms of sexual abuse or violence that are like rape, but do not include penetration. Sexual assault includes such behaviors as groping, grabbing, and touching. In most jurisdictions, a legal distinction is made between sexual assault and rape.
- **Sexual harassment** is sexualized (sexist) behavior that makes someone feel uncomfortable or threatened. It occurs in workplaces, classrooms, hallways, malls, religious institutions, shopping centers, as well as on the street. It has the effect of reminding women that they are unsafe. Some sexual harassment escalates to other forms of assault or abuse.
- **Sexual violence** is the broad term that describes all forms of sexual assault, including rape, incest, sexual harassment, sexual abuse, sexual assault, pornography, and prostitution. Sexual violence certainly includes physical assault but does not require physical contact. In other words, it is possible to be sexually violent to another person without ever actually touching them. Put simply, it is any forced or unwanted sexualized contact.

- **Stalking** involves the unwanted pursuit of a person using a variety of tactics that cause that person to be afraid. The act itself may not necessarily be overtly threatening, but an implied threat is usually involved.
- **Street harassment** occurs on the street or in public transit. Whistling, making catcalls, leering, and so on, are all common examples of harassing behaviors.

Overview of Educational Theory and Practice

Effective education is grounded in solid theory. Before discussing the specifics of how to educate men, you must understand the educational theories upon which they base their practice. What follows is a brief overview of educational theory. The educational theories (and practices derived from them) used as the basis for an educational program are at least as important as the content. Put another way, it is as important to understand *how* to educate (the theories and practices) as it is to understand *what* is taught (the content).

The Traditional Form of Education

Most educators are probably familiar with the more traditional form of education: A presentation is developed, the outline prepared, and the educator stands in front of the class and provides the information that the educator deemed important for the students to receive. Given that this is such a common practice, there is little need to further discuss this method here, other than to say that this is not the most efficient one in engaging men, and it is utterly ineffective in mobilizing men to take action.

Liberating Education

One educational theory is referred to as *libratory* or *liberation* educational theory. This theory is based largely on the works of Paulo Freire (1970, 1973), bell hooks (1994), and Henry A. Giroux (1997), and seems the most appropriate and relevant theoretical foundation to use when educating men to be allies with women to end sexist violence. Libratory educational theory is based on the principle that the art of educating is a liberating experience for the student as well as the educator. As such, it is an inherently empowering process that actively engages participants in the process of the education.

One foundation of libratory education is the development of "critical consciousness" (Freire, 1973). *Critical consciousness* is best understood as examining one's place in the world and one's relationship with others. Most people take their place in the world and their relationship with others for granted, and do not consider how they came to believe whatever it is they happen to believe. Critical consciousness means critically examining the following:

- What one believes
- Where and how those beliefs were founded
- How one interacts with the world and with others as a result of those beliefs

How do men come to understand themselves as men? How do men learn how to relate to and with women? How do men learn to flirt? What is it that men learn about sexism and violence/abuse? By creating educational programs that help men examine these questions (not necessarily overtly, but imbedded in the educational efforts), men have an opportunity to develop their critical consciousness. As a result of asking these kinds of questions, men can begin to reshape their understanding of themselves and begin making more conscious and critical decisions about how they would like to answer the questions.

As Paulo Freire writes, "an active educational method helps a person to become consciously aware of his context and his condition as a human being as Subject, it will become an instrument of choice" (Freire, 1973, p. 56). By educating men through a process that engages them in education, and thereby making them active *subjects* in the process (as opposed to *objects* at whom a lecture is delivered), educators provide a means through which men become more aware of their personal relationship to the forms of sexism or abuse being discussed. Educators can help to develop critical consciousness by engaging in educational methods that encourage dialogue and reflection.

Standing in front of a class, church group, men's club, or other group of men and talking at them about sexism and violence does very little to develop their critical consciousness, nor does it do any good in helping them to *understand* sexist violence and why they should care. Such a passive method may be effective (although even this is somewhat questionable) in transmitting information such as the definition of rape, the incidence of domestic violence, or the Dworkin-MacKinnon definition of pornography. But this method will not result in effectively engaging men to join the movement to end sexist violence, much less encourage men to examine their own behaviors, assumptions, and attitudes about sexism and abuse. (For a detailed definition of pornography, see *In Harm's Way: The Pornography Civil Rights Hearing,* edited by Andrea Dworkin and Catherine A. MacKinnon.)

The process of helping to develop critical consciousness is achieved through engaging with the participants in identifying and examining the contradictions that each person holds. For example, most men argue ferociously that rape is never justified. Given time, most of these same men will also argue, often just as strongly, that there are times when women may share some of the responsibility (they way they dress, or act, or behave when they drink too much, and so on). This is a clear contradiction. Rather then confronting it directly, helping men to develop their critical consciousness means pointing out this contradiction in a supporting environment in which they can struggle with the contradiction. Educating to develop critical consciousness means, in part, stepping out of the role of having all the answers and helping them to understand better. In the midst of attempting to resolve their contradictions (thus developing their critical consciousness), some of the men in the room are moved to act.

It is through this process of developing a critical consciousness that people begin to increasingly notice the harm and abuse that occurs around them. Once this level of consciousness develops, it is a short step to realizing one's relationship within those systems or patterns that either cause the harm or allow it to continue to be ignored. In turn, once this realization is made, it becomes easier to become convinced of a need to act. For example, most people who educate about sexism and violence have experienced a process through which they came to personally understand the enormity of the problem and the relationship of these forms of abuse to broader systems of sexism. This process varies in time for different individuals, but, as a result of it, many educators and activists feel compelled to take action not only for the good of women generally, but also for their own good personally. They have come to take a personal stake in working to end sexist violence.

Men's main belief systems about sexism and violence have been based on a host of assumptions that they have never had the opportunity or need to challenge. Some of these unexamined assumptions include

- What it means to be a man
- A man's relationship to power
- How men experience feelings of power
- When men have the right to use violence (for example, when revenge seems necessary, "property" is threatened, "men's women" are violated, and so on)

Educating men about sexist violence requires, in part, helping men to begin developing a critical consciousness about their understandings of themselves as men, how they present themselves as men in the world, the ways they practice being men, and their relationships with and to women, as well as to sexism and violence.

Libratory educational theory understands that the people being educated are active *agents* in the world. All of us are in a constant process of redefining ourselves based on our environment and our place within this environment, as well as redefining and recreating our environment. Each person enters different settings and slightly "remakes" him or herself.

CASE STUDY

For example, Steve (not his real name) will likely present himself in a different way at work than when he's at a bar or at home with friends having a cook-out. Even at the work setting, he will present himself slightly differently when he's with colleagues he knows fairly well than with the president of the agency or board members. All people do this. The often-missed dynamic is that how Steve chooses to present himself also impacts the other people around him and the environment. If Steve were to present himself at work as he does at home having a cook-out, his workplace would have to adjust. Granted, that shifting is more subtle and may be short-lived. If he's immediately fired, then the adjustment isn't so long-lasting, but there is an adjustment. The choice-making that one goes through in determining how to present oneself is one example of "agency."

One goal of educating for critical consciousness is to bring this sense of personal agency to greater awareness. Men make decisions about how to act towards women and with other men about women. Engaging men through an educational process that treats them as agents within that process means that educators challenge men to make more conscious decisions. How do they *want* to treat women? How do they want women to be treated? How do they want to be as men?

Popular Education

"Education for Empowerment means the opening up of possibilities: to take risks, to struggle for a place in the decision-making process, to acquire knowledge in a critical manner, beyond one's immediate personal experience, and to imagine versions of the future world."

ELISHEVA SADAN, 2002, P. 129

The libratory educational theory described earlier is put into practice through what is called "popular education." Popular education, as distinct from more traditional educational practice, assumes that knowledge is co-created between the participants and the educator, and that it is through a dynamic process that information is shared. Popular education is also driven by an understanding of educating for a purpose, that purpose being primarily social change. As such, popular education practice based upon libratory educational theory is the best suited practice for educating men about sexism and violence.

Popular education requires that people be *actively* engaged in the educational process rather than talked to or at (i.e., given a lecture). Traditional models of educating assume that the educator has the information to provide to the "audience," and the most effective means to *provide* that information is to talk to the audience. Even the language describes a distinct division between the educator and audience. Note, for example, the difference in the way traditional practices refer to an *audience* as opposed to *participants*. The term *audience* suggests a passive taking in of information and a dynamic that is led almost entirely by the educator. The term *participants,* on the other hand, suggests more active engagement in the educational experience, and that the dynamic of educating is a shared process between the educator and those being educated.

The traditional model often seems particularly appealing when educating men, given how unfamiliar *any* information about sexist violence is for most men, and given that the various forms of violence are connected and are sexist. Most men have not given the definition of rape a second thought, so providing them with "*the*" definition of rape may seem like a crucial educational goal.

Using the old model, an educator stands in front of a group of men and tells them what the educator thinks the men should know. The appeal of this model is that it is far easier to come up with an outline of what to tell men without allowing for different experiences that men may have. But given that one of the goals, perhaps the key goal of educating men, is to motivate men to become more involved and change, the traditional model provides very little because it does not motivate men to take sexism or violence personally. This model keeps sexism and violence in the realm of the intellectual.

Popular education demands that men examine and understand what the definition of gender-based violence means to *them* in *their* lives. Just having a definition means very little unless men can translate that definition into their lives and create something meaningful out of that definition. Simply knowing how to define rape or domestic violence, for example, is of little value. The value is for men to create a personal understanding of what rape or domestic violence means for them in their lives. A definition offers a starting point, and the meaning of that definition comes later. Educators have a responsibility to assist and support men in creating this meaning.

In addition, popular education understands that men already have their own understanding of sexism and violence. The process of popular education allows men to look within themselves and use their own experiences to better understand sexism and violence. Through this process, they can better understand their relationship with sexism and violence and are more likely to move to action.

Creating meanings of the terms related to sexism and violence is a process that involves at least these two processes: developing critical consciousness and expanding one's awareness of each person as an agent. The practice or "praxis" (the marriage of practice and theory) of education is to create an environment in which dialogue occurs. It is in the process of the dialogue that learning and critical consciousness occurs. It is through dialogue rather than lecture that education really happens.

The point of educating men about sexism and violence is, in part, to politicize them. Sexist violence is inherently political. As described in this manual, the impact of men's violence against women is to restrict women's lives, movement, actions, and voices in ways that men's lives are not restricted. That is political! In order to effectively combat and end sexist violence, men must be motivated to act not only to confront the sexism and abusiveness in their own lives, but also to address and confront the institutional sexism, racism, and homophobia that help to maintain violence and abuse against women as an option for men.

Using libratory educational theory as a foundation for educational efforts also helps educators set more realistic and attainable goals. Using popular education allows educators to more realistically identify and achieve the goals in educating men. The goals should not necessarily be to make men pro-feminist activists, or even for them to adopt an anti-sexist lifestyle after one presentation. This may be a hope, but it is not a realistic goal. The goal of educating men is to encourage them to make one step towards a more pro-feminist, or anti-rape, or anti-violence perspective. There are many more steps that follow. If educators can design educational programs that successfully urge men to take just that first step, then the educational efforts are effective. Because popular educational tactics encourage men to look within themselves to better understand sexism and violence, they then become much more motivated to take the steps that follow.

Inherent in this is the aim of examining the process as much as the goal of any educational program. When educating a group of men, simply engaging them in a critical dialogue about sexism and violence is an appropriate goal. Engaging in a critical dialogue is not only more likely to be more meaningful for the men, but it is also a more achievable and empowering goal than convincing them of a particular definition or perspective.

Using libratory educational theory and popular education techniques informs educators not only about how to do educational programs with men, but also how to achieve one's goals with men. If two of the main goals are to change men's attitudes about sexist violence and encourage men to be more involved in efforts to stop sexist violence, one-time educational efforts are probably not the most effective tactic. A one-time educational program can provide information, and people can choose to use that information to change their attitudes, but, in general, it is unlikely that there will be a dramatic change in attitudes as a result of one educational event. Liberation educational theory and popular education practices suggest that if educators want to mobilize men to take action, then a longer-term process of engagement with the men must take place during which education occurs.

Consider your own experience in changing a deeply held attitude. One person talking to you one time with some new information is likely not what changed your attitude. Rather, it was probably a series of events that reinforced the same or similar message that forced you to challenge a previously held belief and to begin considering a new perspective.

The same is no doubt true for men in general; that is to say, if the goals include attempting to change men's attitudes about sexism and sexist violence, more strategic, long-term, and meaningful tactics are required. One-time educational workshops will not change men's attitudes and are even less likely to motivate men to join the movement.

DOING YOUR WORK: *Thinking About Your Own Attitude*

Take a few minutes to consider your experiences that have resulted in changes in your awareness or your development of critical consciousness.

Think about a time when you have felt motivated to act based on a teacher or educator.

What was your relationship with this person?

How did they treat you?

How did they treat themselves?

What did you perceive was their relationship with the issue?

How did you come up with that notion?

What did you do as a result?

Obviously, using liberation educational theory and popular education techniques requires more time, effort, and different skills than more traditional forms of education (where educators go in with a set outline, defined goals, and predetermined knowledge or information that the men will get from attending a presentation). Ultimately, using popular education techniques is more effective. As educators continue to develop their skills, understanding, and knowledge, it is worth examining how to incorporate some of these principles and practices into even short one-hour presentations. While far from ideal, this can improve the impact of the educational efforts dramatically.

The following questions, developed by Ross Wantland, Coordinator of Sexual Assault Education at the University of Illinois, Champaign-Urbana, are very helpful in thinking about how educators can begin educating using a liberation educational perspective.

QUESTIONS FOR REVOLUTIONARY SEXUAL VIOLENCE PREVENTION EDUCATION

- Am I aware of my limitations and hot button issues? How will I deal with these limitations? How will I maximize strengths?
- Am I telling the group what to think, or am I creating a space where they can come to their own conclusions?
- Do I know (or am I able to hear) where they are in their process? Can I take these needs and work with them from where they are?
- Am I approaching them as the problem or the solution?
- Am I paying attention to the emotional process and space the students need to understand this information?
- Am I giving them skills for practical application and reintegration?
- Am I creating an opportunity for them to engage in social change?

Education—No Panacea

As suggested in the previous section, education in and of itself is not a panacea. Changing behaviors requires a much more concerted and broad-based effort than education alone. National experiences with drunken driving, smoking, and drug use clearly demonstrate that education cannot be counted on to change people's behaviors. Education can and does provide a means to effectively share information. Education has also been demonstrated to effectively change people's attitudes to a limited degree (although rarely does education alone change one's attitude). Education has rarely been shown as an effective tool to change behaviors. The goal of changing men's behaviors (to stop acting in abusive or sexist ways, to act more supportive of women or men who are victimized, to actively engage in their own healing, to become allies of women in the work to stop sexism and violence, and so on) cannot be realistically achieved by using educational methods alone.

It is beyond the scope of this manual to address the multiple tactics that could be used (support groups, community organizing, public awareness campaigns, and so on) in great detail. Examples of men taking action are offered later in the manual in order to demonstrate some of the tactics and strategies that educators can use in conjunction with a comprehensive education campaign. The point is to consider educational efforts targeting men as but one array of tactics that are part of a much larger system of efforts for engaging men.

In educating men, it is important to begin with the premise that all forms of men's violence (rape and sexual harassment, partner abuse, pornography, prostitution, and so on) are completely preventable. Sexism and violence are preventable in three main ways:

- Sexist violence is preventable by men choosing to stop being violent against women, children, and other men.
- Sexist violence can be prevented when the men who are not violent or abusive stop allowing sexism, abuse, and violence to occur around them.
- Sexist violence is preventable by working to transform society to institutionalize gender respect and justice rather than gender inequality and oppression.

Those men who aren't violent or abusive can be described as *bystanders,* the men who "stand by" while other men say demeaning things, use pornography, make sexist comments, relay rape-jokes, or in other ways act in ways that suggest attitudes that support sexist violence. *Allies* are men who take a stand for gender and sexual justice and against sexism and abuse, even when women are not in the room.

In all these areas, education has a role. Education can be used with men who are violent or who have acted in sexist ways to help them understand that violence is a choice and to recognize the patterns of sexism and violence and the harm that results from their actions. Education can be used to help men who are bystanders understand their role in the perpetration of sexism and violence and to move them from bystander to ally. Education is also one important tactic for institutional and social change.

It is not readily apparent to most men why they should be involved in working to stop sexism and violence. Most men do not see their behaviors as abusive, are unaware of the women or men in their lives who have been abused, and do not see any relevance to their lives. Strategic and well-conceived educational efforts (programs and campaigns) are a crucial means to achieve these goals:

- Reach potential allies
- Inform them that they do have a role in ending men's violence
- Encourage them to take action
- Identify possible actions for them to take

Men are actively engaged in leadership in a wide range of social justice and human rights efforts, but are glaringly absent from the work for gender justice. In order for men to be more involved, they need to better understand how rape, domestic violence, stalking, and other forms of men's violence are human rights/social justice issues. This effort, obviously, does not necessarily mean that men will begin lining up to join the movement, but experience suggests that educating men about sexist violence as a human rights issue increases the likelihood of men becoming involved.

The Rebound Effect

In doing educational work to change attitudes, it is important to be aware of the so-called *rebound effect.* Not only is this important in providing educational programs, but it is particularly important in *planning* programs. In addition, it is worth exploring ways to connect educational models with other forms of grassroots organizing and activist tactics that can augment educational programs.

The basic notion of the rebound effect is based on an understanding of the dynamics of attitude change. The rebound effect suggests that if a group of people's attitudes towards an issue is tested (for example, smoking) right before a presentation and then retested immediately after the educational program, more than likely they will show a demonstrative shift in their attitudes about smoking. If they are tested again some period of time later (for example, six weeks), however, there will likely be some rebound back towards their original attitudes. In most cases, the scores six weeks after the event are still better than they were before the program, but they are not as good as they were immediately after the presentation.

This dynamic makes perfect sense and should come as no real surprise. It takes a long time for people to develop their attitudes about any topic. A presentation may challenge those attitudes with new information. Most people take new information in and wrestle with it for a period of time. They also try to figure out what it is that the presenter wants them to think. When the program is over, they continue to grapple with the old attitudes and beliefs as confronted with the new information, as in,

> "I know smoking is bad for me and that I should give it up, but I really like smoking and I'm really healthy in other ways. I don't eat meat, and I exercise regularly. Besides, I don't smoke all that much."

Those longer-held beliefs and attitudes begin to erode the new information. The result is that people may have more and better information and a deeper understanding of the issues, but their attitudes are likely to have changed only a little.

The rebound effect is also in play when educating men about sexism and violence. When educating about sexism and violence, the rebound effect that is seen suggests that men's attitudes and beliefs about sexism and violence is actually worse after a one-time presentation than prior to the presentation. The main difference between the rebound effect related to other social issues and the rebound effect for men in relation to sexism and violence is that men's attitudes and beliefs about sex, power, entitlement, privilege, women, what it means to be a man, and so on are probably much more deeply engrained, strongly held, and socially supported than their attitudes and beliefs about smoking. Because these beliefs are likely more strongly held by the men, and more socially supported, then educators' efforts need to be that much more thoroughly prepared. When preparing for presentations with men, educators should expect and plan for there being some degree of rebound to previously held attitudes and beliefs after the program is completed and the participants go back to their lives and behaviors.

Very little research has looked at the long-term impact of educational efforts on men's attitudes. However, the research is very telling. The research findings demonstrate fairly consistently that men's attitudes four to eight weeks after the presentation are actually worse than their attitudes before the presentation (Heppner, et al, 1999, and Schewe and O'Donohue, 1996). This research reinforces what was suggested earlier, that is, that one-time presentations with men may do more harm than good.

The ways that the rebound effect is played out with men in regards to sexist violence has a number of possible explanations. First, men may figure out early in a presentation what it is that the educator wants to hear and there is likely a motivation (both conscious and unconscious) to give the "right" answers. So some men may answer a posttest based more on what they think the presenter wants them to believe than what they actually believe. After a period of time, the influence of the educator diminishes and they are more likely to answer with their true thoughts and feelings.

It is also unlikely that educators have the opportunity to educate men as an identified group, in other words, a group of friends who continue to interact after a presentation. Educators typically speak to a class, a workplace, a church group, or some other group in a formal setting. After the presentation, the men go back with their friends and may discuss what they've just heard in the presentation. Their friends, who probably did not take part in the educational program, will likely respond strongly and negatively to the new information, not only reinforcing the previous attitudes, but also pressuring men to reassert their masculinity by voicing their rejection of the new information. Many, if not most, men are openly challenged and criticized for any suggestion that they are coming to accept the "feminist line" about sexism and sexist violence. Men exert a strong pressure on each other to keep traditional views about sexist violence because it maintains male privilege. It benefits men to continue to blame women for being victimized, and, as a result, men pressure each other to hold on to those victim-blaming attitudes. This pressure, then, can force men to feel as though they need to reassert their masculinity by claiming a more victim-blaming or anti-feminist perspective.

The information that one-time presentations may do more harm than good should not be taken as a reason to stop educating men. Rather, it suggests a re-examination of how educators develop educational programs for men. Rather than conducting one-time educational programs for men, multiple educational programs seem to be called for. Programs must be designed for the long haul and the hard work of really changing someone's attitudes and beliefs. In fact, the only demonstrated program that has shown an improvement of men's attitudes has some methodological concerns and really measures only one area: men's belief in rape myths (see Foubert and Marriott, 1997; for a critique of Foubert's research, see Berkowitz, 2001a).

Resources

Web

Amnesty International. AI has recently launched a campaign against violence against women. www.amnestyusa.org

Communities United Against Violence Network (CAVNET). An online resource and listserv addressing violence against women. www.cavnet2.org

Equality Now. Works to end violence and discrimination against women internationally. www.equalitynow.org

Legal Momentum. Formerly the NOW Legal Defense and Education Fund. Provides legal advocacy and resources on legal advocacy. www.legalmomentum.org

Tahirih Justice Center. Addresses and responds to violence against women internationally. Develops advocacy efforts and offers resources. www.tahirih.org

United Nations Development Fund for Women (UNIFEM). Has a host of resources on ending violence against women, including *16 Days of Activism Against Violence Against Women—Information Packet*. www.unifem.org

UNIFEM also organizes the International Day to End Violence Against Women. Information at www.unifem.org/campaigns/november25/

V-Day. The web site supporting local activism against violence against women. Founded by Eve Ensler, author of the *Vagina Monologues*. www.vday.org

Vital Voices. An organization that addresses and provides resources to respond to trafficking of women. www.vitalvoices.org

World Pulse. International magazine and media resource addressing the activism and women and youth. www.worldpulsemagazine.com

Print

MacKinnon, C. (2005). *Women's lives, men's laws*. Cambridge, MA: Harvard University Press.

O'Toole, L. L., & Schiffman, J. R. (Eds.). (1997). *Gender violence: Interdisciplinary perspectives*. New York: New York University Press.

Spindel, C., Levy, E., & Connor, M. (2000). *With an end in sight: Strategies from the UNIFEM Trust Fund to eliminate violence against women*. New York, NY. United National Development Fund for Women. Available from www.unifem.org.

United Nations Development Fund for Women (UNIFEM). (2003) *Not a minute more: Ending violence against women*. New York: UNIFEM. Available at www.unifem.org/attachments/products/312_book_complete_eng.pdf.

CHAPTER 2

Determining the Goals of Educating Men

At some point, in the process of discussing how to most effectively educate men, it seems significant to ask what may seem an overly basic question and spend some time examining the answers: Why is it important to educate men? Although educators and activists may all agree with the idea of educating men, before actually beginning, it seems constructive to begin by outlining *why* it is important. Individual educators and the programs or agencies for whom they work must also spend time discussing this point before beginning any specific or sustained efforts to educate men and at various times throughout these efforts. This discussion can surface important theoretical points that can continue to ground the work and inform the efforts.

Historically, the primary goals of the educational efforts of the movement to end violence against women were (and continue to be) to educate, empower, and liberate women. For most rape crisis centers, battered women's shelters, and other agencies who educate about these issues, the first and most important objective is to educate the community about these issues so that women are empowered. Why, one could ask, bother to educate men about sexism and violence? How does educating men empower women? What is the role of men, even educated or sensitized men, in working to end men's violence? These may seem to be obvious and unnecessary questions, but they speak to the core of the efforts of education and social change.

Without answering the basic question about why we should educate men in the first place and the other related questions, those who work to stop sexism and violence may begin educating men or creating programs that, inadvertently, aren't grounded in their own philosophy. As with anything else, if the actions taken are not grounded in a common understanding, they can become less than strategic and can be disingenuous or even harmful. Therefore, when considering developing or expanding educational programs for men, it is crucial that educators take the time to examine these questions and reflect upon both the agency setting and the community context (neighborhoods, campuses, populations served, and so on). The answers to these questions help guide the work to more effectively reach local men and to address and respond to sexism and violence.

Establishing the Goals in Educating Men

There are two levels of goals when considering educating men: the global (what is the general goal in educating men?) as well as specific goals to each educational program (what is the goal of *this* educational program with *this* group of men?). Both of these levels of goals need to be examined in the process of planning to educate men.

For the most part, the goals of education are to

- Inform
- Empower
- Enlighten
- Change attitudes
- Mobilize men to do something with the information they have received

These goals probably look familiar, even if unstated, for they are (or should be) common with any population one is educating. Each of these goals often includes a multitude of sub-goals. For example, the goal of *informing* men could include all the following and much more:

- The legal definitions of sexual assault
- An advocate's definition of sexual assault
- The impact of a sexual assault
- How a person might respond to being sexually assaulted
- The impact of sexual assault on the loved one of a person who has been assaulted
- How to best support a loved one who has been sexually assaulted

It is virtually impossible to achieve all these goals in one educational program, so before doing any kind of educational program with men, it is important that educators think clearly about the audience and choose one or two goals for that particular effort. This, then, leads into a discussion about defining the overall purpose for educating men.

Defining the Main Goal

In general, most educators would agree that it is important to educate men about sexism and violence. Beyond this general (and rather vague) goal, educators need to clearly define *why* it is important to them, as educators, as well as why it is important to the organizations for whom educators work. Additionally, educators need to examine what they would like to achieve by educating men.

Whether an educator is planning an educational program or developing a campaign for men, it is important to begin by thinking through the *main goal* for educating men. Before exploring *how* to educate men in a local community, the goal needs to be clearly defined. Each community and program is unique, and although there may be some broad general principles that are more universal, every educator's and every program's goal will be specific to

- The community
- The needs of that community
- The strengths within that community, including those of the men, to meet those needs
- The men who are being focused upon
- The specific goals to be achieved by educating men

DOING YOUR WORK: *Defining the Goals*

Before beginning a program, an educator or agency should write clear answers to all the following questions:

What do you want to accomplish by educating men?

What do you want men to know?

Which men do you want to educate?

How do you want to educate the men?

What do you want men to do with the information once they have been educated?

How will educating men help you achieve your goals in your community?

What are the possible drawbacks of educating men?

These questions are designed to assist educators in *beginning* to think more thoroughly about the main goal and other goals of educating men and the achievements that are desired as a result of educating men. By better understanding and articulating why educators want to educate men, the educational programs that are developed and designed will be more effective and productive. In addition, examining the various answers to these questions leads one towards developing a comprehensive educational program for men.

For example, one accomplishment of educating men may be to alert them to the support services and resources that are available in the local community for women or men who are victimized. Designing an educational program or campaign for men to raise men's awareness about the services and resources can probably be achieved fairly successfully by using a mix of media campaigns and public speaking efforts. Developing posters, flyers, commercials, and other tools that specifically speak to men about the resources that are available and why they may want to know of the available services, coupled with educational programs designed for men throughout the community, would likely raise men's awareness. Each of the questions listed in the worksheet can be answered from the desired accomplishment, now that it has been stated.

Defining the Action Goals

Included in this discussion about the goals of educating men are the questions related to what men are being educated to do. Presumably, the goal is not simply to educate men so that they are better educated about sexism and violence. One of the main goals of educating men is for them to be better educated so that they will turn that education into action to either respond to sexist violence or work to stop it. For example, educating men on how to better respond to a friend or loved one who has been victimized includes turning the experience of being educated into the action of supporting that friend or loved one.

This is an important, but also challenging, task. Most agencies and advocates have a long list, usually unstated, of what they want men to be educated about and what they want men to do after they are educated. Add to this the perceived pressure of having only one opportunity to talk with a group of men, and many educational programs for men are overflowing with expectations and goals for what the men who attend that presentation will come away with. It is not realistic to think that one one-hour presentation will achieve all the following:

- Increase men's awareness of
    - The issues in general
    - How the issues link to sexism
    - The dynamics and forms of gender-based violence
    - The effects on women

    - The reality of men's victimization
    - The laws and their inadequacies
    - The resources available
    - Why sexism and violence are men's responsibility
- Increase men's empathy for
    - Women or men who are victimized
    - Women in general
    - Themselves
- Mobilize men to take action
    - To better support their friends when they are victimized
    - To confront sexist comments
    - To support the work of local programs
    - To take action in other ways

This is a daunting list! It is not uncommon for educators who work with men to want to achieve all of these, and probably more, at one time. While that is certainly a desire, it is impossible in one educational program (or even one educational campaign). Furthermore, if educators walk into a room to do a presentation with a list of goals this long, whether these goals are stated, the result will be that both the educator and the men in the room will be overwhelmed.

DOING YOUR WORK: ***Listing the Goals for Educating Men***

Take some time right now to list your own goals that you have when you are given an opportunity to educate men. It is likely that you will come up with a list much longer than the one above.

Educators will be most effective if they pick one or two goals for each presentation and focus on these throughout the discussion. If there is more than one goal, there needs to be more than one educational program. As educators continue to develop their skills in this area, related goals and purposes can be linked to create an educational campaign using a variety of education techniques to focus on different groups of men to achieve broader results. To effectively achieve the goal of reducing men's use of sexism and violence requires a multi-year, multi-method educational campaign that is culturally relevant and one that specifically targets the different populations of men in any community.

There are multitudes of goals that any educator or agency may develop in terms of educating men. What follows is a brief exploration of three broad goals. Educators are encouraged to examine these, but also to explore what other goals may be more relevant for the agency, the community, and the educator.

Goal 1: To Reduce the Rate at Which Men Perpetrate Sexism, Violence, and Abuse

One goal of educating men is to reduce the rate at which individual men perpetrate sexism and violence. Although it seems that it should be obvious to men when they are acting in abusive or harmful ways, they often do not recognize that they are perpetrating abuse. In order for men to know when they are acting in sexist, abusive, or harmful ways, they need to be better educated and sensitized about the more subtle expressions of sexism and about how these subtle expressions of sexism relate to other forms of gender-based violence.

EFFECTIVE STRATEGY

Challenge men to examine the sexism they perpetrate and explore forms of sexist abuse that is not considered violent.

Most men understand that hitting a woman with a fist is not acceptable (although most available evidence suggests that many men do so anyway), but men perpetrate many forms of abuse that, while not physically violent, are still harmful. While one realistic expectation is to reduce the incidence of physical violence in order to end sexist violence, men must be challenged to examine the various forms of sexism that they perpetrate and to explore the forms of sexist abuse that are not necessarily violent (and thus fall under the radar of men's awareness) but which are still harmful. For example, later in the manual is a discussion of street harassment. While some forms of street harassment are egregious and overtly harmful, many forms are relatively subtle and the harm is easily unrecognized. Most men do not see talking loudly about how a woman is dressed on the street as abusive or harmful.

Goal 2: To Increase Skills in Supporting Victimized Loved Ones

Another goal may be to increase men's skills in supporting loved ones who are victimized. Men in general do not know how to support their women or men friends when they are victimized. Most men have learned to express anger, to take control of situations, especially in crisis (which means, in part knowing what to do, or at least acting like they know what to do even when they don't), to stay emotionally disengaged and "rational," and to attack the person who harmed a loved one. These are not the actions that most victimized women or men find supportive.

EFFECTIVE STRATEGY

Educate men about the forms of trauma, the impact of trauma, and how to best support loved ones who are victimized.

An educational program such as this could address what the trauma is (including the various ways that sexism or violence affects someone) and how people respond to trauma. Men know very little about these issues, and as such, know almost nothing about how people respond. Educating men about the effects of and responses to sexism and violence can be very valuable. Finally, this kind of educational program would include information for the men themselves. Caring for someone who has been victimized is painful. Educating men about supporting a loved one includes some information about how to care for themselves.

Goal 3: To Educate Men to Become More Active in the Work to End Sexist Violence

Yet another goal is to educate men to become more active in the work to end sexist violence. In order for men to become more involved in community activism and social change, they must be educated to better understand that sexist violence is a form of oppression; how and why it demands male attention, energy, and activism; ways they can be involved to end sexism and violence; and the reasons why they should be involved.

> **EFFECTIVE STRATEGY**
>
> Challenge men to accept response-ability to work to end sexism and the violence that comes from it.

Talking with men about becoming more active requires that men not only understand sexism and violence, but also understand that they can do something to combat sexism and violence. For many men, addressing sexism and violence is an overwhelming task, and one that they feel ill-prepared to take on. These kinds of educational programs would provide men with enough information to feel like they know what to do, and also enough passion and motivation to feel like they should.

After you have determined your main goal and the actions you desire the men to take, you are ready to begin developing a program.

Conceptualizing Educational Programs

One way to conceptualize educational programs for men is under four main categories. This list is not prioritized in any particular order and will be discussed in further detail below. Educating men to increase men's knowledge, awareness, and sensitivity, and to promote change in their behavior about

- **Sexism and Violence in General.** Men need more information in general about the dynamics of sexism and sexist violence. In order to be better human beings, men need to better understand how sexism and violence impact all people, how sexism and violence impact differently on women and on men, and how sexism and violence has a different kind of impact on different women and on different men.
- **Male Victimization.** It is important to educate men about the issues of male victimization because men are victimized too. Educational efforts can focus on men's risks of being victimized and how to reduce those risks. For men who have been victimized, the focus, as with women, is to offer information that promotes healing.
- **Significant Others.** It is also important to educate men to be more sensitive and responsive to the needs of women, children, and other men who are victimized by

sexist violence. When someone that a man cares about is victimized, he too is hurt. Therefore, educational efforts provide men with the information and tools to be supportive of the person(s) in his life who are victimized, as well as with the tools to take care of his own needs.

- **Men's Response-abilities to Act.** Sexist violence is men's violence. Therefore, the efforts to end men's violence will not stop until men stop perpetrating violence. Educating men, then, involves educating men as to their individual and collective responsibilities to work to end sexism and violence. Efforts to motivate men to become more involved require educating men both as bystanders and as activists, which are not mutually exclusive. Overall, an important goal of educating men is to encourage them to take the initiative to end their own abusive behaviors and become active in the movement to end all forms of men's violence.

Increasing Men's Knowledge, Awareness, and Sensitivity

With the attention that rape and domestic violence have been given over the past few years, it is safe to assume that most men know something about these issues. This "knowledge," however, is likely some mix of accurate information, misinformation, and myths. Furthermore, the "knowledge" that men do have rarely translates into increased awareness or sensitivity. Therefore, the responsibility of educators is to provide the information in ways that are more likely to make the knowledge that men do have (and the additional knowledge that they will presumably gain from the presentation) translate into becoming more aware and sensitive.

Knowledge, awareness, and sensitivity are closely related, but they are different. Increasing knowledge is mostly intellectual, awareness is a mix of the intellectual and the heart, and sensitivity is mostly heart. Because this is true, educators need to think of developing educational programs that focus on one or two of these areas (in other words, men's knowledge and awareness, or men's awareness and sensitivity).

These distinctions are also important because they have implications for how educators implement the program. As discussed earlier, there are various forms of educating. On one extreme is the lecture style; on the other extreme is a facilitating dialogue in which the facilitator actually says very little, encouraging as much conversation amongst the participants as possible. Another distinction is the number of exercises and activities that are part of a presentation. Increasing awareness can occur effectively in a format that is more lecture-based and with fewer activities, but this format is unlikely to increase men's sensitivity or awareness.

Ultimately, these efforts are aimed at educating men to change their attitudes and behaviors, and increase their skills to respond to and confront sexism and violence. There is little evidence that increasing awareness or knowledge alone results in behavior change or increased skills.

This is not to say that increasing men's knowledge, sensitivity, and/or awareness are not meaningful goals in and of their own right because they certainly are. If educators hope to change men's behaviors or increase men's skills, however, then different kinds of educational programs need to be developed.

These kinds of programs are more intensive and long-term, and they involve role-playing, exercises, and other tactics as a way to assist men in developing and practicing new skills or behaviors. One example of this is what many campus-based programs use frequently, namely, male peer educators. Training men to be educators about sexual assault on campuses, for example, takes a different form than the education that these men provide on the campus. The training for men to become peer educators requires a longer duration and is designed to give men specific skills about how to educate. The education that these men turn around and provide to the campus community is typically designed to increase knowledge and awareness.

EFFECTIVE STRATEGY
Design intensive, long-term, interactive programs.

Educating Men About Sexism and Violence in General

Educating men about sexism and violence means that you provide detailed information about the specific forms of sexism and violence. Such educational efforts can be understood as building the foundation for further, ongoing activities. These educational activities should focus particular attention on definitions, dynamics, and impact.

Debating the Definition

Men will often want to have in-depth conversations about the precise definition of the form of violence being discussed (rape, for example). If the educator has created an environment in which the men feel comfortable in asking questions, they will often ask very detailed questions about what is or isn't abuse. This is an important conversation for educators to engage in. While it can be frustrating, it is worth allowing time for it in this process.

Ultimately, there is no one definition of any of these forms of violence and abuse. As mentioned above, there is always a gap between the legal definition and a victim-centered definition. Furthermore, there are likely differences in definitions even amongst people on the same staff. One key point to try to get across to men about the definition is that violence and abuse (from an advocate's perspective) is best defined based on the experience of the person who was victimized. This cannot be externalized or intellectualized into a universally acceptable definition. If a woman feels harmed, threatened, violated, disrespected, confused, angered, shocked, and so on in relation to a sexual experience, then she probably was raped, regardless of what some definition somewhere says.

One aspect of this debate about definitions that is worth exploring with men relates to abusing people in ways that aren't illegal. One of the underlying themes in men's efforts to define **a** precise definition is to examine how close they can get (or have gotten) to perpetrating some form of abuse without breaking the law. If they know precisely what the definition of rape is, for example, then men know exactly how much pressure, coercion, manipulation, and force they can get away with using before they get into trouble. One question to ask men during a presentation when you feel like you can't move beyond the definition debate is, "How come you want to know so precisely what the definition is? This sounds like you want to know how much you can hurt someone without getting into trouble. Seems to me, when talking about rape, domestic violence, stalking, etc., that men would want to behave in ways that are the complete opposite." This kind of statement can help move men away from focusing so much on the definition.

EFFECTIVE STRATEGY

A sample outline for a presentation on Rape and Sexual Assault follows. It is unlikely that educators will have an opportunity to discuss the topic "Sexism and Violence in General" with a group of men. More likely, educators are presenting on specific topics to a group of men (Introduction to Rape/Sexual Assault, What Is Domestic Violence, What Is the Harm of Pornography, Understanding Stalking, Defining Sexual Harassment, etc.). The discussions above are offered in a general way that can be applied to the specific forms of sexism and violence that educators may be presenting on. The sample outline on the next page is an example of what this kind of general discussion might look like as applied to a Rape 101 presentation.

Focusing on Intent

Men also often focus more on the intent of an action. They often would rather discuss both the intent of the person who allegedly hurt someone and the intent of the person claiming that they have been harmed. Again, this can be a very frustrating process, but it *is* worth discussing to some degree. This is a real question that men have, and in order to keep them engaged in the conversation and to respect where they are coming from (rather than where an educator would like them to be), it is important to allow some time for this kind of conversation to occur.

In the process, educators are given a ripe opportunity to identify and confront the myths that are exposed as a result of this conversation. Inherent in the questions about intent include, "What did she do to deserve the violence or abuse?" and "How is she to blame as much as he is?" As described earlier, when educating men, it is important to not only address the literal question asked, but also the questions beneath the literal question. Engaging in a conversation about intent is just such an opportunity.

Redirecting the Focus Towards Impact

At the same time that it is important to engage in a conversation about intent, it is also crucial to redirect the discussion to a focus on impact. While intent is an important aspect, focusing on the impact will prove more beneficial and be more to the point. Furthermore, focusing on impact is a great way to increase men's sensitivity.

All people have experiences in which they have felt harmed, abused, victimized, mistreated, or disrespected in ways that did not necessarily fit a definition. Reminding men of these kinds of experiences can assist them in understanding the importance of impact over intent. In addition, all men *can* understand that there are differences between definitions and experiences and the importance of focusing on a person's experience over any definition. This will not totally assuage their concerns and arguments, but it will substantially help to move the conversation forward.

SAMPLE OUTLINE: ***Rape and Sexual Assault***

(Italics indicate words the presenter says.)

I. Introduction of Presenter

Hello, my name is (supply your name) and I'm here to talk with you from the Anytown Rape Crisis Center. The Anytown RCC offers 24-hour services for people who have been victimized by rape or sexual assault. This includes a 24-hour hotline, crisis counseling, hospital and court accompaniment, and ongoing counseling and therapy (both individual and group). All our services are offered free of charge.

I have been invited to come and talk with you about rape and sexual assault.

II. Introduction of the Topic

Would you agree, in general, with the statement that rape and sexual assaults are more damaging and harmful than a physical assault is? That if I were to leave here this evening and get raped, I would probably be more negatively affected than if I were to leave here and get beat up by somebody?

(Allow discussion)

Why?

(Discussion)

Who each of us is sexually is perhaps the most profoundly personal and sacred part of us. If we have control over nothing else, we have control over who we are sexually, how we express our sexuality, and what we do sexually. When someone else attempts to take control of that, regardless of how "gentle" that attempt may be, it is by definition a violent act. This is why we always refer to rape/sexual assault as a violent crime regardless of how physically violent the act may or may not have been.

III. Defining Sexual Assault

If we were to define for ourselves what rape/sexual assault is, what would that be? What are the key elements of our definition?

(Have them throw out ideas and list them as they verbalize them.)

(continued)

(continued)

You will find, eventually, that they will come up with (you can assist them in this direction) key elements of forced or unwanted sexual contact.

Okay, for our purposes, sexual assault is any forced or unwanted sexual contact? What does that mean for real?

Here's the scenario. A heterosexual couple is making out. And they are really getting into it—they're sharing some tongue and there's some bumping and grinding and some moaning and groaning... He massages her breast. She stops him and says that she's really into making out but does not want to go any further. They re-adjust and pretty soon are back to some heavy making out. He touches her breast again.

Based on our definition, is this a sexual assault?

(More than likely, there will be lots of discussion and some disagreement as to whether this was a sexual assault with some folks in the room saying yes, while others arguing no. As the educator, take the least popular position. If need be, argue that this is not a sexual assault.)

So we're not in any agreement in this room. What about if it were the 4th time that he touched her breast and she says no a 5th time? Would it be a sexual assault yet?

(More discussion—some folks will begin asking "well, why is she still with him? Shouldn't she get up and leave? Doesn't she have some responsibility here?")

For the purposes of this conversation, let's stay focused on his behavior.

(More discussion)

The point is, there really is no one definition. The first thing that we need to know is to what degree does she feel afraid, disrespected, harmed, afraid, sad, angry, confused, or any other feelings that can be associated with being harmed. Chances are, she is not feeling any of these things in this scenario, but if she is, than this is a sexual assault.

Secondly, how common is this? More than likely, every man in the room has done this.

(Male educators can easily include themselves in this and acknowledge that they have done this too. Female educators can likewise acknowledge how common it is for them to have experienced this).

What does it say about how he respects her, or how men respect women in general, if her "no, I'd rather not do that" gets translated in him to become "try again later."

IV. Legal Definitions

(Discuss briefly the state laws of rape/sexual assault.)

V. Impact of Rape/Sexual Assault

What effect do you think being raped has on a person?

VI. Resources

Educating Men About Male Victimization

Most educators have experienced male audiences that respond to any presentation with something like "But men are raped (or battered, or prostituted, or harassed…) too." While this is certainly true, this argument is often used as an attempt to derail the presenter as well as undermine the arguments made. It is assumed, for example, that if men are raped too, then rape is not a sexist act. When this argument is raised, it is with the mistaken belief that men are victimized by women, suggesting that if men are victimized by women the same ways that women are victimized by men, then the violence cannot be based on sexism.

If (and this is a big "if") it were true that both men and women are victimized at roughly the same rates and by both men and women, then the argument could possibly be made that these forms of violence are not sexist acts. The fact is, women and men are not victimized at the same rates, and when men are victimized, they are most often victimized by other men, not by women. The experiences of men who are victimized by the forms of violence discussed here mirror, in most ways, the experiences of women who are victimized. Similarly, the dynamics of the violence perpetrated against men are often very similar to the dynamics of these forms of violence when perpetrated against women. As such, the victimization of men, like the victimization of women, is an expression of sexism.

In most cases, educators only address male victimization within the context of a general presentation (for example, when educating about dating abuse, a sub-conversation about men who are abused by a dating partner). It is important for educators to be prepared ahead of time for these questions to arise and be able to answer them quickly and thoroughly without allowing the conversation to get sidetracked. It can be tempting to enter into a dialogue about male victimization in the midst of a presentation, but it's important that educators stay focused on their main agenda for the presentation. It is also worth developing specific educational programs designed to address male victimization. By developing specific educational programs on male victimization, educators fill a need, and also discover that they are better prepared to respond to questions about male victimization when they do arise in other presentations. Educating men about male victimization involves many of the same basic skills used when talking about female victimization.

Gender-based violence is based on power and control, not sex, although sexual organs may be involved. In most rapes, for example, the penis is used as a weapon, and many times the sexual parts of a man are the target of the violence towards him. Regardless of the kind of sexist violence, the perpetration of the violence may appear to be motivated by other feelings, most typically sexual desire and anger. It is crucial that educators keep the focus that all forms of sexist violence are perpetrated by the desire to control. Men, like women, use a variety of tactics to resist the violence, to defend themselves, and to minimize the degree of violence used and harm experienced. Sometimes not responding physically is the smartest and safest form of resistance.

EFFECTIVE STRATEGY

Begin a presentation on this topic with statistics and a general overview.

A presentation about men victimized by rape, domestic violence, stalking, harassment, pornography, or prostitution is a complicated and challenging mix of information, feelings, and responses from both the participants and the educator. It is helpful to begin with statistics and a general overview of the dynamics particular to men's victimization patterns (some statistics and a general overview is offered in the section on sexual assault).

In general, it is safe to say that unlike women, whose risk for being victimized remains fairly constant throughout their lives, it appears that men's risk of being victimized decreases as they reach adulthood and then continues to decrease as they get older. This is generally true for every form of sexist violence.

Overview of the Dynamics of Male Victimization

Men who are victimized, like women, suffer a great deal. Sexist ideas about what men are and should be, such as the following, abound.

- "REAL MEN don't allow themselves to be victimized."
- "REAL MEN don't ask for help."
- "REAL MEN don't talk about their experience of being victimized."

Because of these ideas, men are often more reticent than women to disclose their victimization, which means the issues and dynamics are more shrouded in secrecy and shame. It is important for educators to be sensitive and talk about men's victimization in ways that empower the men in the room who might have been victimized, while educating all men about the issues involved.

Another issue that often arises when educating about issues of men who are victimized is the shame and stigma that surrounds male victimization. Socio-politically, the issues of male victimization are roughly 10 to 15 years behind where society is in dealing with the victimization of women. Fifteen or so years ago, there were few programs for women, and those that did exist were severely under-resourced. The information "on the streets" was even more victim-blaming than it is today:

- "Be aware of how you are dressed."
- "Know your surroundings."
- "Get a dog."
- "Buy a gun."

The current state of information about male victimization is similarly filled with myths and half-truths. It is still true for women who are victimized, but was much worse 15 or more years ago, when society as a whole, and men in particular, held victim-blaming attitudes. For example, historically, women have been faulted for their victimization. Today this view is very strong with male victimization. The belief is still very common that somehow men are at fault if they "allow themselves" to be victimized.

Most men have some rudimentary understanding about male victimization. Men know that men are also victimized but often assume that it is women who perpetrate the violence that men experience, or that gay men are more likely to be either the person who perpetrates or the person victimized.

For example, it is a common misperception that men who rape other men are gay, and/or that the men they rape are gay. Most of the time, men who rape other men are heterosexual, and although gay and bisexual men do appear to be somewhat at higher risk to be sexually victimized, largely as a result of sexual assaults during gay bashing, the higher risk does not mean that the crime is sexually motivated. Rape and other forms of sexist violence, be it against women or other men, is motivated by power, control, and entitlement, not sex.

EFFECTIVE STRATEGY

Address misinformation and myths.

When educating men about the issues of male victimization, it is important to be prepared to offer presentations that counter the misinformation and myths while working to assuage men's defensiveness and discomfort. In part, this means educators being somewhat comfortable with men having and expressing their discomfort with this topic. Men may (depending on their age and development) laugh, have side conversations with other men in the room, and otherwise appear to disengage or disrupt the conversation. Unless they are overtly disrupting, much of this behavior can better be understood and responded to as men's genuine discomfort with the topic and coupled with recognizing and acknowledging their own vulnerability. It's important to maintain a general tone of respectfulness for the men in the room who have already been victimized, but it is also important to allow some room for men's discomfort and "acting out" as a way to express this discomfort.

EFFECTIVE STRATEGY

Acknowledge homophobia.

Acknowledging that most men are victimized by other men often fuels homophobic responses amongst heterosexual male audiences. This provides another opportunity for educators to yet again reinforce that sexist violence is motivated by power and control. Most violence against men (with the exception of dating and domestic violence, gay male pornography, and prostitution) is perpetrated by heterosexual men, regardless of the sexual orientation of the man victimized. Thus, the violence or abuse is not sexually motivated. Heterosexual men often sexually assault gay or bisexual men during a gay bashing. The sexual violence is motivated by a desire to punish or humiliate, not for sexual pleasure. Many of the dynamics, motivations, and impact are the same regardless of the gender of the person victimized.

EFFECTIVE STRATEGY

Address men's perceptions of emasculation.

Because many men feel that being sexually victimized is (or would be) an assault on their masculinity, educators must address the issues of perceived emasculation. Men are no less "male" as a result of being victimized by sexist violence. Men who target men may well target their masculinity during the assault, but being victimized does not make men less masculine. The only thing that being victimized does is make men survivors of some form(s) of victimization. Men's experiences of being victimized by sexist violence is no more connected to their masculinity than women's experience of being victimized is connected to their femininity.

EFFECTIVE STRATEGY

Discuss the language used by perpetrators.

Exposing the language used by men while perpetrating this abuse is probably the clearest way to demonstrate that these are sexist acts. Regardless of the gender of the person who is targeted, men who perpetrate violence use the same kind of sexist and degrading language during the commission of the violence, such as gender slurs, using feminine descriptors towards the person they are victimizing, and so on.

Because of the interplay between sexism and homophobia, educators themselves must be comfortable with issues of homosexuality and bisexuality or at the very least not *un*comfortable about it. The degree to which educators may be uncomfortable about or opposed to homosexuality is the degree to which educators will act in ways that inhibit the discussion when talking about male victimization.

EFFECTIVE STRATEGY

Respond to questions about lesbian abusiveness.

During the conversation about men's victimization, often as a result of exposing the same-sex nature of these forms of violence, men may raise questions about women who perpetrate these forms of violence against other women. A part of the motivation for these questions is curiosity, mixed with an attempt to derail the focus of the presentation.

While it is certainly true that these forms of violence and abuse occur in lesbian and bisexual relationships between women, the focus of an educational program with men is examining the issues of *men* in relation to sexism and violence. In this context, any discussion of lesbian violence is, and needs to be understood as, an attempt to sidetrack the discussion. Don't allow this to happen. Educators must stay focused and work to keep the group focused on the topic at hand. Asking men "Why, in the context of educating men, are we talking about lesbian violence?" can be one effective way to shift the conversation back to the main points. Men can do very little to effectively stop abuse and violence in lesbian relationships. If the questions are asking about how to respond to lesbian friends or loved ones who are victimized, then an educator can respond by addressing the needs of people who are victimized and how to best support them. There is little to be gained, in educating men about sexism and violence, by engaging in an in-depth conversation about lesbian violence.

Services for Men Who Are Victimized

A common misperception is that rape crisis centers and battered women's programs exclude men. While, for obvious reasons, programs may put some limitations on the ways that men are served (for example, not putting battered men in the shelter or not including men in female-only rape survivor support groups), services are available and provided to men. In fact, rape crisis centers, domestic violence programs, and support services for those who are prostituted have been the first and are still on the front lines of reaching out to men who are victimized. It has been, in fact, the same feminist women who were in the forefront of arguing for protections for women from sexual harassment, who have argued most ferociously for men to be protected as well (for example, Catherine MacKinnon).

The fact that men make up a minority of service recipients of most victim/survivor support services does not necessarily reflect a lack of openness of these programs to work with men. It more likely suggests that men who are victimized are uncomfortable or unable to seek the services that are available.

As has been made clear through experience, men are extremely reluctant to seek counseling or support services for any reason. In general, men tend to seek counseling or support services either because their partners demand that they do, judges order them to, or they hit rock bottom. Men are not more likely to seek services if they have been victimized than for other issues. They are simply unlikely to seek services for any reason. This is not to "blame" men for not accessing available services; rather it is to acknowledge the efforts by feminists to provide necessary services that men who are victimized so rightly deserve.

DOING YOUR WORK: ***Identifying Available Services***

Educators need to be aware of available local services for men who have been victimized and should be prepared to address the following questions:

Are there support groups in the area for men who have been victimized?

What kinds of specialized services are available for men?

If there are services addressing people who are prostituted, stalked, or harassed, how would men access those services?

Educators need to know what is available and, if possible, have copies of flyers, brochures, or other written material available to hand out when making a presentation on male victimization. It is also important that educators know the local laws and how they may be different for male victims than for women (for example, whether same sex couples can get a restraining order or whether the legal definition of rape is limited to vaginal penetration).

Educating Men About Male Significant Others

Most men's first contact with gender-based violence occurs when they realize they know someone who has been victimized. Because men tend to receive such limited information about sexist violence, especially related to responding when a loved one is victimized, they are often severely disadvantaged when faced with such a situation. Educating men about how to respond supportively to loved ones provides a urgently needed service. In addition, approaching men from this angle provides a less-threatening way to address sexism and violence. By discussing issues related to being the significant other of someone who is victimized, men can be motivated to take action and become allies in the movement to end sexist violence.

EFFECTIVE STRATEGY

Be aware of your beliefs of men's roles in relation to their significant others who have been victimized.

When educating about significant others, educators need to be aware of what they believe in terms of men's role in relation to women or men who are victimized and how men should express this role. Some educators believe, for example, that men's expression of anger is an act of support for women or men who have been victimized. Men's anger can be supportive of their loved ones who have been victimized, but it can just as likely be a diversion. Women and men who are victimized often express concern with how their male loved ones will respond to the knowledge that they have been harmed. Whatever educators believe about male significant others, they must be aware of these beliefs *before* doing presentations to ensure that these assumptions or beliefs do not interfere with the educational programs. Also, one must be careful of assuming that male significant others only have female loved ones who are victimized. Men also have male friends and loved ones (including lovers) who are victimized.

Men want to know *how* to care about and support their loved ones. As will be discussed in greater detail later, each expression of sexist violence has its own healing process. As such, educators need to design an educational program for male significant others for each form of gender-based violence. That being said, there are similarities in how men tend to respond, as well as in the ways that men can learn to respond that are supportive of their loved one's healing process. The first step in educating male significant others (after providing some basic definitions and an overview) is to explain the process of victimization, what it does to the person who was victimized, and how people heal.

Healing is a circular process. People who have been victimized frequently proceed through several stages of healing, only to return back to stages they have previously dealt with. They may also appear to skip some stages of healing or proceed through them in a manner that makes little sense for others. One of the key points in educating men regarding being supportive to someone who has been victimized is to prepare them for this circular process and help them better understand it, thus being better prepared to care for a loved one.

Secondly, educators need to compassionately relate that individual men have their own unique responses when a loved one is victimized. When one person is victimized, many people are harmed. Male significant others need to have their own pain acknowledged.

As such, educators need to encourage male significant others to take care of their own needs and heal from the pain they have experienced, while at the same time respond supportively to their loved one. Following is a list of common responses from men. Educators need to simultaneously educate men about what their loved ones will likely go through and educate men about what they themselves are likely to experience. With knowledge and information, men are better able to respond supportively.

Some of the more common responses that male significant others have to a loved one's victimization include

- Need to be (or perceived to be) in control
- Desire to protect
- Anger
  - At themselves for not "protecting" their loved one
  - At their loved one for being victimized
  - At the perpetrator(s)
  - At society
  - At the police for not "doing their job"
  - At advocates for "getting in the way"
  - At the situation
- Victim-blaming attitudes
- Feelings of
  - Self-blame
  - Shame/embarrassment
  - Relief (that the violence or harm caused was not any worse)
  - Eroticism of the attack (this is particularly true for sexual assaults), which often feeds their self-blame and shame
  - Being overwhelmed
  - Inadequacy
- Difficulty in identifying and expressing those feelings

Most men aren't taught how to identify or express their feelings, and are allowed to express even fewer. In general, men are taught to express three kinds of feelings:

happiness, anger, and sexual arousal. When someone close to them is victimized, men often feel a much greater variety and degree of emotions than these three. Therefore, when educating men, one must explore the full range of feelings and responses that men are likely to experience, thus, helping men to prepare for this overwhelming emotional onslaught.

EFFECTIVE STRATEGY

Talk with men about the range of emotions they will feel and how to respond to the emotions.

Educators can talk with men about the range of emotions they are likely to experience and provide them with some suggestions about how to respond to those feelings. Men who have a loved one who is victimized by sexist violence often have a wide range of emotional responses—so many that they may feel overwhelmed. Because of the ways that men are generally socialized, men often have a lack of access to how to identify, much less express, this range of emotions they experience. Most easily accessed is the anger, but there is much more going on for male significant others than their anger.

Whatever men feel in relation to a loved one's victimization is their own experience. It is no one's right to judge these feelings, and it is important for educators to affirm this when addressing male significant others.

Male significant others are responsible for their own feelings and for addressing these feeling. This can be challenging for many men, as traditional masculinity suggests that men should "take care of" others (fix the problem, protect their loved one, get them the help they need, etc.) before or instead of responding to their own feelings. As such, *how* men act towards others can be understood as men's efforts to take care of themselves. By taking over, men are taking care of their feelings of inadequacy and guilt. The problem is, however, that this form of self-care is at the expense of healing the person who was victimized. Rather than taking care of their own needs by acting out on behalf of the persons victimized, men need to separate these two responses. Educators can help men to begin to understand how to do this.

Men's primary responsibility to a loved one who has been victimized is to be a support and ally. Therefore, male significant others must also accept the full responsibility to take care of their own feelings and meet their own needs.

CASE STUDY

Ron's reaction on learning that his loved one, Jeff, had been victimized was the desire to know as much as possible about what happened. This need to know "all the details" was *Ron's* need, not Jeff's. Ron's need, in fact, ran exactly counter to the need of Jeff, the person who was victimized. In order to be truly supportive in the healing process, Ron had to distinguish between his need to know the details, and the needs and rights of Jeff to tell what happened to him at a pace with which he was comfortable. The process of listening to Jeff tell his story at his own pace was frustrating for Ron, yet it was one of the most empowering and healing things that he could do for Jeff (even if it meant sitting silently by while Jeff also remained silent).

Addressing the Urge to Take Control

Men are also taught to take control, especially in crisis situations. When a loved one is victimized, she or he does not need someone else, especially another man, to take over. In fact, this is inherently disempowering and can inhibit healing. What that person needs is someone to support, love, and be an ally as she or he proceeds through a healing process that is uniquely that person's.

When men do not take control, they are often at a loss about how to respond. There are at least two other dynamics that occur that further complicate this process for men. A crisis situation often triggers a heightened need to be in even greater control because of the degree to which they feel out of control. In addition, any guilt men experience for failing to protect their loved one from being victimized in the first place often generates a desire to step in and take over.

EFFECTIVE STRATEGY

Discuss strategies for being supportive without trying to control the victim's feelings.

When educating men, educators need to talk with men about how to be supportive without taking over. For example, many people want to put their arms around and hold a loved one who has been victimized. Recognizing that this was a horribly traumatic event, men often want to provide comfort. One way to do that (especially for men) is to offer a hug. Women or men who have been victimized by sexist violence may not want to be touched at all, and certainly not by another man. This may also be exactly what they want, but the decision to be touched and how to be touched, even in comfort, needs to be left to the person who was victimized.

Rather than hugging a loved one who was victimized, holding her hand, or putting a hand lovingly or "supportively" on his back or leg, it may be experienced as more supportive for a man to lay his hand, palm up, on his own leg or on the arm of a chair. This subtle gesture allows loved ones to recognize that men are there for them and will hold them if that is what they want, while leaving the choice about being touched, and the power, to the one being comforted.

Learning to Handle the Anger Appropriately

One of the emotional responses to which men do have access is anger. Anger, even rage, is a completely appropriate and understandable response to having a friend or loved one raped, beaten, harassed, stalked, or prostituted. For most men, the first response to thinking about a loved one being victimized is rage. Not only is men's anger completely understandable, it can also be a great source of support and validation for loved ones who are victimized. The issue is not whether men have anger, but rather how men express their anger in ways that can be experienced as supportive by their loved ones. (See the poem "Spittin' Nails" in Appendix C. This was my attempt to capture men's responses to a loved one who was sexually victimized.)

Women, in particular, tend to be concerned about how their male loved ones express anger at the attack and often internalize men's anger as being directed at them. Women's concerns about men's expressions of anger are, in fact, one of the main reasons that women give for not disclosing to their male loved ones that they have been victimized. Talking with men about how to be angry, which is their right, and how to express their anger in a way that is supportive is vitally important. For example, during a presentation, an educator could say something like:

> *Men's anger is completely understandable, and it is important for men who are significant others to have room to express their anger at having a loved one harmed. Men also need to understand that they need to be aware of how they express their anger.*
>
> *One of the reasons that women or men who are victimized state that they do not report their victimization to their male loved ones is fear of anger. Not necessarily that the anger will be directed at them, but that he will "lose control" and "do something stupid" (or violent).*
>
> *The desire to want to rip the throat out of the man who rapes my niece may be very strong, but acting on those desires not only places me at increased risk, but also diverts my niece's attention away from her healing to worrying about me and what I'm going to do.*
>
> *The best that men can do to support their loved ones is to allow themselves to be angry, but express that anger in ways that do not hinder their loved one's healing.*

As presented in the preceding commentary, the anger that male significant others feel often has a wide variety of sources and targets. It is important when educating men about being supportive of their loved ones who have been victimized to clarify this range and talk with men about ways to relate their anger to the source. It is not uncommon for male significant others to feel anger from all these sources converging at once, and to target those feelings in one direction: the police, the counselor, or even the person who was victimized. Educating men to understand this range of anger sources can provide them with the knowledge they need to be better able to direct their anger should they ever be in such a situation.

Overcoming the Myths

Male significant others, as with much of the male population, have been misinformed by the myths and lies about sexist violence, especially in regards to the degree of responsibility of the person who was victimized. These beliefs don't change just because a loved one is victimized. Men still have at least some of these attitudes:

- "Why were you out so late?"
- "I told you he was no good. Why did you go and marry him?!?"
- "Why did you get so drunk?"

- "You were wearing that?!?"
- "Why did you make him so angry?"

The blame and accusations are self-evident in these statements, as are the myths upon which these statements are based. Educating men about being a victim's significant other presents an opportunity to expose and counter these myths. Assuming that men want to actively support their partners, educators can explain how men who act out of these myths will inadvertently do things that will further harm their loved ones.

In an educational program, provide opportunities to talk about myths by asking questions, creating scenarios, and using some of the exercises offered in Appendix B. Myths can be countered and real information provided. Reinforce this by emphasizing how acting based on mistaken beliefs is victim-blaming and will be harmful to their loved ones.

Addressing Men's Sense of Responsibility

Male gender training teaches that men are responsible for protecting their loved ones. The closer the person who is victimized is (lover, daughter, mother, and so on), the greater a man's sense of responsibility. When men's loved ones are hurt, men often feel that they have failed in their duties to protect. Men often blame themselves for not protecting their loved ones, or for not seeing the signs earlier and doing something. During educational programs with men, this issue must be addressed. Facilitators can remind men that they are not to blame for the actions of the perpetrator(s) any more than the people who are victimized are to blame. The crucial point is not the degree to which they "failed" their loved one, but how they can best be supportive of her or him now.

Confronting the Sense of Relief

As paradoxical as it may sound, men often feel some sense of relief when a loved one is assaulted and survives. Some women and men are killed by assaults, and regardless of how brutal or bad the attack, at least their loved one did survive. This sense of relief, in turn, suggests that men know that the assault could have been much worse. Male significant others are relieved that the assault *was not* worse. However, when an assault occurs, there is so much horror, anger, and pain that men may feel uncomfortable identifying and acknowledging their sense of relief, and therefore, may deny it.

When educating about significant others, educators need to make men aware that this sense of relief is a part of a natural response for both significant others and people who have survived, that it is common, and that their acknowledging this sense of relief can be beneficial to their loved one because it acknowledges the real threat and very real fear that she or he experienced.

Addressing the Eroticization of the Violence

For male significant others of loved ones who are sexually victimized, there is an additional, often troubling dynamic that must be addressed. Men frequently eroticize aspects of a sexual assault. Because sexual violence has so effectively been ingrained into men's psyche as a sexualized crime, and, in part, because of what pornography does to men in terms of eroticizing inequality (see Dines, Jenson, & Russo, 1998, for a further discussion), men often focus on the sexual before, beyond, or in addition to the assault.

Addressing the eroticization that male significant others often experience not only makes men aware of this part of their response, but also provides another opportunity to confront the sexualizing of violence and inequality. The eroticization of sexual violence is a complicated issue and is often rife with other emotions and responses, not the least of which are defensiveness and denial. It does not take much exploration, however, to identify the ways that sexual violence is eroticized. When talking about this with men, it is important to approach it from a non-judgmental perspective.

Preparing for the Questions

When educating men about being a significant other of someone who is victimized, educators must be prepared for a series of likely questions. This is more complicated than it sounds, for with each question asked, there are also likely to be underlying issues that need to be brought to light. For example, at a program for fraternities at Whittington College in Washington, one man asked incredulously, "You mean I'm just supposed to sit there and not do anything?!?"

This question derives from at least two underlying issues: the need to take control and actively respond (to protect) when someone a man knows has been hurt, and the need to express anger through physical action. When answering this kind of question, an educator must answer both questions simultaneously. First, educators need to answer the question asked. An appropriate response might be

> *Yes, I mean you are supposed to sit there and be supportive as your friend or loved one defines being supportive.*

Second, an educator needs to address the underlying feelings exposed by the question, as done in the following response:

> *Like most men, having a loved one sexually attacked is an outrage. You should be angry. It is good that you are angry. But you need to be able to express your anger in a way that doesn't divert your loved one's attention from her own healing. If you were to "go after the guy," your loved one would likely be worried about you rather than focused on her needs.*

In this way, men are better prepared to respond to their loved ones. In addition, by engaging both questions directly, educators effectively connect more strongly not only with the person who asked the question, but with the entire audience.

Addressing Men's Reactions to Delayed Disclosures

Although this section focuses on the issues of male significant others in the context of an immediate disclosure (in other words, the assault(s) has happened fairly recently), the issues are not terribly different for disclosures of incidents in the past. There are many reasons that women or men who have been victimized may wait to tell their male loved ones that they were assaulted. For male significant others, however, their reactions to learning of the victimization will likely be very similar. For them, it is still a crisis and an outrage. Their loved one may well have worked through a lot of their crisis issues by the time they disclose, but for male significant others, finding out is still hurtful. The one main difference may have to do with men feeling some sense of anger or frustration at not having been told sooner about the assault(s).

EFFECTIVE STRATEGY

Men's focus needs to continue to be on how to best support their loved one.

When educating men about being a significant other, educators can remind them that people share their stories of being traumatized and harmed at their own pace. The person who was victimized knows when it is best to tell of their experience(s) and how it is best to share these. They should not be rushed in any way, and any need that men have to "find out what happened," or "learn all the details" is the need of the men, not the need of the person who was victimized. While it is understandable that men are disappointed, frustrated, and perhaps even angry that they were not told immediately, men's focus needs to continue to be on how to best support their loved one. Whatever feelings they have need to be attended to but not necessarily by their loved one.

In short, when working with male significant others, it is important to talk with them about the need for them to get support for their experience of having a loved one assaulted so that they can better be available and able to support their loved one.

DOING YOUR WORK: *Thinking About Your Reactions*

Think about someone that you care very much for—a family member, a best friend, or a partner. Now consider that they have been hurt in some kind of devastating way. You find out about how your loved one has been hurt.

What is your first reaction?

What do you want to do?

What do you want for your loved one?

What do you think your loved one wants from you? How would you find out?

What do you need in order to be the best support person you can be?

SAMPLE OUTLINE: *Reactions to Significant Others' Experiences*

(Italics indicate words the presenter says.)

I. Beginning Activity

Most men, at some point in their lives, will come to realize that they know or love someone who has been raped or sexually assaulted in some way. For most men, this will be a crisis.

Exercise—Act Like a Man

II. Expected Responses to Rape

Given what men have learned about what it means to "be a man," how is a "man" (referring back to the description within the box) supposed to respond when someone they know and love has been raped?

(Allow time for answers.)

A "man" is supposed to protect, take charge, "fix" the situation (i.e., get her to the hospital, find and beat up the perpetrator, get the law enforcement to respond, and so on). But these reactions, as natural as they are for most men, are not what women or men who are raped need or deserve.

These reactions will likely only divert her attention away from her own healing in worrying about what her male friend will do.

III. Supportive Responses to Rape

So how can a man respond?

Describe ways that men can respond in ways that are supportive, encouraging, and caring.

IV. Men's Reactions...

Men who love someone also have feelings connected to having a friend or loved one raped. Some common reactions include

Anger

At the perpetrator

At the situation

At the person who was victimized

Fear

Sadness

Shock

Confusion

Concern

And more...

Men who have a loved one who's been raped have the right to their feelings as well. The challenge becomes how men can take responsibility for their own feelings without getting in the way of their loved one's feelings or healing process.

V. What Men Can Do

VI. Resources

Developing Male Allies

"As members of the human race, we have an obligation to work to expand human rights for everyone."

Rus Ervin Funk

Educating with the goal of motivating men to be allies is, for many educators and activists, *the main point* of educating men. For the entire history of this movement, every step forward is the result of women's efforts: developing local centers and resources for people who have been victimized, creating hotlines, writing new laws and working to get those laws passed, organizing marches and pickets, training professionals, creating an entirely new arena for professional development, organizing communities, and so on. Rarely have men been integrally involved in the efforts to respond to these issues. It is time for men to become part of the solution.

The Two-Level Call to Action

Becoming part of the solution requires that men take action, *personal* action. As discussed earlier, men's violence takes place in a sexist environment. To end sexist violence, men need to work to end sexism. That's social change work. Just as men are active in other social change/social justice issues, they should be active in this movement. Part of educating men is to define sexism and violence as social issues that require and are responsive to social change efforts. As social justice issues, sexism and violence are issues for which men have an obligation to help eradicate.

Just as it is true with other forms of social justice, becoming an ally with women requires that men work on two levels simultaneously:

- The personal level to challenge their own sexism and abusiveness
- The collective or political level to change the institutional expressions of sexism and abuse that allow and encourage individual men to act in sexist or abusive ways

"Women have a right to walk down a street and not be accosted, to sleep in their own beds and be safe, to live in their own homes and not be beaten, to walk into convenience stores and not see images of themselves displayed as men would like to see them, to spend a day at work or in school and not be harassed."

Men should be involved in working to end men's sexist violence as a social justice issue because men are part of the human community. As members of any community, each person has a responsibility to the other members of the community. Women have a right to walk down a street and not be accosted, to sleep in their own beds and be safe, to live in their own homes and not be beaten, to walk into convenience stores and not see images of themselves displayed as men would like to see them, and to spend a day at work or in school and not be harassed. These are rights—rights that men have taken from women. Men have an obligation to work alongside women so that women can experience and celebrate these rights.

Educating men to become more mobilized involves a combination of assisting men to understand why it is better for men if women are free from the threats of sexism and violence, and to understand the moral or ethical issues relative to men's violence and women's human rights. Thus, working to end men's violence is understood as both in men's self-interest, as well as a moral obligation. Educating men about both of these increases the likelihood of men taking action.

The Benefits for Men of Working to End Sexism and Violence

The benefits gained from ending sexism and violence are many. This section discusses three.

- Freedom from the threat of a significant other experiencing sexist violence
- Freedom from worrying about friends and loved ones perpetrating the violence
- Freedom from women fearing men

Working to end sexism and violence benefits men because the women who are harmed are the same women men know and love. If, roughly speaking, one out of two women is victimized by some form of gender-based violence, most men know and love a woman who has been victimized. Reducing the incidence of sexist violence means that women are less likely to be harmed, which in turn means that men are less likely to know and love women who have been harmed. It personally benefits men to have the women in their lives at less risk. Morally, all women should experience the same reduced risk.

If women and men are most likely to be victimized by the men they know, and men know and love women and men who are victimized, then it is likely that men also know men who perpetrate sexist violence. There are no reliable guesstimates as to the number of men who perpetrate sexist violence, but it seems safe to assume that a large portion, if not most, of men perpetrate some forms of sexist violence. As painful as it is to consider that the women or men in men's lives may be victimized, it is just as painful to consider the *men* in men's lives who are *causing* this harm and perpetrating these forms of violence.

DOING YOUR WORK: ***Considering the Harm Caused by Sexist Violence***

Take a moment and think about three men that you know, love, and respect. Consider that one of them may have perpetrated rape, or domestic violence, or harassment, or used a prostituted woman or man. Consider the harm that these behaviors cause, and think (and feel) about that man that you love and respect causing that kind of harm.

What is your initial reaction?

How does your view of this person change?

(continued)

(continued)

How does the knowledge that this person perpetrated an act of violence impact your feelings for him?

What would you say to him if you could?

For most people, this exercise causes a great deal of discomfort, perhaps even pain. Some men know all too well the pain that results from knowing a man who has perpetrated sexist violence. When men end sexism and violence, they are less likely to have to face the thought and the reality of their fathers, brothers, nephews, best friends, uncles, or sons perpetrating these forms of violence or abuse.

As a result of sexist violence, women must, at some level, fear men, or at least be wary when men are around. Since women cannot tell the difference between "those men" who would never do such a thing and "these men" who might, they must, to some degree, be wary of all men in order to be safe. This wariness and fear probably does not rule their lives, and most women have become so accustomed to the fear and wariness that they themselves are unconscious of it. Men, however, experience women's fear.

It is not at all uncommon for men to experience times when women are afraid of them. A man walking down a street towards a lone woman (especially at night), standing in an elevator to have the doors open to a lone woman, or walking in a largely deserted parking garage is aware on some level of that woman being afraid. Even if only aware peripherally, men tend to notice women's fear and to interpret women's fear as the woman being afraid of them. Though they have done nothing overt to warrant women's fear, most men know the experience of seeing a woman cross the street, lock her doors, not get on an elevator, and so on in response to their presence.

These experiences, of course, are magnified for men of color and men from poor or working class backgrounds. Although these experiences are discussed in more detail later, the convergence of racism, classism, and sexism with gender-based violence reinforces the myth that men of color or poor men pose a greater threat to women than European American men or men from middle or owning/upper class backgrounds. Men of color and poor or working class men often have even more experiences like these than do European American and wealthier men. Regardless of the differences in the frequency or severity, all men experience women's fear of them to some degree. By working to stop sexism and violence, men work to create a world where women do not have to fear them.

There are dozens of additional reasons that it benefits men to work to end sexist violence. In addition, it is important for men to reflect on the ways that they individually and specifically benefit from working to end sexist violence. When educating men to be allies with women, it is helpful to address these benefits and work to encourage men to identify the ways that they will benefit.

DOING YOUR WORK: ***Imagining a World Free of Violence***

Imagine, for a moment, what it would be like to live in a world free from sexist violence—a world in which there is no rape, domestic violence, harassment, stalking, pornography, or prostitution.

How would your life be different?

How would it be improved?

How would men's relationships with women in general be different?

How would men's relationships with specific women (consider the women closest to you, one at a time) be different?

The Morality of Working to End Sexism and Violence

In addition to the benefits for men of being involved in working to stop sexist violence, men's involvement is also the morally right thing to do. Sexism and violence are, at the core, issues of human rights. Just as men are involved in other human rights issues, they should be involved in working to address sexism and violence.

The rationale is the same. Men are involved in human rights issues to some degree because of self-interest, but also because they feel compelled to be involved, because they define whatever the issue is in a way that, morally, they can't *not* be involved. People are involved in Amnesty International, or Human Rights Watch, or are against the death penalty, or for animal rights, or for any number of other causes because of a sense of ethical responsibility.

Sexism and violence and the impact of sexist violence on women are no different. Men have an ethical responsibility to women, to other men, and to themselves to work to end sexism and violence.

STRIKING A BALANCE

It is in this area of educating men that another key balance must be struck. One goal is educating men to take action against sexism and violence by taking these actions more personally, to take a personal stake in making the world a better and more just place. However, men who take acts of sexism and violence too personally may descend into self-blame or self-pity and become inhibited from taking action. Men have a responsibility to address sexism and violence, but they are not responsible for all sexism and violence.

From Bystander to Ally

One of the clearest ways for men to act as allies for women is to change the role of bystander. A *bystander* is someone who stands by while sexism or violence occur. (The notion of bystander also applies in other areas of social justice.) An example is when a man in a locker room is talking about the woman he dated the night before in derogatory ways, and the men around him silently listen. The men standing around as he talks about his date and the woman are bystanders. Bystanders are those men in a bar who are silent when one man harasses a waitress or who listen to other men tell rape jokes.

The role of bystander is a powerful one and creates a unique opportunity for men to take action as allies for women. By remaining silent when acts of sexism occur, men offer their tacit consent and support for these attitudes and the behaviors that follow. The person who is acting in sexist ways "reads" the silence of other men as encouragement to continue, and in some cases, to escalate.

By speaking out in these situations, men provide a powerful challenge to men's sexism and abuse. This is true not only because they do not remain silent in the face of sexism, but also because it is *men* challenging other men. Furthermore, it is men challenging other men in a setting that has traditionally been a place where men have felt comfortable in talking in sexist or abusive ways about women. The dynamic of a man challenging other men about the derogatory ways they talk about or act towards women raises men's awareness of their behavior and is often a more meaningful challenge because of men's relationships with other men.

EFFECTIVE STRATEGY

Define the term *bystander* and the fear associated with taking a stand.

Educating men about acting as an ally involves defining *bystander*, followed by discussions designed to encourage men to act. This part of the discussion includes exploring the difficulty of acting as allies—for example, fear of being ostracized, not wanting to seem "uncool" or "nerdy," not knowing what to say or how to say it, and so on. When men are encouraged to label and list the barriers to their acting as allies, educators can turn the discussion towards overcoming these barriers.

Women do not need men to speak up for them when women are around. They are perfectly capable of speaking up for themselves. It is much more powerful, however, when men speak up for women when women are not in the room. Some men are made uncomfortable by the sexism and abusive language or actions of another man in their vicinity. A man acting as an ally by speaking up to say that sexist language offends him or that he doesn't appreciate those actions challenges other men to consider the way they talk about and treat women. A woman challenging men's language or behavior is not experienced by most men in the same way as when other men challenge their behavior. Men tend to put more weight behind the opinions of other men than they do the opinions of women.

Men have many beliefs about what it means to "fit in" and the dangers that they face if they choose to act in ways that do not fit in. As Michael Kimmel (1996) and others have described, being a man is in part performance—one that men often put on with other men. Men define themselves as men based in part on how other men see and relate to them. So men often, perhaps constantly, compare themselves to other men to see the degree to which they "measure up." Acting as allies for women runs directly counter to this performance that men often believe that they have to play in order to be accepted by other men.

Part of men's performance includes disrespecting women, or so it seems. Watching preadolescent boys is instructive in this regard. Part of the way that boys bond with each other is by disrespecting girls. This can be most easily seen in group settings and tends to escalate as the boys continue to interact. If a boy acts too "girlish," is too "friendly" with girls, or defends girls from the ways that other boys are talking about them, these boys often become targets and are subject to ridicule and harassment that sometimes borders on abuse.

These dynamics continue into adolescence and adulthood. When educating men about moving from bystander to ally, it is important to keep these dynamics in mind. It can be threatening for men to consider acting in ways that are counter to these kinds of experiences. Encouraging men to act as allies may feel like encouraging them to act in ways that will result in being ridiculed, harassed, or abused, just as they were or they witnessed when they were boys. Educating men about acting as allies for women, then, requires that educators appreciate the dilemma that they are asking men to face.

EFFECTIVE STRATEGY

Breaking the silence about sexism provides opportunities for other men to speak out about their discomfort.

Men are not alone when they feel uncomfortable about sexist or abusive comments made in their presence. Many men feel this discomfort. These men are silent largely because of the reasons discussed earlier and because of the mistaken belief that the other men around them agree with the one man making the comments. By breaking the silence, men not only act as allies for women but also provide an opportunity for other men to speak out about their discomfort as well.

Next, it is important to talk with men about *how* to act as allies. Being an ally is, after all, far easier said than done. Educators should encourage men to speak for themselves, not for women. For example, rather than saying, "that's offensive to women" encourage them to say "I find that offensive because...." Men cannot (and should not) speak for women, and as soon as one man tries, another man will claim that he speaks for women, too.

Regardless of how women may or may not feel, the truth is that the man in the situation is made uncomfortable about a comment or behavior. Encourage men to challenge other men by speaking clearly and gently. It does not help to grab another man by the collar, jam him up against a wall, and yell in his face that he could be talking about a sister or daughter. That will likely only escalate things. It is more likely to be effective if men clearly state that, "I don't agree." Obviously, the nature of the relationship and the context of the situation affect how direct and confrontational a person can be. Asking a man to repeat his remark is often a rather easy and nondirect tactic that can get men to notice what they're saying. Humor can also effectively challenge men's sexist words or actions.

EFFECTIVE STRATEGY

Assure men that the awkwardness in confronting sexism will dissipate as they find their own style.

Finally, educators need to remind men that they will likely feel very awkward and artificial the first few times they challenge other men. There may be times when it won't work. The important thing to remind men is that it is crucial that they begin, and that by continuing to challenge other men, they will develop their own style and their own skills in being allies for women. And they will like themselves better for trying.

ACCEPTING MEN WHERE THEY ARE

Educating men to be allies involves some different perspectives and emphasizes distinct points. Men are likely to have a wide range of responses and varying levels of commitment. The theme of "accepting men where they are" applies here just as it does when educating men for other reasons, perhaps even more so. While it is certainly one responsibility of educators to motivate men to increase their efforts as allies, educators also have the duty to accept the level of motivation that men may have. This balance of accepting men from where they are and challenging them to do more is difficult to maintain, but it is crucial. Men have different interests in terms of how they want to act as an ally, as well as varying levels of energy to apply to the efforts to end sexism and violence.

DOING YOUR WORK: ***Thinking About How You React to Sexism***

Consider a time when you have been among a group of friends. You are hanging out, having a good time—laughing, joking, and enjoying each other's company. One of your friends makes a comment that he clearly thinks is funny, but which you find discomforting. The comment is racist or homophobic, or in some way offends you.

How do you react?

What would it take for you to challenge your friend?

What do you fear would happen?

What do you hope would happen?

What do you expect would be the most likely response?

If you chose to challenge your friend, how would you do it?

SAMPLE OUTLINE: ***Moving from Bystander to Ally***

I. Assumptions of Working with Men

II. Impact of Those Assumptions on Working with Men

III. Defining an Ally

Comes from social justice work (anti-racism, anti-homophobia, work against Semitism, and so on)

IV. What Men Have Done/Can Do

V. On Accountability

CHAPTER 3

Developing Programs for Men

In many ways, providing educational programs to women makes perfect sense. After all, women make up the vast majority of those who are victimized by sexist violence, and women have historically provided the primary force behind any and all efforts to combat sexism and violence. Educating women about the ways they can reduce their risks has been a crucial focus of the movement. As a result of all these forces, most educational programs are made up of women talking with women...with men in the room. By not educating men, educators and activists run the risk of having men continue to act in ways that, at the very least, disempower women, and at most, harm women.

Although it is crucial to educate, inform, and empower women about sexism and violence, by focusing *all* education efforts on women, with no real attention or planning specifically with men, the message that is reinforced is that sexism and violence are women's responsibility and women's issues. Yet men commit almost all sexism and violence.

In order to stop sexist violence, both women and men need to be educated, although *what* women and men are educated about and *how* they are educated are different. Educational efforts for women should continue to focus on women's empowerment—both individually and collectively. Educational efforts for men should focus on ways that men can support women's empowerment, as well as the ways that men can take the initiative to end sexism and the violence and abuse that results.

Selecting the Format: Mixed-Gender or Sex-Specific?

There is some debate as to *how* to most effectively educate men. One main area of discussion regards educating men in a mixed-gender or sex-specific format. The research is pretty clear that men benefit more than women from mixed-gender programs, and that mixed-gender programs are less effective for women than single-sex presentations. In other words, making a presentation to an all-women's group appears to be more effective for the women than doing that same presentation to a mixed-gender group. When considering mixed-gender or sex-specific programming, one must consider the primary target audience: women/girls or men/boys. For the purposes of this manual, it is assumed that a primary target of education is men, but educators and activists who have responsibilities to educate both women and men must be aware of the impact of different forms of educational programming on the various audiences.

Research on the effectiveness of mixed-gender versus sex-specific programs for men focuses almost exclusively on educating men about sexual violence. There is limited data on educating men about domestic violence or dating abuse, and almost none on educating men about stalking, harassment, pornography, or prostitution. There is reason to believe, however, that the research on rape and sexual assault is applicable to educating men about all forms of sexist violence.

The short answer to the question of whether to educate men in mixed-gender or sex-specific venues is that it depends on the main goals of the presentation. The research suggests that mixed-gender programs are more effective in increasing men's empathy for women or "victims" of men's violence (see, for example, Lonsway, 1996). If the goal is to encourage men to accept ownership of working to stop sexism and sexist violence, or to move from bystander to ally, then sex-specific venues seem to be more appropriate. If the goals include creating an opportunity for men to listen to women, and/or for women and men to enter a dialogue, then mixed-gender formats seem indicated.

Educating Men in Mixed-Gender Venues

Women and men do not need the same information about sexism and violence. Both experience and research suggest that women and men do not receive the same information in the same way, especially about issues as emotionally charged as these. Therefore, it is important when designing programs for mixed-gender audiences, to explicitly consider male participants. Consider, for example, the goals for the men and develop specific information and exercises that focus on the male participants who will attend the presentation. It may be worthwhile to offer an overview of rape (the dynamics, laws, and impact) to a mixed-gender audience, but if the goal is to ensure that male participants actually receive the information, educational strategies must be designed specifically for men within a mixed-gender context.

There are many legitimate reasons to consider mixed-gender programs that encourage men and women to dialogue. It is exceedingly rare for women and men to have an opportunity to have real conversations about sexism and violence. The process of coming to a better understanding of sexism, gender-based violence, and the connection between them, and then beginning to move towards creating meaningful solutions begins with dialogue. This is not dissimilar from addressing racism and racist violence. There is a need for European Americans and people of color to have dialogue and to listen in depth to each other about what racism and racist violence is, what it looks like, its impact, and how to begin creating meaningful solutions.

Similarly, with the issues of sexism and violence, there is a need for women and men to have a dialogue and listen in depth to each other about these issues and the impact that they have on their lives. It is from a shared understanding that men and women can begin joining forces to create efforts to end sexism and violence.

Within mixed-gender discussions, educators must be mindful of the fact that though both women and men are impacted by sexism and violence, there is a significant difference in the influence of this impact. Women are affected more directly and more profoundly than men. Thus, when conducting mixed-gender programs, it is important to challenge men to listen to women's definitions, their experiences, and the impact on women's lives of sexist violence.

EFFECTIVE STRATEGY

Challenge men to listen to the women when discussing the impact of sexist violence.

Because women are the primary targets of sexism and the victims of sexist violence, men should listen to the experiences of women and how sexism and violence affects them before reflecting on how sexism impacts men. "The Fishbowl" exercise in Appendix B is a particularly powerful exercise to begin engaging mixed-gender groups in dialogue.

EFFECTIVE STRATEGY

Anonymously write questions about sexism and violence to the other sex.

Another good way to encourage dialogue is to ask participants to write down questions for the other sex (in other words, men write down questions for the women or vice versa) relative to the topic on note cards and *not* sign them. Facilitators then read the questions and have the other sex respond (the women respond to the anonymous questions asked by the men in the room and vice versa). Educators can then facilitate a conversation about each question.

For a variety of reasons, whenever making a presentation in front of a mixed-gender group, it is most effective to have mixed-gender facilitators.

Educating Men in Male-Only Venues

Just as there are legitimate reasons to educate men in mixed-gender settings, there are also many reasons to educate men without women present. Just as there is evidence that education in mixed-gender groups has some benefits, there is also evidence that male-only educational programs have some benefits. Whereas men tend to show more empathy to women in general, and to women who have been victimized specifically, when they are in mixed-gender presentations, male-only presentations tend to show an improvement in men's understanding of the dynamics of sexist violence and of what men can do to accept responsibility for stopping it (see Berkowitz, 2001b).

Educating men in male-only settings provides a venue in which assumptions, myths, and beliefs that would likely go unstated in mixed-gender settings can be exposed and challenged. Men tend to censor themselves when women are in the room (especially when these topics are covered). This self-censoring can mean that men

- Do not say the things they want to say
- Say things to perform for the other men or women present
- Say things to get a reaction from the women or the presenter

Regardless of the specific dynamics, the end result is that men tend not to speak as openly or honestly when women are in the room and, as a result, their attitudes or opinions that they believe will be unpopular will likely go unstated, and therefore, unchallenged. Talking with men in male-only settings provides an opportunity to talk with men without this self-censoring dynamic.

Male-only settings provide a valuable opportunity for men to explore their real attitudes and beliefs about sexism and violence. Without women in the room, men are often more likely to reach a deeper level of honesty about what they think and feel. This occurs both consciously and unconsciously (and can happen even with a female facilitator). Men often find themselves saying things they didn't realize they believe and they decide to share at a deeper level. Because so much of sexist and abusive behaviors stem from attitudes and beliefs, creating an environment where men can examine their own attitudes about women in general, masculinity, power, and abuse is an incredible educational opportunity.

Male-only settings can also provide a relatively safe forum in which men may be more likely to discuss their sexist or abusive histories. It is common for women to disclose previously unreported experiences of abuse or violence after a presentation. It is not uncommon for men to realize that some of their behaviors have been abusive as a result of a good presentation or program. Designing a program for men only increases the chances for men to talk about these histories and to explore ways that they can accept responsibility for their abusiveness as well as to work to ensure that they don't abuse in the future.*

Talking with men in male-only settings can also provide an opportunity to discuss the particular issues related to men's involvement in ending sexism and violence. In any situation in which allies act in support, special issues arise. These issues come from the dual role of trying to act in support of women while continuing to benefit from the system of privilege that puts women in harm's way. It is not as if men stop being male and thus stop benefiting from male privilege just because they start being active in the effort to end sexism and violence. Educating men in male-only settings affords an opportunity to have this conversation in a way that is unlikely with women in the room.

**I want to be careful not to overstate this possibility. It is still very uncommon for men to disclose their abusiveness. However, it is not unheard of, and as educators continue to develop their skills and expertise—the collective abilities—to make room for men to identify and acknowledge the ways that they have acted abusively, the likelihood of men disclosing more will only increase.*

In many ways, men working against sexist violence are in a unique position. Men often find themselves becoming closer to women or working in mostly or all-women environments, and yet they are not women; therefore, they have a different experience. At the same time, men who become more aware of sexism often find that they no longer relate with other men in the same way as before. In effect, many men experience an "insider-outsider" position both with women and with other men. Educating men in a male-only space provides an important venue for the initial exploration of these issues.

EFFECTIVE STRATEGY

Male educators in male-only settings need to stay in communication with local feminists about the content of the discussions.

When designing male-only educational programs, educators, in particular male educators, need to develop clear and open relationships with the local feminist leadership about what is being discussed and how the discussion will be handled. It is very easy for men who are talking with men to get swayed by the arguments that men use to blame women, often in very subtle ways, for the violence and abuse that men perpetrate. In order to make sure that male educators avoid this pattern, clear lines of communication and an open process must be put in place. In effect, male educators need to ensure that they create relationships with their local feminist leadership that allow for some kind of supervision and insight as to what men are talking about when women aren't in the room. It is crucial that there be some means by which women are able to know the kinds of discussion that men are leading other men through. This will be covered in more detail in the section entitled "Accountability" in Chapter 12.

In short, there are benefits to both mixed-gender and male-only educational programs. Deciding which presentation format to use depends on the situations and the goals. Ideally, a mix of both should be offered to men. This gives them a chance to listen to women discuss the impact of sexism and violence, and thus, to develop empathy, while also providing men an opportunity to discuss with other men what their response-abilities are in working to support women and to end sexism and violence.

Describing Men's Reactions to the Format

Men react in a variety of ways to discussions about sexism and violence. While it is impossible to be fully prepared for men's reactions, educators should be aware of some general practices in responding to these reactions that will make the presentation more effective, more meaningful for male audiences, and less stressful for presenters.

Men's reactions differ to some degree depending on the type of sexist violence addressed and the setting in which the presentation is offered (mixed-gender versus male-only). For example, men's reactions to discussions of rape and domestic violence tend to be somewhat different from their reactions to discussions of pornography and prostitution. The information that follows is a very broad overview that addresses a variety of issues and is not meant to address the specifics of every scenario.

In general, men tend to react to discussions about sexism and violence with some combination of the following:

- Blame
- Defensiveness
- Curiosity
- Empathy
- Sensitivity
- Guilt
- Denial

Men have precious few opportunities to talk about sexism and violence in any meaningful way and are often deeply curious about the issues and how women or men are impacted. Traditionally, men are kept out of the conversations about these topics and do not feel involved even if, or when, they are part of the conversation. The focus tends to be on women. Men are sensitive to the fact that women and some men are victimized, and many already have personal experiences with a loved one who has been harmed. Due in part to male posturing, they may be hesitant or unwilling to express these reactions, but educators need to understand that these reactions are part of what men bring to educational programs. Simultaneous with men's expressions of defensiveness and doubt is curiosity. A good educator can use men's defensiveness as a means to address men's curiosity.

In part, because of the way that sexism and violence have been framed, and in part because men instinctively know but don't want to acknowledge that gender-based violence is, in fact, *men's* violence, men tend to respond to any attempt to raise such issues by feeling blamed. It is important to be aware of this dynamic but remain consistent with the content. Men can handle feeling blamed. Just because they feel blamed doesn't mean that an educator is blaming them.

EFFECTIVE STRATEGY

Rather than argue with defensive men, ask them to identify the information with which they agree.

Related to blaming is defensiveness. Men's defensiveness can perhaps be better understood as, in part, a reaction to feeling blamed. This is a common reaction that many people have when feeling blamed for something. When responding to men's defensiveness, it is important to understand from where it originates. As often as not, men's defensiveness will be framed as questions that raise doubts about the validity of the points an educator makes. For example, men often question the statistics that educators use to describe the incidence of sexist violence. Rather than argue about who might be more right, it is more useful to ask them to identify the statistics they are comfortable with and then use that information as the basis for the conversation. Regardless of whether the statistic is one in three or one in ten women who are battered, it is still far too many. Something still must be done about it, and the men in the room are in a position to do something about it.

As blamed and defensive as men may be, they are also often legitimately curious and empathic. Educators are encouraged to remind themselves of the assumptions offered at the beginning of this manual. These assumptions include the belief that most men *do* want to better understand the issues. Men *do* want to be able to respond supportively when a friend is victimized. The myth that women lie about rape is rampant, and yet men *do* want to understand why some women may lie. They really *do* want to understand why some women stay with or return to the men who batter them. Although their curiosity may be shrouded in bravado and posturing (particularly with adolescent men), the educator must speak to the curiosity rather than react to the bravado. This can be challenging, but it is an important, even crucial skill.

CASE STUDY

During a presentation on sexual harassment to teenage boys, one of the young men, Michael, shouted out, "You know the chicks are really into it. If they aren't into it, they're just uptight."

Rather than reacting to any of the attitudes imbedded in this very loaded statement, the educator thought of the responses he could have by speaking directly to this young man, engaging him directly in conversation with this: "So what kinds of things do you say to women? And how do you know that they like it?"

However, the educator chose a more confrontational response, which ran the risk of shutting down both Michael and other men in the room but, fortunately, was effective this time: "This behavior in this setting is exactly like a lot of harassment. Michael is not making his statement to really engage in a conversation with me. He's making this statement in order to get a reaction out of the rest of you. In harassing situations, this can be one way of telling whether the person engaging in the behavior is doing whatever he's doing in order to engage the other person, or he is doing it to get a reaction of the other guys in the room."

Engaging Michael in the conversation this way provided a means for Michael (and the other men in the room) to directly and more effectively confront misinformation.

Men's Reactions to Female Educators

Men have an interesting and somewhat paradoxical relationship to female educators. Most of men's formal educators, throughout their school experience, have been women, and yet men have been taught not to take women seriously. As a result, men (particularly high school-aged men and men in some typically all-male environments such as police, judges, the military, fraternities, and so on) tend to react with a combination of listening attentively while resisting women's authority and expertise.

EFFECTIVE STRATEGY

Female educators should act as if they expect to be treated with respect rather than directly confront disrespectful behaviors.

Men are also taught to dismiss women's authority and often have thoughts such as, "You're a woman and of course you think that." Female educators need to claim the respect that they deserve just as any expert would expect. It is generally unproductive to directly confront the behaviors that are disrespectful; rather, female educators need to stay grounded in the expectation to be respected. As long as female educators act as if they expect to be treated with respect and continue to engage with questions and comments about the topic, there is no reason why female educators cannot be as effective as male educators when talking with men.

Men may also feel more strongly blamed by a female educator. There is often a presumption that women are blaming men and that women who educate about sexism and violence are feminists who, in turn, are defined as man-hating or man-blaming. Because of this, men may claim that women are blaming them when women are doing nothing of the sort. This is one key reason why educators (especially female educators) need to do the work on themselves, so that when they do get accused of being "man haters" or "blaming men," they are less likely to get hooked by this manipulation and can stay focused on the message. This dynamic is best understood as an attempt by men to dismiss and undermine a woman educator's expertise and position, combined with a sincere fear that the male participants may, in fact, have perpetrated something very much like what the educator is describing.

Men's Reactions to Male Educators

Men also often have mixed reactions to male educators. On the one hand, men often assume that male educators will be more understanding about the "men's side" than female educators. On the other hand, men may be suspicious of male educators and just as defensive and dismissive about the topic as they are with female educators. Some men see men who are sensitive, knowledgeable, and passionate about sexism and sexist violence as traitors and, therefore, a threat to masculinity and a challenge to them. By dismissing male educators, the men dismiss the challenge to their understanding of masculinity.

In general, however, men tend to be more open and appear more comfortable with male educators. A setting with mixed-gender educators is different from one with male-only educators. When it is "just the guys," the conversation is often quite different from one if a woman is present. This suggests that men are somewhat self-censoring when women are in the room in a way that they are not when only men are there. As a result, male educators can probably expect to get a more thorough depiction of the ways that men subscribe to the myths of male violence than when women are present. Discussions that occur when it is "just the guys" provide a unique and powerful opportunity for male educators to challenge deeply held beliefs and assumptions that the male participants may have.

Male educators need to stay consistent with the message and not be swayed by the weight of opinion that may be present. Men experience intense pressure to go along with what other men think, or what they *think* other men think. This pressure is often felt by male presenters just as it is by male participants. Male participants may be inhibited from asking some questions or raising points that suggest that they may be becoming sensitized by the presentation. If male participants think that other men in the room will think that they are "wimpy" or otherwise "less male" for agreeing with the perspective of the educator, then they are unlikely to demonstrate any support for what the educator is saying. This is crucial to keep in mind, namely, some portion of being a man is behaving "manly" in front of other men. Being supportive of women and feminism, and/or empathetic to issues of sexism and violence is rarely seen as "manly." This is one of the dynamics that occurs for all educators, but it particularly surfaces for male educators.

EFFECTIVE STRATEGY

To keep from being derailed in an all-male presentation, imagine a woman colleague, who is also a sexist violence survivor, sitting in the back of the room.

Whenever men are in a room with other men, there is some degree of "performance"; men attempt to make sure that they measure up to whatever vision of masculinity is dominant. To counter this dynamic, male educators must use different practices in order to ensure that they stay "on target." For example, it may be helpful to imagine a woman colleague, who is known by the educator to have survived some form of sexist violence, sitting in the back of the room. Visualizing her in the room and listening to the conversation can help male educators stay focused on the important points they want to make, which are the main points that she would want him to make. Thinking "What would she want me to say?" "How would she want me to respond to that question or point?" and "What main points would she want me to focus on?" can help male educators steer clear from inadvertently bonding with the male participants at the expense of getting the key message across. Although male educators may change *how* they say things in an all-male setting, *what* they say must stay consistent. Male educators need to remain consistent and accountable to the message they try to convey and to the women who are harmed.

Men's Reactions to Mixed-Gender Educators

Male-female co-educators provide a powerful opportunity in educating men. By working together in a partnership, mixed-gender educators can provide a model to male participants of interacting respectfully and sharing power and authority. A mixed-gender educating team also provides an opportunity to challenge men's reactions in ways that rarely arise with only a male or a female educator.

It is not uncommon for men, when presented with male and female co-educators, to engage exclusively or primarily with the male educator. Even when clarifying a point that the female educator has made, male audiences will frequently engage the male educator. (This dynamic is also true, although to a lesser extent, with female audiences.) This happens, in part, because men are taught to listen to men as the authority more than to women, and, in part, because it is still somewhat of an anomaly for men to present about the issues of sexist violence.

EFFECTIVE STRATEGY

Male educators support their female counterpart by deferring to her when questions are posed.

In these situations, the male educator has the responsibility to gently but firmly point out this dynamic and the underlying sexism that it represents. Male educators need to demonstrate their support for female's authority by deferring to the female educator when questions are posed by the audience, even if they are posed to the men directly. For example, when making a presentation with a female colleague, it is helpful for the male co-educator to physically step back while she is speaking to ensure that the female speaker is "front and center." Even this subtle action sends a message about who is control of the dynamics and to whom the men should listen.

CASE STUDY

In a mixed-gender, educator-led workshop on sexist violence, the men in the room consistently ask the male educator, Tom, questions. Tom thought about visibly turning to JoAnne, the co-educator and asking her thoughts. However, the behavior was so obvious that Tom directly (though gently) challenged the behavior by saying, "I've noticed that you all ask me all the questions even when you ask a question about something that JoAnne has stated. Why is that?" Tom wasn't trying to "nail them" for their behavior, but rather to point out the subtle expressions of sexism and encourage the men to notice what they were doing, probably without even being aware of it.

Men's Reactions in All-Male Settings

As mentioned previously, it is not uncommon for men in all-male settings to "act up" a bit. (This is especially true of high school- and college-aged men). This acting up can include laughter, talking with each other while the educator is talking, moving exaggeratingly slowly when asked to move to participate in an activity, making smart remarks, and so on. Educators need to be ready for and willing to allow for some level of "organized chaos" when educating a group of men. These are highly-charged topics and ones that men have had very few opportunities to discuss. Because of the discomfort, it is likely that men's anxiety will be quite high. Men acting up during a presentation does not necessarily mean that they disrespect the educator or are not taking the topic seriously; it is likely just a way that they peel away their layers of anxiety.

One of the main jobs of educators is to create an opportunity for men to have a real and honest conversation about sexism and violence. This means creating a space where men can get in touch with the feelings of anger, outrage, fear, anxiety, sadness, and so on that frequently arise around topics and experiences of sexism and violence. Understanding men's acting up as ways that men are expressing these feelings is important for educators, as long as it does not interfere with the goals and process of the education.

> **EFFECTIVE STRATEGY**
>
> To minimize chaos when working with a rowdy group, be very careful in selecting the types and number of exercises or group discussions.

Educators need to know their own comfort level with varying degrees of chaos. Some educators are able to continue to provide content with a higher degree of chaos than others. In addition, with experience, educators tend to become better able to proceed through the content despite increasing degrees of chaos. Educators need to understand their comfort levels with chaos and then set up the structures that limit the chaos to allow for the content to be offered. For example, limiting the number of exercises or group discussions can minimize the chaos. Regardless of the level of chaos, educators must maintain some sense that they are in control of the conversation and that they are the expert.

These chaotic reactions, though normal, are often also influenced by men's common practice of competing with each other. Men often feed off each other in terms of acting up, and, in these kinds of situations, their acting up may escalate. Men may feel compelled to act in response to other men's acting up, or they may strive to demonstrate the degrees to which they may better understand or be more knowledgeable than the other men in the room. These kinds of competition amongst male participants can hinder their participation as well as their getting anything meaningful out of the discussion.

It is important for educators to be attuned to signs of competition and to minimize it by reminding the men who are participating that this is not about anyone being more sensitive or aware than the others. Rather, the conversation is focused on how each man can become more respectful of the women in their lives and be more supportive when a loved one they know has been harmed.

Finally, and as a last resort, educators have the right, the authority, and indeed the responsibility to "call out" men who are intent on disrupting the program. Educators should use this option with some hesitation, but when an educator becomes convinced that a male participant is interested only in undermining the educational experience, then the educator certainly can and should describe what is going on, explain to the man in question and the rest of the participants, and move forward—silencing him in the process.

CASE STUDY

Mark continually interrupted the presentation with questions. On the surface, they seemed to be legitimate, but K.J., the educator, began to sense that Mark was in competition with another fellow in the room. Turning to Mark, K.J. said, "I have answered your questions several times, and it appears to me that you're asking questions not because you are really interested but because of it's your intent to dismiss me and/or the presentation. The other people taking part in this conversation *are* interested in participating, so I am not going to call on you anymore and will respond to other participants who have questions or comments."

Men's Reactions in Mixed-Gender Settings

In mixed-gender settings, the two main dynamics to be aware of are men's tendencies to self-censor and heterosexual men's attempts to get the attention of the women in the room. Whenever women are present, there is a tendency for heterosexual men to watch what they do or to censor their remarks so as not to look bad, "say the wrong thing," or incur women's anger. In these kinds of situations, educators can use what they have heard, or male educators can use their own experiences or beliefs, as a way to engage the men.

It is not uncommon in a mixed-gender presentation for male participants to say very little or nothing at all. Educators must prepare opportunities through exercises, small-group discussions, videos, pointed questions, role-plays, use of plays or skits, or other ways for men to stay engaged in the discussion. Although it is important for men to listen to what women have to say and to hear what women's experiences of sexism and violence are, this can also be an invitation for men to disengage completely. In order for men to stay present and engaged in the conversation, it is important to find ways to keep them talking.

Flirting is a constant possibility. Heterosexual men may "check out" the women in the room to find one that they are attracted to and will look for ways to engage in the conversation in a way that will draw her attention. There is not necessarily anything wrong with this dynamic, but it can have an impact on the dynamics of the educational program and, therefore, is something for which educators need to be prepared.

CASE STUDY

In a mixed-gender presentation, the men were obviously censoring themselves. The educator needed to directly identify this dynamic and encourage the men to participate. He said, "I've noticed that the men in the room are particularly quiet. I assume that some of the men either feel like they don't have anything to contribute (which I doubt) or they are worried that they're going to be judged if they say what they're really thinking. We are not here to judge anybody! We are all here to learn together, and, as men in the room, you have some things that we can all learn from."

Men's Reactions in Multiracial Settings

As rare as it is for men in general to talk about sexism and violence, it almost never happens that men of color and European American men have the opportunity to sit together and discuss anything of substance. This, coupled with the legacy of how sexist violence has also been used as a weapon of racism, has led to some particular barriers in talking with men in multiracial settings.

EFFECTIVE STRATEGY

European American educators working with multiracial groups should directly address the issue of sexist violence being used as racism.

What typically happens, especially with European American educators, is that men of color silence themselves. A vital role for educators in this situation is to ensure that men of color have a voice and that their voices are heard in the discussion. To do this, it is incumbent on educators, especially European American ones, to point out that the men of color are being silent, and that they have perspectives that are important for everyone to hear. In addition, educators need to take the initiative to identify the ways that sexist violence has been used as a weapon of racism and has been used to maintain, enforce, and sustain white supremacy. (More explicit information about how to best do this is offered in Chapter 9.)

THE MOST EFFECTIVE STRATEGY FOR WORKING WITH MEN

In any situation in which educators are educating men, it is helpful to point out dynamics as they occur, not in a judgmental or "gotcha" way, but in a curious, noticing way. For example, simply noticing and pointing out that more women are engaged in the conversation than men can bring to consciousness this dynamic as it occurs. This act provides permission to all the participants to engage differently; the women to not speak up quite so much and the men to speak up more.

Developing Programs for Specific Groups of Men

Men are not all alike. When developing programs for men, it is important to think about which men one is preparing to educate. Although there are lots of similarities, each group of men has some differences in their relationships to sexism and violence. This section explores the issues of educating men by looking at some demographic categories as well as attitudinal differences amongst men in regards to sexism and violence.

Factors That Impact a Program's Goals with Specific Groups

Educating high school men is different from educating college men which, in turn, is different from educating professional men. There are differences among men based on the following factors:

- Educational background
- Ethnicity
- Class
- Religion/spirituality
- Sexual orientation

The core material or information being presented will likely be similar, but the *specific* information and *how* it is presented will have to change based on the specific audience.

Different groups of men have different relationships to and interactions with sexism, male privilege, and gender-based violence. Although all men do benefit from sexism, not all men benefit in the same kinds of ways. In order to effectively reach men, it is important to design educational programs specifically for the population of men present for the program.

Gender-based violence is aimed not only against the individuals who are victimized, but also at various classes of people. As such, gender-based violence is not only a weapon of sexism, but it is also a weapon of racism and homophobia. Sexism and violence not only harms individual women who are victimized, but also harms women as a class. Similarly, gender-based violence not only harms individual women of color or lesbian or bisexual women, but also harms people of color as a class, and gay men, lesbians, bisexuals, and transgender people as a class. In order to effectively talk with, mobilize, and organize men, the ways that sexism and violence specifically impact men from various groups and populations need to be overtly included as part of the discussion.

EFFECTIVE STRATEGY

With men of color, discuss how sexism and violence have been used to harm women and men of color.

For example, in an attempt to educate and mobilize men of color, it is important to examine and discuss how sexism and violence have been used to harm women *and men* of color. This is a challenging task, because men of color are not *a* group. There are differences and similarities among African American, Latino, Asian, and Native men in terms of how they've been affected by sexism and violence. As such, educators are encouraged to do the research in the communities in which they are educating to become more aware of how these differences are manifest.

Men of color are more likely to be arrested, charged, and convicted of committing crimes than European American men. Similarly, women of color are more likely to be victimized and less likely to receive services or to successfully convict their attacker than European American women. Educators need to develop an analysis and educational practices that incorporates racism and sexism within the context of gender-based violence so that they can articulate how working against sexism and violence is not only working for gender justice but is also working for racial justice as well as justice for other groups of men.

Looking at Differences Amongst Men's Attitudes

In addition to these broad differences, there are additional differences among men in terms of their attitudes and beliefs about sexism and abuse. For example, consider preparing an educational program for a fraternity that is forced to attend because of allegations of sexual assault compared with making a presentation with a group of male members of the National Organization for Women (NOW). While it would be dangerous to assume that all the fraternity men are going to be hostile to the presentation, and that all the male NOW members are going to be welcoming, it does seem safe to assume that, as a group, the NOW group will be more open to a discussion than will the fraternity brothers. Therefore, educators need to consider how much content to prepare and how to present the information differently for these different groups of men. While this example demonstrates two extremes, whenever an educator is preparing a presentation, it is worth getting some background information on the audience to better prepare both the material (what as well as how much) and the exercises for that specific group of men.

When preparing educational programs for a group of men, have some understanding about who that group of men is so that an educational program can be designed specifically for them. Doing so is certainly more work, but it also increases the likelihood of having a successful educational experience.

DOING YOUR WORK: ***Preparing for a Presentation***

Think about a random group of men that you are planning to do a presentation for. You do not know anything about them—all that you know is that you have a group of men who have requested a presentation.

What do you imagine this group of men to look like? What is their age, race/ethnicity, class background, sexual orientation, are they (as a group) "conservative" or "liberal"…

What groups of men would you feel more comfortable talking to?

(continued)

(continued)

What groups of men would you feel less comfortable talking to?

Why?

What do you need to do to make yourself more comfortable with those groups of men you're less comfortable talking to?

Educating Men from Where They Are

It is helpful to think about men and their attitudes about sexism and sexist violence as existing along a continuum. Imagine, if you will, a speedometer. Along the bottom of the speedometer (really a continuum) is men's degree of support for anti-sexism. At each "mile mark" are different attitudes men have. For example, on the far right are men who are engaged and ready to get actively involved; on the far left are men who are overtly hostile to any message about these forms of violence and abuse and a pro-feminist analysis (these may be, for example, men in a group for men who batter, are convicted sex offenders, or men who are pimps or johns). As one proceeds along the speedometer (starting from the left), every "10 miles" represents a group of men who are one degree more supportive of anti-sexism work and activism. Men at the half-way mark are ambivalent. Continuing along the speedometer, men are increasingly supportive of gender equity and gender and sexual justice.

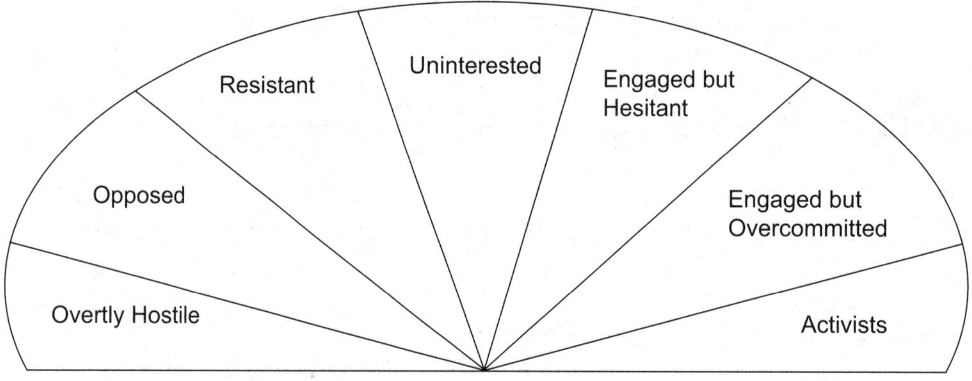

Figure 3.1: The continuum of male attitudes towards sexism and sexist violence

These categories are meant only as descriptive examples to clarify the metaphor of the continuum. The point is to consider that every man and every male audience is at some point along this continuum. Educators should not focus on trying to make all men activists as a result of one one-hour presentation. Rather, one goal of a presentation is to try to move men one step along this continuum.

Educators need to keep in mind where men are when designing educational programs; they should create a design and share the information to reach men where they are. Consider the audience while choosing the specific topics, the information about those topics, the goals, and the process (exercises, discussion format, and so on) for each presentation. Try to make those decisions strategically and in a way that will increase the likelihood of success with each group of men.

CASE STUDY

When designing an educational program on sexual assault to be presented to a group of men in prison for domestic violence, one could safely assume that the men's knowledge about the dynamics and impact of sexual assault is somewhat limited and that the men's attitudes about sexual assault as a weapon of sexism are probably negative. Rather than trying to convince this group of men that sexual assault is a weapon of sexism and ask them how they can work actively (once they are released) to stop sexual assault, it may be more effective to focus solely on the dynamics and definitions of sexual assault, with the goal of increasing their empathy for rape victims.

On the other hand, when planning an educational program to be presented to a group of students at an all-male Catholic high school, an educator could probably safely frame sexual assault as a moral issue and use this frame as a basis to encourage men to not only treat women with greater respect, but also possibly to motivate men to get actively involved in working to stop sexual assault. With this population, focusing too strongly on sexism as a foundation of sexual assault may well turn them off and undermine the effectiveness of the program.

The point of considering the group of men to which an educator is speaking is *not* to over-generalize or lump similar kinds of men into one category. Rather, it is to encourage educators to think about the group of men they are educating and to plan strategically to deliver the *content* to that group of men in a *process* that will help to increase the effectiveness of the educational program.

Each presentation should be designed not only for a specific group of men where they are on the continuum, but the educational program should be designed to move them, at most, one place along the continuum. One presentation will not move men from ambivalence to pro-feminist activists. One presentation, if designed carefully for a specific audience, *might* move a man one step closer.

Determining the Process

Many different strategies and formats can be used when educating men. The appendices at the end of this manual provide samples of the kinds of activities that can be done during a presentation to engage men and emphasize certain points. It is important to consider these three factors when developing a presentation:

- What does the educator hope for as a result of men getting motivated?
- What do the men want to accomplish?
- What is the best way to accomplish those goals?

Educators also need to know some concrete information about the presentation and the participants:

- How much time is available for the presentation?
- How much physical room there is to move around? Can the room be re-arranged if needed?
- What is the age, racial, and developmental range of the participants?
- Is there access to av and/or other visual equipment?

A half-hour presentation with 100 men will be designed very differently from a week-long training with 10 men. But every presentation deserves and requires careful consideration about how to best get across the main points and to achieve the goals for the presentation.

After educators have this basic information, they can begin thinking about which tactics to use to achieve the goals of the presentation. Some educational tactics include

- Mini-lectures (small lectures within the overall presentation)
- Q&A (question and answer)
- Movies/videos
- Panel discussion (bringing in small groups of experts on particular topics)
- Demonstrations (attending public demonstrations organized by other groups, or offering demonstrations of some key points)
- Role-plays
- Personal stories (the educators sharing their own stories, relaying the personal stories of survivors [with their permission], and/or developing ways for the men to share their own personal stories)
- Jokes/humor
- Use of overheads
- Debates (having the men take different positions on a topic so they can debate their positions)
- Skits
- Brainstorming
- Small group discussions

People tend to have an attention span of about 10 minutes. Plan to change the subject slightly approximately each 10 minutes by throwing in an exercise or activity, asking a question, or using some other tactic to take advantage of this natural pattern.

As discussed earlier, the audience will raise some opposition and disagreement to the main points of the presentation. This is okay. It is important to allow men to disagree and to be uncomfortable with the information. One example of a way to introduce the topic with men is the following:

> *This is a terribly uncomfortable topic. Be prepared to feel uncomfortable (angry, sad, frustrated, disgusted, and so on). If we have a conversation about these issues and you do not feel something, then I have not done my job, and you are being dishonest. It is not my job to make you feel uncomfortable, but neither is it my job to make rape (or domestic violence or any of these issues) easier for you to talk about.*

This introduction reinforces the assumption outlined earlier that educators believe that men can handle their own feelings that arise from a presentation. As an educator, one must make room for the men to feel whatever they may feel, so long as it doesn't disrupt the presentation.

Overcoming Barriers

Most educators who work with men express a great deal of apprehension and frustration about attempting to educate men. Educators often report feeling as if the men are not listening, do not take the educators (or the topics) seriously, don't care, blame victims, are antagonistic, or act in other ways that educators interpret as men being hostile. What follows is a brief discussion of the more common barriers to engaging men and some recommendation for how to address the barriers.

Rather than interpret the men's behavior as hostile, it is helpful to understand that these behaviors are expressions of the barriers that men face as they are challenged to address sexism and violence. Defining these behaviors as "barriers" may be a challenge for many educators because doing so may seem to be making excuses for men's behaviors or their choices. Seeing them as barriers, however, makes these behaviors more understandable and provides an opening for engagement. It is very hard to penetrate "hostility," but barriers can be overcome. Perhaps the two biggest barriers are

- Men's struggles with the definitions
- The enormity of the issues

The Barrier of Definitions

The process of educating men suggests this: If what educators are saying about the definitions of sexism and violence and the frequency with which they occur is true, then most men perpetrate some forms of sexism, violence, or abuse.

For good reason, few men are willing to identify their own behavior as acts of violence or abuse, so minimization and denial are common reactions. It is important to understand this minimization and denial, in part, as men trying very hard to not accept these definitions and reports of their frequency in order to maintain images of themselves as good and decent. This dynamic is not all that different from the experience of educators when talking to women. It is quite common for educators to talk with women about sexism and violence, after which women disclose that although they never identified it as abuse before, they now realize that what happened to them was indeed abuse.

It seems likely that some of the men listening to these presentations have internal dialogues that go something like this:

> *If what they are saying is true, then maybe the sex I had last night (or last week or last month…) really wasn't consensual, maybe I raped her.*

This is a difficult realization to face and one that men, understandably, will work very hard to keep from accepting. The easiest way to avoid accepting this is to deny what the educators say. People generally, and men are certainly no exception to this, want to see themselves as good people. It is difficult, if not impossible, for people to see themselves as good people, and acknowledge that they may have raped, or beaten, or otherwise abused someone else. The two main ways to manage this disconnect is to either deny that what one did was abusive or blame the person that was harmed in some way.

EFFECTIVE STRATEGY

Normalize the experience.

To respond to this problem, educators should normalize the experience and acknowledge the difficulty in identifying the ways that someone has hurt someone else. This is one area that male educators *may* be more effective than female educators.

DOING YOUR WORK: ***Normalizing the Experience of Having Harmed Someone Else***

Remember a time when you have hurt someone you cared for, either inadvertently or intentionally, knowing beforehand that what you were going to do would hurt that person.

If you use the preceding short exercise with men, it can make room for them to acknowledge that they do act in sexist ways and also begin to reduce the denial. Do not allow participants to answer out loud. They should just think of a time and recall the feelings that they had. Most people will easily recall not only the memory, but also the feelings associated with the memory. Remind the participants that although they feel bad about what they did, they are not inherently bad people; there is much more to them than that behavior.

Admittedly, raping, battering, buying prostituted women or men, or otherwise perpetrating the kinds of abuse that are described here is substantially different than "hurting someone you care for." This exercise *can* run the risk of minimizing abusive behaviors, or allowing men who have been abusive to deny the harm they've caused. However, in the context of a full presentation, the exercise can be a useful tool to explore why some men who abuse may deny or minimize their abusiveness.

The Barrier of the Enormity of the Problem

A second barrier men face is the enormity of the problem. Any one of the issues discussed here are enormous problems at any level. On the personal level, rape, domestic violence, harassment, stalking, pornography, and prostitution cause devastating trauma. For the people who are close to people who are victimized, these forms of abuse and violence result in intense feelings of confusion, anger, and so on. Further, on the social-political level, sexist violence is an overwhelming issue to attempt to get one's brain around and come up with solutions. On any level, men (like all of us) understandably can feel besieged by the sheer enormity and complexity of the issue. It is not an uncommon reaction at all to respond to being overwhelmed by choosing not to react at all. When a person doesn't have the slightest clue of what to do in response to a problem that they are faced with, it is far easier to do nothing than to be overwhelmed.

The Barrier of Homophobia

Perhaps the greatest barrier to men hearing the information presented and to men's engagement in working to end sexism and violence is homophobia. Men's homophobia is manifest in a number of ways, but early in most men's experiences, any indication that they are not acting "manly" enough subjects them to verbal and even physical taunting. As described, part of manhood is performance. Any suggestion that men are less than "manly" leaves men vulnerable to questions about, or attacks upon, their masculinity.

Becoming an advocate for women is certainly one way that men have their masculinity questioned. Most men experience, as a child or adolescent, multiple examples of being taunted, picked on, and perhaps even assaulted, for being "too friendly" with girls. Indeed, research increasingly suggests that being friends with women is one of the leading causes of male youth being bullied (Epstein and Johnson, 1998; Mac an Ghaill, 1994; Martino, 1999; Nayak and Kehily, 1996; Phoenix et al, 2003). When boys are friends with girls, they tend to be taunted and perhaps assaulted for not being manly—"real men don't have female friends" goes the mythology. Educators are, in effect, asking men to become friendlier with girls and women; in fact, educators are asking men to go one step further—to become advocates for women. Thus, educators are asking men to do the very thing that may well have caused them to experience, or witness, violence. Understanding this is an important aspect of educating men.

There are few models of masculinity that include advocating for women's rights. The primary models that do exist are those models that project men as being the protector and defender of women, implicitly and often explicitly suggesting that women can't protect or defend themselves. Men as protectors are either protecting "helpless" women or violently attacking other men. Neither of these options are the model that educators are encouraging; these models do not ask men to challenge other men to end sexist violence. Nor are they models of men supporting loved ones who have been victimized. Engaging men to work to combat sexism and men's violence is asking men to do something for which they don't have very many clear models and asks them to do something that, in their past, has resulted in their masculinity being questioned and challenged.

EFFECTIVE STRATEGY

For one-session programs, it is best to just acknowledge the barrier that homophobia creates and then move on.

Homophobia is a challenging issue to address in the context of a presentation on sexism and violence, particularly if an educator has only one presentation with men. Homophobia will also likely come up in somewhat different ways depending on the focus of the presentation. For example, when educating about rape dynamics, homophobia will likely arise in the context of addressing male rape; when educating about responding to a loved one, homophobia will likely arise in the context of challenging men to not react with violence or aggression. In these kinds of situations, the best that an educator can likely do is to acknowledge that this dynamic exists and move on. Label the attitudes that men are exposing as a form of homophobia, acknowledge how it is acting as a barrier, and continue with the focus of the topic.

If more time is available, then educators can explore the issues of homophobia and how it relates to men's involvement in more depth. It is best if these issues are addressed in male-only settings, as men are less likely to openly discuss the issues of threats to their masculinity with women present (unless in a longer-term situation in which the trust between males and females can be fully developed). In addition, this discussion is most relevant in conversations focused on getting men more involved in the efforts to combat sexism and violence.

Although it is important to acknowledge and directly challenge the homophobia that surfaces during a presentation with men, labeling the behavior as homophobia may (and often will, depending on the audience) become more of a distraction than a way of moving through the barrier and continuing the conversation. Therefore, it is important to use other language to raise the points. "Sounds like you're saying that if you respond without aggression, some of your friends may challenge your masculinity. That's an important point to consider..." will likely have a better chance of acknowledging what is being said while still moving forward than a direct challenge to the homophobia.

Other Barriers to Facing Sexist Violence

Some other barriers that men often face include

- Lack of role models
- Not knowing what to do
- Not wanting to "look foolish"
- Appearing too "feminine"
- Appearing too sensitive
- Not fitting in with the men they know
- Feeling hesitant to challenge others about behavior that they themselves may have done just last week, or last night
- Guilt
- Fear of
  - the intensity of the issues
  - giving up male privilege
  - facing men's anger
  - being a traitor
  - being labeled "gay" (when men stand up for women, they are often baited with being called gay)
- Anger
  - about the issues
  - at themselves
  - at other men

The preceding barriers present some common reasons for men's lack of engagement, regardless of which specific topic is addressed. However, some specific topics evoke specific barriers. Discussions of pornography, for example, often generate some barriers that domestic violence or sexual harassment do not. Men's defensiveness is related to the degree to which they experience those feelings, among others. The stronger the men react defensively, the stronger they are feeling something. For men, feeling *something* about these topics and the conversations is a good thing.

Confronting Myths

When educating men, it is not uncommon for them to overtly expose the myths they hold. They may not mean to expose their beliefs openly, but they will likely express their opinions, utterly believing that they are speaking the truth. What follows are a few examples of common myths and possible responses. These are not the only responses, and as educators become more competent and confident in their ability to respond, they will undoubtedly develop their own responses. One of the key things to notice about these possible responses is how they acknowledge the kernel of truth in each myth, and then proceed to debunk each myth. These responses also do not contain judgment or defensiveness. The tone that is most effective in debunking myths is conversational, relaxed, and easy-going. The more defensive, aggressive, or harshly an educator responds to myths, the less likely the person(s) who hold those myths will change. In fact, such a response may increase others' degree of belief in a myth.

EFFECTIVE STRATEGY

Responding to myths is an opportunity to reemphasize the main points of a presentation.

Please note that more specific details of myths and how to combat them are addressed in the following chapter.

Myth: Why Do Women Lie About Being Raped?

Response: There is indeed an issue of women lying about rape, although not in the way that you think. What we know to be true, based on data from the FBI, is that the incidence of false reports of sexual violence is about the same as the incidence of false reports of any crime: between four and eight percent (4%–8%). What is also true is that rape is the most under-reported crime. The issue is not so much why women lie that they have been raped when they haven't, but more that women lie and say they have not been raped when in fact they have.

A second and related point about this belief that women lie about being raped is that this question never gets asked when discussing men who are raped. For whatever reasons, we think it more likely for women to lie about being raped than for men to lie about being raped. Why do you think that would be?

Myth: What About When Women Lead You on or You Are at That Point When You Just Can't Stop?

Response: At times, all of us, women *and men*, play sexual games or aren't as straightforward as we should be. If you are feeling led on, it is important to stop the process, ask what is going on, and clarify your needs and wants.

It is also true that women, like men, may sometimes feel ambivalent about being sexual with someone. This is part of what gets so difficult. Instead of being forceful or reacting negatively, check in with your partner and talk about what is going on.

As far as men "getting to the point of no return," imagine that you are 16 and making out with your girlfriend on her couch. Imagine that you're at that same point (clothes are off, touching is happening, and so on) and her father pulls into the driveway. How able are most men at getting themselves back under control?

(This response can be used in a very humorous tone that gets the point across but still allows people to recognize the absurdity of the so-called "point of no return." Just because there is laughter does not mean that the point is being lost or dismissed, or that the issue being addressed is not being taken seriously.)

Myth: Can Men Get Raped?

Response: Yes, men can get raped, and it is as much a tragedy, horror, and outrage when men are raped as when women are raped. Most men who are raped are raped by other men—almost always by heterosexual men.

As underreported as the rape of women is, male rape is even more underreported. Men face many of the same barriers that women face when reporting that they have been sexually assaulted. In addition, the fear of others' reactions and of their masculinity being questioned acts to keep men who are raped silent.

For men, the risk of being sexually victimized goes down as they reach later adolescence and adulthood; for women, on the other hand, the risk of being raped remains about the same throughout their lives until they reach their mid-forties, at which point the risk begins to go down. Throughout their lives, women's risk is substantially higher than men's risk.

Myth: Don't Women Sometimes Just Ask to Get Hit? You Know, They Get You So Mad That You Can't Do Anything Else!

Response: Those of us who are in relationships know that sometimes you are in a bad mood and want to make your partner angry. We all have the ability to act immature from time-to-time. However, provoking my partner's anger and "asking to be hit" are two very different things. No woman asks to be hit, ever! She may behave in ways that make her partner angry, but she does not behave in those ways to make her partner hit her.

Put another way, a woman can provoke a man, but nobody can make another person choose to hit, call names, or make her feel bad about herself. If someone makes me mad, how I express my anger and what I do with my anger are my responsibilities.

(This question also implies that a man is not in control of his actions or behaviors. It suggests that a man needs a woman to change so that he will decide not to hit her.)

Myth: Don't Women Use Violence in Relationships as Often as Men Do?

Response: This is a key question and one that needs some time to explore. Yes, the statistics do suggest that women use violence in relationships as much as men use it. However, when exploring domestic or dating violence, it is important to also explore the reasons people use violence and the impact of their use of violence.

Women tend to use violence in self-defense whereas men tend to use violence to reassert their power or control in the relationship. In addition, women react to men's violence with fear and self-blame, and are often harmed; men tend to react to women's violence with anger or disregard.

To understand domestic violence, it is important to look for a pattern of power and control in which physical violence is just one tactic.

Myth: Don't Girls Harass Boys as Much as Boys Harass Girls?

Response: Recent research suggests that in some situations girls do behave in similar ways to boys. However, before we call that harassment, it is important to examine the context and the impact. When girls are harassed by boys, girls tend to feel threatened, fearful, and self-conscious. When boys are harassed by girls, boys tend to laugh it off, and feel flirty and self-conscious. Harassment is never okay, but there are very real differences between girls' experiences of being harassed and those of boys.

Most boys who report being harassed and bullied (two very similar dynamics) indicate that the perpetrators are other boys, not girls.

Myth: Don't Prostitutes and Women in Pornography Choose to Be Involved?

Response: Choice is an interesting concept and not at all as simple as it first appears. To truly have choice, one must be able to freely choose to do something or choose not to do something. To truly have choice, people must know that they can stop doing something at any point.

Most women who are involved in pornography and prostitution have no choice. Based on research (certainly internationally but also within the U.S.), the vast majority of women who are involved in pornography and prostitution got involved at very young ages (the average age is 14) and do not have the choice to leave. Most are forced to participate in pornography and/or prostitution because of lack of other available supports and resources. Most women who try to leave cannot because of the coercion and violence used by male "promoters," "managers," or pimps.

Myth: Aren't Prostitution and Pornography Just Alternative Ways for Women to Make Money?

Response: Prostituted women and women who are involved in pornography rarely make enough money to survive adequately. The notion that this is an economic "ace in the hole" for women is a myth. Most women or men who are in prostitution and pornography are still poor and cannot get out mainly for economic reasons.

Myth: If a Woman Doesn't Want to Be Harassed, She Wouldn't Wear Short Shorts and Halter Tops.

Response: First of all, people have the right to wear whatever they are comfortable wearing. Just because someone is wearing something does not mean that someone else has a right to respond inappropriately.

Secondly, women (and men too for that matter) often dress in ways because they want to be noticed and want to have other people pay attention. There is a world of difference between wanting to have a man (or men in general) pay attention and being harassed. This last point, of course, can be developed much further.

Strategies for Overcoming Barriers and Confronting Myths

Overcoming barriers and confronting myths requires a balance of understanding with conviction combined with the skills to address these concerns. The following sections share strategies that have been effective in educating men.

Remember the Educator's Role

As discussed earlier, it is not the job of an educator to make men feel guilty, but neither is it an educator's responsibility to make sexism and violence something that is easy for men to talk about. Men *should* feel something and feel intensely when sexism and violence are brought up. These are not topics that should be allowed to evoke idle curiosity.

Feeling intensely about sexist violence demonstrates the degree to which men are connecting with the actualities being discussed—namely, an appalling human trauma and social injustice. Often people feel something for the first time when they feel uncomfortable. It is much easier to blame the person who "caused" the feelings and to deny the degree to which it is an issue than it is to look at the issues that cause the discomfort.

Because men have so rarely had any opportunity to take part in a serious conversation about sexism and violence (a formal educational experience may be their first opportunity), the educator will often take the brunt of the blame for men having these feelings. Recognize this dynamic when it occurs and do not accept the responsibility for the feelings that men may experience.

Chapter 1 of this manual provided a list of assumptions for educators when educating men. One of these assumptions is that men can handle their feelings. It is when facing men's defensiveness and attempts to blame the educator for their feelings when educators are most challenged to recall this assumption. Unless an educator is doing a poor job of educating, it is not the educator who is making men feel blamed—it is the nature of the topic and the reality of sexist violence that makes men feel negative emotions. When being accused of blaming men, educators are encouraged to step back and allow men to accept the responsibility for these feelings of being blamed.

EFFECTIVE STRATEGY

Expect men in the group to feel blamed, but ask them to identify the source.

Most people, including men, confuse responsibility with blame. If men are complaining of being blamed for sexist violence, ask this question: "*What have I said that blames men?*" Encourage men to consider the source of the feelings of blame. Are they coming from what the educator said, or are these feelings coming from the men themselves? Remind men of the difference between blame and response-ability, and state that in order to begin working towards solutions of something as socially entrenched as sexism and violence, one must begin by accurately defining the problem. Saying that men perpetrate almost all sexism and violence is *not* blaming men. It is stating fact.

Do Not Back Away from the Main Points

Personal experience and the available research suggest that the process of overcoming such barriers and confronting myths is best achieved by remaining true to the main message and addressing the barriers and myths as they arise in the conversation. The degree to which men feel defensive should not be taken as evidence of an ineffective presentation. Men are very likely to feel defensive. Being able to proceed through the topics of the presentation in spite of men's defensiveness or to use men's defensiveness in a constructive way are better measures of a successful educational experience.

One effective way to handle barriers and myths is to repeat the main points. For example, while giving a presentation on acquaintance rape, if men continue to ask questions related to the myth of women's false reporting (which is very common), continuing to re-state the main point that there is no evidence that women are more likely to lie about being raped than men are or than other crime victims, is one effective way to continue to move through the presentation goals and not be sidetracked. In addition, the more this point gets reinforced, the better.

Use Humor to Combat the Barrier of Lack of Knowledge

Although it may be true that men are often unsure how to respond to sexist violence, and therefore, choose not to respond at all, it is worth pointing out that men often do things even though they do not know what to do, from building a wall, to replacing plumbing, to working on the car. It is even a common theme in sit-coms that men take on projects they don't know anything about, so not knowing what to do should not be a barrier to men's involvement in responding to sexism and violence. Educators can remind men that they do this all the time. This is one place where humor can be used effectively to continue to engage men.

Men *can* learn what to do and how to be supportive. The men who already are involved are still learning what to do. It is an ongoing process. There is no magic or quick answer. Getting involved really is as simple (and as complex) as taking a first step.

Point Out That Guilt Is Neither Helpful nor Empowering

As men learn more about the dynamics of sexism and abuse and the myths surrounding them, they may experience guilt, which likely arises from a number of sources. As men are confronted with the facts and dynamics of sexist violence for the first time, they may realize that some behaviors that they've engaged in (behaviors they originally believed to be mutual or consensual) were in fact abusive. Another source for men's guilt may be recognizing the degree to which they have eroticized abusive behaviors. Both of these reactions likely result in guilt.

Male activists often experience a period of guilt as they begin uncovering and accepting responsibility for the ways that they have acted in sexist and abusive ways. Often men also experience periods of guilt as they realize how much work women have done while men have remained silent. They may experience some levels of guilt for not taking action sooner. After all, it is hardly possible that men have been able to be completely unaware of rape, domestic violence, and harassment.

When confronting men's guilt, it is necessary to point out that guilt is neither helpful nor empowering. Guilt, in fact, only keeps one immobile. While it is important for people to feel whatever they are feeling at the time that they feel it, including guilt, it is also important that they challenge themselves and each other about some of those feelings. Frankly, there simply is not enough time for men to feel guilty. As Andrea Dworkin (1988) stated in a speech to men, "You have the time to feel guilty. We don't have the time for you to feel guilty. Your guilt is a form of acquiescence in what continues to occur. Your guilt helps keep things the way they are" (Dworkin, 1988, p. 165).

Although men often feel guilty in response to the issues of sexist violence, it is important to educate men to move through the guilt. While acknowledging that these are feelings or thoughts that men may well have as they begin taking action to address sexist violence, remind them that guilt is not transformative and achieves little in terms of actually ending sexist violence. No program or political agenda is worthwhile if it requires that people feel guilty in order to be involved.

Prepare Men for the Fear and Anger They May Feel

Fear and anger tend to work closely together and can prove to be a huge barrier to men's involvement in confronting sexism and violence. It is scary to step out of the box of how one has become accustomed to acting and into a new direction. It does not take long for men to realize that acting against sexism and violence is acting against the norm of masculinity, which is something that most men are loath to do. When educating men to become active, educators must prepare them for this probability. Men will likely make changes and very well may lose some friends as a result of those changes. As men become more aware and active, they often find that the kinds of things that they used to enjoy are not as fun anymore or have become downright offensive as a result of their increased consciousness.

The best preparation that men can have is to know that these kinds of reactions happen and are relatively common. Unfortunately, there are no short cuts, no way to go through the process without this particular part of the process. It is hard. It is difficult. However, most men who have become involved find that they have become more empowered, more sure of and happier with themselves, and more self-actualized as a result. It **is** worth facing the fear and anger!

Encourage Men Not to Wait Until They're Perfect

Another common barrier particularly relevant to talking about ways for men to take action is men feeling like hypocrites. How often men say,

> *How can I talk to other men about their sexism and abusiveness when I continue to confront my own and learn more about the ways that I act in sexist and abusive ways?*

No one expects men to be perfect, and if people are waiting for men to be perfect before they begin taking action, they will be waiting a long, long time. Actually, the fact that men are still on the path of becoming more aware of and working to end their sexism and abusiveness makes the work educators do that much more authentic and honest. It adds to the legitimacy of what educators do. It does not take anything away.

Allow Room for Men to Struggle

Educators need to remind themselves that learning about and addressing sexism and violence, and the associated myths, are struggles. Every man has his own struggle to go through as he comes to understand the issues and begins to take personal responseability to address them. It is not the responsibility of educators to relieve men of their struggles.

Preparing for the Outcome: Men's Response-Ability*

"The most radical step you can take is your next one."

JAMES BALDWIN

As discussed earlier, one of the most common reactions men have to any conversation about sexism and violence is that they feel blamed. This reaction tends to correspond to the degree to which educators present the information from an overtly pro-feminist perspective.

The Ineffectiveness of Blame

However, blame is not the point of working with men and certainly not the point of any presentation. Blame is not healthy, is not helpful in generating real solutions, and results only in someone's self-esteem being battered. Blame is not an effective motivation to be more compassionate and does not result in men being better able to care for their loved ones who are victimized. Blame is useless and is decidedly not an effective method of producing social change.

An inherent dilemma that educators face is encouraging men to take sexism and violence personally (in that they feel personally motivated to do something about it), but not to feel that they, personally, are to blame for the existence of sexist violence. This line between encouraging men to accept personal responsibility without encouraging blame is very faint, thin, and elusive. But this is exactly the line that educators dance along in educating men. It is helpful while dancing along this line between blame and responsibility, to remind men of the model of taking personal responsibility by taking the keys away from a drunken friend who is threatening to drive. People are responsible for trying to stop a friend from drinking and driving, but if the friend goes driving anyway and gets into an accident, the people who tried to stop the drunken driver are not responsible for the accident.

This line is further blurred by the baggage that educators bring to the educational relationship. Everybody has experiences with men in the past that have triggered thoughts, feelings, and beliefs about how men may respond to the issues of sexism and sexist violence. Educators need to check their preconceptions (which may be based on experience), both positive and negative, about educating men and allowing every man and every group of men the opportunity to attend a presentation with a clean slate. Just as it is unfair for men to come to a presentation with preconceived notions about anti-rape educators, it is also unfair for educators to come to a presentation with preconceived notions about the men.

**I first developed this notion of response-ability in my book* Stopping Rape: A Challenge for Men *(1993).*

In order for people to feel engaged and motivated to take part in creating something new, individuals must feel empowered. In order for people to work together to create a world in which everyone is and feels safe, and everyone has the ability to live their lives strong and free, each person must feel a personal stake in creating such a world. Educators cannot make anyone feel anything, and it is certainly impossible to make those who participate in educational programs feel a personal responsibility to address sexism and violence.

Educators *can* create an environment in which participants are offered some new information, develop a deeper understanding, expand their knowledge, and perhaps learn some new skills. Taken together, new information, a deeper understanding, expanded knowledge, and new skills might increase the motivation and ability of participants to become more engaged. After all, that is one of the main points of educating men. In short, educators can't make men care.

Given this, it is important for educators to offer men a way to learn more about sexism and violence in a way that nudges them closer to accepting personal responsibility to do something. This process often can get misconstrued as blame. In all fairness, there are times when educators get frustrated and anxious and may resort to tactics that run counter to the goals strived for, such as blaming.

CASE STUDY

There have been plenty of times when I have been educating men and because I have been tired, frustrated, or anxious ("there isn't enough time"), I resorted to using blaming tactics in a presentation. Since blame is, in part, a dynamic of pointing fingers and separating oneself from the participants, when I become aware that I am blaming, I must take a step back and refocus on working *with* the men in the room. I must take a breath and reconnect with the men by putting into practice the understanding that coming to a better understanding of sexism and violence is a process. I must take men from where they are, not from where I want men to be.

From Blame to Response-ability

EFFECTIVE STRATEGY

Reframe response-ability as the ability to respond.

An effective way to stay focused on where men are (instead of where one may want them to be) as well as to urge them to accept personal responsibility without feeling blamed is to reframe response-ability as the ability to respond. Every man, and men as a group, has an *ability* to respond to sexism and violence and to the women and men who are harmed by sexist violence. Every man has the ability to respond caringly and supportively to loved ones who have been victimized. These abilities are inherently creative, intelligent, and unlimited. So far, this is an ability that few men have realized, and one that men as a group have done little with, but it *is* an ability. Each man has the ability to ensure that he treats every woman with respect and can challenge himself to push the envelope about what respect looks like. Each man has the ability to work to combat the foundations of sexist violence by challenging sexist language, donating money to a local rape crisis center, volunteering with a local feminist anti-pornography organization, and so on. Collectively, men have the ability to stop sexist violence.

Ability speaks much more about empowerment than it does guilt or blame. This is what social change is all about: people using their abilities, both personal and collective, to make the world a better and more just place. This value goes to what is probably the core purpose for educating men—to support men to reach towards their individual and collective ability to stop sexist violence. Ability speaks to the ways men can reach toward an end to sexist violence

Perhaps the main reason for focusing on the point of men's ability to respond is to counter the notion that men are being blamed and to counter men's guilt. These two are probably *the* most common responses from men. By focusing on response-ability rather than guilt or blame, educators re-claim the energy of the conversation and focus on the main purpose. It benefits no one, and does nothing for the movement as a whole, for men to feel blamed or guilty for the incidence of men's violence. Guilt and blame are both, frankly, just a big waste of time. It *is* valuable to emphasize that there are ways for men to be part of the solution to men's violence and to encourage them to take some initiative.

There are several specific ways in which educators can talk with men about response-ability. The first is to insist that men be fully response-able for their reactions and feelings during the presentation. Educators tend to want to create an environment in which participants are comfortable, especially when discussing emotionally-charged topics such as sexism or violence. This desire, rightfully, comes from the experience of educating women, when educators want to create a comfortable space where people who have been abused can feel more comfortable and safe enough to potentially disclose. There is a belief that in order for people to be able to take in new or challenging information, they need to feel comfortable and at ease. While to some degree this is true, it is also true, as discussed earlier, that sexism, violence, and the harm that results are inherently disturbing topics. Some degree of discomfort reflects the degree to which the educator and participants are engaging in an honest and real conversation about sexism and violence and the realities of the harm caused.

A second way for educators to talk with men about response-ability is to discuss how we all have learned to take responsibility. Most children learn how to take responsibility through a process something like this: a child does something wrong, a parent (who is two or three times bigger than the child is) catches them in the act, gets angry, and tells the child (usually shouting) to "take responsibility." People can easily resonate with this experience and know the real lessons that children learn through this. These lessons are to feel ashamed for themselves and be blamed for whatever they did.

As such, when educators use language such as "take responsibility," some part of most men reverts back to being seven and having just broken the cookie jar and having mom or dad yell at them. Moving from this discussion to redefining response-ability helps move men beyond this subconscious reaction and keeps them engaged in the conversation.

A third way to discuss response-ability is to focus on the abilities that men, individually and collectively, have to respond to sexism and violence. Focusing these abilities shifts the focus off of blame and guilt entirely.

Allowing men to be fully response-able means allowing and trusting—*really trusting*—that men can handle whatever feelings are brought up for them as a result of a presentation. Men can handle being angry as well as sad, frustrated, and even blamed. Good educators will not necessarily end a presentation with men feeling angry, sad, frustrated, blamed; but neither will good educators work to take those feelings away from men. Feeling these things is part of the process of men taking it personally, and often is part of the process of men becoming mobilized to take action. For example, most educators, activists, and advocates, indeed most of the people who are involved in the movements around sexism and violence in any way, are involved because they *feel* personally about these issues. This is not the kind of profession that one enters blithely. It's a movement that people join because they *feel* (often passionately) about it. It is these feelings that keep those who are involved, involved. It is these feelings that educators are trying to stir in men.

EFFECTIVE STRATEGY

When someone feels blamed by the presentation, gently suggest that the feelings may be coming from within themself.

Going through all the strategies in reframing response-ability does not necessarily mean that men won't still feel blamed. When men claim that they are being blamed during a presentation, it is important to hear and acknowledge that they may feel blamed, while simultaneously restating the main points. Men often feel blamed regardless of what one says. If this is the case, gently suggest that the feelings of blame they are having may be coming from inside themselves, not from the educator or the message. Or they may feel blamed from recognizing, perhaps for the first time, that sexist violence is, in fact, men's violence. Men may also feel blamed because they may be questioning whether acts that they thought were okay were perhaps violent or abusive. The point is for educators to be clear about the message and not to take responsibility for blame that men may feel as a result of what is said. Allowing men the fullness of their feelings is part of allowing and encouraging them to accept (and *feel*) their ability to respond.

PART 2
An Overview of the Issues

Part 2 provides a brief overview of various forms of sexist violence. Chapter 4 examines rape and sexual assault and the ways that rape and sexual assault impact on people. This chapter starts off by providing a working definition of rape and a discussion of the ways that educators must operate with at least two definitions simultaneously—the legal definition of rape and sexual assault within their state, territory, or other jurisdiction; and a feminist or "victim-centered" definition. Both of these definitions are important to bring into educational programs with men. Chapter 4 also examines Rape Trauma Syndrome and explores ways that men can be supportive of women and men who they care for who've been raped through their healing.

Chapter 5 examines several forms of sexual harassment. This chapter begins by examining the difference between the legal categories of "quid pro quo" and "hostile environment" harassment and the implications of educating men about these forms of harassment. As with rape, harassment is often perpetrated and experienced in ways that are beyond the definition provided by law. As such, educators need to be aware of the impact of harassment and the contextual nature of harassing behaviors. Chapter 5 also includes street harassment and explores how street harassment is similar to and different from other forms of sexual harassment. In educating men about harassment, one of the most important aspects to discuss is the difference between impact and intent—that regardless of whether or not a man intends to harass a woman or other man, if another person feels harassed, then they are.

Chapter 6 examines stalking. Although there has been an increasing amount of work done around stalking, it is still perhaps the least understood form of sexist violence. As a result, Chapter 6 is one of the shortest chapters in this book. That being said, stalking appears to be one of the fastest growing and more pervasive forms of sexist abuse. Educating men about stalking requires talking with them about the subtle forms of stalking and, like harassment, the difference between intent and impact.

Chapter 7 looks at domestic and dating violence. There is a discrepancy between the legal definitions of domestic violence, which focus on incident, and the lived experienced of domestic violence, which is a pattern of interconnected behaviors that are strategically used to maintain power and control in a relationship. The "Power and Control Wheel" is offered in this chapter as a way to understand (and an effective tool to use when educating men) how these different behaviors are used in concert to abuse partners. Chapter 7 also examines the "Cycle of Violence," which provides another way of understanding how people who are abusive create a pattern to maintain their control in a relationship. Chapter 7 goes on to examine why women stay, why men hit, and the impact of domestic violence. Finally, this chapter briefly exposes the gendered nature of domestic violence and dating abuse. Domestic violence and dating abuse are perpetrated by men against women and other men. It is not gender symmetrical; in other words, the myth that women are just as abusive as men is simply that, a myth.

Chapter 8 examines issues that are rarely conceived of as forms of sexist violence or abuse—pornography and prostitution. This chapter provides a framework for understanding pornography and prostitution as forms of sexist violence, and as interconnected with the other forms of violence and abuse discussed in this part. Not only do pornography and prostitution hurt people, but they also reinforce a mindset and a socio-cultural environment that allow (some would argue encourage) other forms of sexist violence. Educating men to end sexism and violence includes educating men about the harms of pornography and prostitution.

Finally, Chapter 9 explores the ways that racism and homophobia are also a part of any conversation with men about sexism and violence. The forms of violence and abuse discussed in this part are not only used as weapons of sexism, but are used as weapons of racism and homophobia. In other words, one of the ways that men's dominance over women is maintained is due to sexist violence. These same forms of violence are also used to maintain white people's dominance over African American, Latino, Asian, and Native American people; and heterosexuals' dominance of lesbians, gay men, bisexuals, and transgendered people. This chapter explores ways to talk with men about these interconnections, how to talk with men in multiracial settings, and how to respond to men's homophobia that may be unleashed in a conversation with men about sexism and violence.

CHAPTER 4

Rape and Sexual Assault

"Rape, and our society's attitude about rape, affects every woman in this country...Women have the aspirations and the promise of freedom of a new generation, but the fears of our mothers and grandmothers."

MEDEA AND THOMPSON, 1974, P. 3

"The threat of rape and the fact that it does happen to some women, creates a climate of fear. All men benefit from the fact that some men rape women."

KELLY (REFERRING TO BROWNMILLER), 1988, P. 23

Rape and sexual assault, as topics of conversation, often cause visceral reactions in people. The reactions often are based on whatever people think of when they hear the word *rape*. However, rape and sexual assault actually include a full range of behaviors. This chapter addresses the breadth of rape and sexual assault, examining the definitions, dynamics, and impact, and, of course, how to address these topics with men.

A Note About Language

It has become increasingly common to refer to some forms of rape as *date rape*. This is a gross misrepresentation and minimization of the harm, the violence, and the issues. Educators and advocates are strongly urged to drop this phrase from their vocabulary. First, the term *date rape* did not come from the movement. It came from the media who created this phrase as a catchy way to draw readers or viewers. More importantly, the term *date rape* does not accurately reflect the true experience of people who are raped. For the person who experiences a sexual assault, the date stopped when the rape began.

Similarly, the date stopped being a date and became a rapist the moment he or she initiated the violence. Furthermore, the term *date rape* is not taken as seriously or seen as harmful as the term *rape* when it does not have a qualifier. Thus the question becomes this: Should educators use a term that was created by the media which minimizes the harm and does not reflect the experience of people who are victimized? No!

Instead of using the term *date rape,* educators are encouraged to make no distinction between kinds of rape. Rape is rape. The relationship between the perpetrator and the person being victimized matters very little, especially during a presentation. In cases in which educators feel they must categorize, the phrase "rape perpetrated on a date" more accurately describes this experience.

Towards a Definition

One of the common struggles educators have when defining sexual assault is the need to simultaneously work with two definitions:

- The legal definition, with which every educator needs to know and be conversant
- The movement's definition, which comes from the experiences of people who have been assaulted and the people who work most closely with them

Legal definitions vary in many ways, having very different language and covering different acts. The movement's definition is also somewhat influenced by the local "flavor" but tends to vary less than state or legal definitions.

This duality of definitions frequently causes some confusion for participants in educational programs. The law says one thing about what is a sexual assault, but the law's definition fails to reflect the experiences of people who are victimized. For example, in most states, rape is legally defined as *vaginal* penetration, meaning that by law men cannot be raped. The act of forced anal or oral penetration is covered by other legal terms (sexual assault, forced sodomy, sexual violence, and so on), but it is not legally labeled as rape. The *experience* of men who have been sexually assaulted is that they have been raped. There are many ways that, from an advocate's perspective, the law falls short in its definition of sexual assault.

"There are forms of sexual assaults that are not considered a crime and yet still cause harm to women or men who are victimized."

There are forms of sexual assaults that are not considered a crime and yet still cause harm to women or men who are victimized. This is one of the most important aspects of sexual assault for educators to address. For the purposes of educating men, which generally includes a goal of increasing their empathy for women or men who have been harmed, educators must emphasize the ways that people are harmed by behaviors that are not illegal. Just because an act is legal does not mean that it does not cause harm and is not a sexual assault.

Sexual assault is best understood as any forced or unwanted sexual contact. This includes attacking a person's sexual parts, as well as attacking other parts of the body in a sexual manner. Sexual assault does not necessarily involve physical contact. For example, sexual harassment (which is discussed in more detail in Chapter 5) is a form of a sexual assault that may involve verbal comments, whistles, or leering. A woman who may not have been touched while experiencing the harassment may very well *feel* assaulted.

For the purposes of this manual, the term *sexual assault* is understood as a broad category of behaviors that include rape, forced sodomy, and other forms of forced sexualized contact. (Conceptually, sexual harassment, pornography, and prostitution can also be understood as forms of sexual assault, but since they are covered more specifically in this manual, they are not covered by the umbrella of sexual assault here.)

Sexual assault, at its core, is about power and control. A person's sexuality, which includes their gender identity (male, female, androgynous, transgender), sexual and affectional orientation (gay male, lesbian, heterosexual, or bisexual), as well as the kinds of sexual behaviors one enjoys, is perhaps the most sacred and intimate part of who a person is. In sexual assault, another person or persons takes control of these aspects of a person. One's personal power over a very intimate part of the self is taken.

In general, not being listened to when one says "No" is an extremely disempowering and humiliating experience. For example, many children have the experience of being tickled and at some point having enough and wanting the tickling to stop, only to have the person tickling them ignore them and keep tickling. This common experience often makes the child feel powerless, frustrated, and humiliated. When placed in the context of one's sexuality, the experience of having one's power stripped is magnified. It is this dynamic that defines sexual assault as violent. The degree of physical violence has little impact on the person's experience of the rape as violent. It doesn't matter so much whether or not he hits—the experience, even if no physical violence is used, is that it was a violent assault. This is why educators refer to rape and sexual assault as violent crimes, even when the level of physical violence is relatively low.

DOING YOUR WORK: *Considering Your Own Definition of Sexuality*

Take a moment to think through this activity.

Think about who you are as a sexual person. Consider not only the kinds of sexual experiences you enjoy, but also how you define your own gender and your sexual orientation.

Now consider how you express your sexuality. How do you dress, walk, interact with others, and to what degree are these decisions influenced by your self-definition as a man or woman; as gay, bi, or heterosexual, and so on.

(continued)

(continued)

Now imagine that someone else is controlling this part of who you are. Imagine that you no longer control how you express yourself sexually.

How powerful do you feel?

What venues of your life are not affected?

What areas of your life do you still feel that you have some control over?

When doing a presentation on rape/sexual assault, it is generally best to begin with a discussion of definitions. This is a good way to bring the participants into the discussion immediately, as well as to begin addressing the differences between the legal definition and the feminist or victim-centered definition. The implications for the differences between these definitions will have an impact throughout the discussion. Be careful of trying to convince men of a particular definition. It is unlikely to be successful, and you probably will only generate an argument about whose definition is the most accurate—especially in a one-time presentation. Offer definitions in a way that engages men and encourages dialogue. Through the dialogue about definitions, a good educator can provide valuable information.

EFFECTIVE STRATEGY

Do not try to convince men of a particular definition; engage them in dialogue about the definition.

The most widely reported and duplicated studies indicate that roughly one in four women are victimized by completed or attempted rape during their college years (Koss, Gidycz, and Wisniewski, 1987, and Warshaw, 1994). Overall, it is assumed that about one in three women survives a completed or attempted sexual assault in her lifetime. The vast majority of sexual assaults are perpetrated by an acquaintance, someone known to the person. For high school- and college-aged women and men, most of these sexual assaults occur on dates or date-like situations. (See the exercise "What Would You Do?" in Appendix B as a way to effectively make this point with men.)

Understanding sexual assault as "any forced or unwanted sexual contact" fails to explain much about the specifics of sexual assaults. The phrase "forced or unwanted sexual contact" can be too global and too general to be easily understood, especially by men. As educators, it is important to be as concrete and specific as possible about what this definition actually means and looks like in behavioral terms. The exercise, "Is This

Consent?" in Appendix B is an effective activity to use to begin clarifying this definition. The point is not to suggest that all men are bad or that all men are rapists. The point is to reinforce that sexual assault is common and that any definition is based on the experience of the person who is being forced.

The term *force* cannot be defined in a vacuum. It is *always* contextualized in the situation and in the relationship of the people involved. Men frequently want a very clear definition of what is (and what is not) sexual assault. Sexual assault is based on the experience of the person being forced. If the person felt forced (coerced, manipulated, threatened, cajoled, and so on), then there was force. It matters little if someone else who was not in that experience at that time doubts that she or he would feel forced. What matters is that the person *in the situation* felt forced. Whether individuals or the law agree is irrelevant. The person's experience was real and needs to be validated.

As educators, this is one area of focus in educating men: to push them beyond an over-reliance on legalized definitions and encourage them to empathize with *real people's real experiences.* It can be helpful when examining issues of force to reexamine the definition of consent using the definitions offered in the "Address Consent" section later in this chapter.

Rape Myths

Unlike most other crimes (except for those described throughout this manual), there are a multitude of myths that surround sexual assault. These myths are based largely on misinformation but continue to plague women or men who have been assaulted. Clearly, the presence and acceptance of these rape myths have an impact on educators.

Although myths were generally discussed in the previous chapter, there are some particular myths related to rape. There tend to be more myths associated with rape than with the other forms of violence discussed here, and, in many ways, rape myths are more integrated into our cultural messages than are some of the others. Because of these factors, it is important to address myths specific to rape.

Educators should be aware of the myths that are common (in general and in the particular area in which one is educating) and how these myths manifest themselves. Educators also need to be prepared for these myths to arise when educating men, and be prepared with some "myth busters" as part of a presentation. Men tend to believe more myths and to hold onto those myths more strongly than do women. When educating men, it is important for educators to create an environment where men can say what they really believe so that the myths can be exposed and thus countered. Otherwise, male audiences will hear whatever educators say through the filter of these myths. By using some of the exercises described in Appendix B and remaining open to whatever men have to say, educators can create environments where men can say what they truly believe.

The "Women Lie" Myth

The most common and prevalent myth is that women lie. Not only is this myth extremely common, it is also gender based. This myth tends to come up only in the context of talking about the rape of women and never when discussing the rape of men. The myth that women lie about being raped can be seen almost every time well-known men are accused of rape. Immediately, questions are raised about the women and the motivations for accusing men of rape.

The myth that women lie is based on the assumption that women can get something—fame, money, or revenge, for example—by accusing men of rape. The false reporting rate for sexual assault is about the same as the false reporting rate for any crime, between 4 and 8 percent (depending on the study). This means that from 96 to 92 percent of the time men should believe women when they disclose sexual assaults.

The dynamics of sexual assault in a sexist environment create such shame for women that the issue of false reporting is actually the reverse. Most women falsely report that they have not been raped when in fact they have.

Another point to consider is this: Alan Berkowitz has described "men's false fear of women's false reporting" as a way to tease out men's fear and point out that men's fear of being falsely accused, which is at the heart of this myth, is not based on actual data. It is the fear that is false, not the rate of women's reporting.

The "Rape Is Sexually Motivated" Myth

A second myth is that rape is sexually motivated. This is actually a more complicated myth than it appears. Rape is about power and control with sex as the weapon. Accountability requires that educators use the experience of women or men who are raped as the foundation for any discussion offered. Because of this, educators need to focus on an understanding of rape/sexual assault as being about power and control.

While the need to focus on power and control is true, it is also true that for most men who rape, the desire for sex and desire for power have become intertwined. This seems particularly true for people who perpetrate the most common forms of rape/sexual assault. Men who perpetrate rape often feel entitled to the sexual act (he paid a lot of money on the date, he got extremely turned on, she looked at him in such a way, he was flirting with him, she made out with her, she went up to his apartment, she took her own shirt off and so on). As a result of feeling entitled to the sex, people who rape also then feel entitled to use force (or coercion, or manipulation, or any other means) to get what they want. The motivations for sex, to fulfill a feeling of entitlement and for power and control, all get fused together in the perpetration of a rape/sexual assault. For the person who is raped, the rape is an act of power and control, not sex. Sex is used as the weapon or the means to feel power and control, but the true motivation is not sex.

The "The Woman Could Have Stopped the Rape" Myth

Another related myth is that if women really did not want to be assaulted, they could stop it. This myth is exposed in comments such as "Why was she wearing that?" That question suggests that she could have gotten out of the situation if she really wanted to. While it might be true that women, like men, want to feel attractive and may dress in ways to attract attention, it is not true that women want to be forced into sexual activity.

A common myth often depicted in movies and popular songs is that women can be and are "turned on" to a sexual act initiated through force, which then becomes something that women enjoy and ultimately want. The myth that women enjoy being forced is based on male fantasies that are reinforced and fueled by pornography. While it is certainly true that there are times when people may change their mind about being sexual (not really wanting to but changing their mind, or initially wanting to and deciding they really don't), force is not part of the equation. What is more common, based on research, is that women give in to men's pressure. But giving in is not true consent.

"However a person responds to the threat of being raped is exactly the right response. The way they responded, including giving in, is the response they needed to give in order to survive the attack."

In responding to this myth, it is helpful to refer back to the definition of consent, and distinguish between giving in and true consent. Additionally, it is important to point out the level of fear and threat that is inherent in a sexual assault, regardless of how "mild" it may appear from the outside of the situation. People respond in the way that makes the most sense to them in the moment. *However a person responds to the threat of being raped* is exactly the *right* response. The way they responded, including giving in, is the response they needed to give in order to survive the attack.

The "Women of Color Accept Violent Sex" Myth

Racist myths are rampant in relation to sexual assault. These myths are both general to all women and/or men of color (depending on the myth) and are specific to certain racial or ethnic groups (African American women, Latina women, Asian women, and so on). These racist myths suggest either that women of color are more accepting of violent sex or that they are more likely to lie about being raped. As with most rape myths, neither of these misconceptions have any basis in what is known about women of color who have been victimized. In fact, it appears that women of color are even more hesitant to report rape to the police or to rape crisis centers than are European American women.

African American, Latina, Asian, and Native American women are just as unique and distinct as European American women. There is no way to justly generalize any characteristic as being true for an entire group of people. Women from all backgrounds enjoy different forms of sexual behavior.

There are two false premises that converge in this myth. First of all, women of color as a group like or accept certain behaviors—in this case, violent sex. There is no evidence to support this belief. The second false premise here is that because women "accept violent sex," then somehow raping them is more acceptable or less harmful. Sex, by definition, is mutual. So even if it is "violent" or rough, that is categorically different than rape.

The "Black Males Are Rapists" Myth

The myths are not just confined to victims. There are myths related to men who rape. Probably the most common and virulent is the myth of the Black male rapist. This myth will be discussed in greater detail in Chapter 9, "Racism, Homophobia, Sexism, and Men's Violence." At this point, it is important to recognize that African American men, or any men of color, are no more likely to rape than any other group of men.

The "Homosexual Rape" Myth

A myth commonly held about men who are raped is that they are gay, or that same-sex rape is "homosexual" rape. This will be discussed in more detail later. While there is some evidence that gay and bisexual men may be at increased risk for being sexually victimized (in part, as one aspect of a hate attack), they *are* victimized and do not enjoy the attack any more than women do.

There are a plethora of other rape myths. This section discusses only a handful. The main point about this discussion is how educators can effectively respond to myths when they arise in a presentation. As educators develop their educational skills and become more competent and confident, they will develop a full array of responses to myths as they arise.

The Impact

Before reading this section, please think through the following activity.

DOING YOUR WORK: ***Ranking Trauma***

Take a moment to answer the following question.

Is rape/sexual assault, in general, more traumatic or harmful than a physical assault?

Why?

(This is also a very good exercise to use with a discussion with men.)

Experiencing a sexual assault is one of the most traumatic experiences that anyone can have. Sexual assault is so devastating, in part, because it is so invasive. It can and does harm people on several levels: emotionally, physically, spiritually, socially, mentally, and sexually.

The Medical and Psychological Impact

The medical and psychological implications for being sexual victimized can be long-lasting and severe. Some physical and mental health effects of rape/sexual assault include

- Chronic pelvic inflammation or discomfort
- Chronic Irritable Bowel Syndrome (IBS)
- Chronic constipation
- Headaches
- Night sweats
- Depression
- Post Traumatic Stress Response
- Nightmares

Of course, this list could be expanded to include even more effects.

A sexual assault is both physically and emotionally traumatic. Although most sexual assaults involve less severe physical violence, they are still forced acts involving very tender and sensitive parts of the body, most commonly the vagina, anus, mouth, and breasts. There are cases in which women, for example, have had parts of their labia major (the outer part of the vagina) ripped during a sexual assault or had their breasts squeezed so hard they were left with bruises. Men have had their anuses torn. Regardless of whether the physical violence is that extreme, the act of a sexual assault involves touching someone's body against the person's will, which by definition means the use of some form of force (coercion, manipulation, actual force, or other means). During a sexual assault, the vaginal or anal walls are tensed against the intrusion and the body has usually not lubricated the area. Because of these conditions, a sexual assault is often physically painful.

"Regardless of how 'gently' an unwanted sexual act may be done, the act is inherently violent."

Regardless of the severity of the physical trauma, the emotional harm resulting from a sexual assault often has greater impact than the physical force. A sexual assault is the act of someone else taking control of the most sacred, most personal part of another person. Regardless of how "gently" an unwanted sexual act may be done, the act is inherently violent. Because it is disrespecting people's rights to decide who touches them, this level of utter disregard for their personal autonomy is abusive. The impact on the person assaulted is profound.

The degree of the impact may vary depending on the dynamics of the actual sexual assault: how long it happened, how many attacks occurred, the relationship with the perpetrator, and the severity of the physical violence, but the attack is always a profound one. Women and men often feel loss of control, shame, sadness, fear (they often report that they were afraid that they would die), anger (at themselves, at the perpetrator, at the situation), relief (that it was not any more violent or no worse), and a myriad of other emotions.

It is commonly believed that men who rape are somehow easily identifiable and thus easily avoided. This belief, which is also often held by women or men who are raped, is associated with the fact that most women and men are raped by men they know, like, and may have invited home with them. All these factors result in increased feelings of responsibility, guilt, and self-blame. Those who are raped often feel that somehow they should have "known better," "not gotten into that situation," "defended themselves better," and so on.

Rape myths impact the degree of harm that women or men who have been raped experience. Most rape myths have to do with victim culpability, or the notion that those who are raped are in some way responsible for being raped (they should have been more careful, less drunk, more aware of their surroundings, and so on). Unfortunately, people who are raped often believe, to some degree, these same rape myths and turn these myths back on themselves, which only reinforces the self-blame and guilt.

These feelings of responsibility fuel the shame stemming from, in part, the feelings of self-blame and the inherent humiliation of the assault. This shame not only has detrimental effects on the healing process but also results in the low rates of reporting.

It is also important to understand that sexual assault is not just a physical act; there are verbal components as well. When men rape, they are not silent. They talk during the assault. They frequently verbally abuse the person they are victimizing during the assaults, with comments such as:

- "You like this, don't you?"
- "You know you wanted this."
- "Doesn't this feel good to you?"

Frequently people who rape use even more extreme and verbally violent language. This verbal violence can be just as damaging as the sexualized physical violence. The verbal violence reinforces feelings of shame, self-blame, and horror that the victim experiences.

The Low Reporting of Sexual Assaults

One effect of the impact on women or men who have been sexually victimized is the low reporting rate to the police. Rape and other forms of sexual assaults have the lowest reporting rate of any crime. It is estimated that less than 5 percent of rapes are reported to the authorities (Sampson, undated). There are a number of reasons why people who have been raped choose not to report. Some of these reasons include

- They don't label their experience as rape
- They feel
    - embarrassment
    - shame
    - fear of publicity
    - fear of reprisal from the assailant
    - fear that they won't be believed (from friends, family, police, prosecutors, and so on)
    - self-blame

Helping men to understand why women or men don't report is an important aspect of educating men about the issues of rape and sexual assault. (The "Disclosure" exercise described in Appendix B is very effective in addressing this issue.)

Strategies for Presenting on Rape and Sexual Assault

The sections that follow suggest successful strategies for presenting on rape and sexual assault.

Use RTS: The Stages in Coping with a Sexual Assault

Rape Trauma Syndrome (RTS) is a model developed to describe how rape impacts a person. It is based on Post Traumatic Stress Response and, as such, recognizes that rape is inherently traumatic. Trauma can be understood as an event or series of events that overwhelms a person's coping mechanisms. Rape Trauma Syndrome describes the process that a person may go through as she or he heals from a sexual assault.

As the movement to respond to rape/sexual assault has continued to develop the theories around rape/sexual assault and to better understand how people who are victimized respond, they have further developed RTS. One version of RTS consists of three stages with several issues arising within each stage. Based on this work, Pam Remer and the Kentucky Association of Sexual Assault Programs developed the *Stages of Coping with a Sexual Assault*, which better reflect the full experience of someone who experiences rape/sexual assault. (The original Rape Trauma Syndrome is duplicated in Appendix C. Appendix A contains an outline of a presentation on RTS.)

STAGES IN COPING WITH A SEXUAL ASSAULT

Pre-Sexual Assault. What are the feelings and beliefs about rape/sexual assault, personal life experiences, coping skills and strategies, support systems, and so on? This includes any information they have about sexual violence, attribution of blame, level of acceptance of rape myths, feelings, or beliefs about law enforcement and the judicial process, and so on. These attitudes and feelings impact the ways the person recognizes danger and responds to the sexual assault. This stage also impacts the feelings and behaviors during the next stage and the choices made about reporting to the police, disclosing to others, calling a hotline, and so on.

Sexual Assault Event. At some point, people become aware that they are going to be raped.

A. **Immediate Pre-Assault—The events before the assault.** What is going on immediately before the sexual assault? What danger signs are victims aware of? Any awareness of risk or danger often starts as rather vague and then increases. How do people cope with the increasing threat?

B. **Sexual Assault—The time during the assault.** Many people report feeling that their lives are in danger and their primary consideration becomes how to survive. How do they react to the knowledge that they are imminently going to be raped? How do they survive the actual assault? Many people who are raped describe dissociating or "leaving their body" during the assault. These immediate coping strategies have implications for the ongoing healing.

C. **Immediate Post-Assault—The moments immediately after the assault.** How did the person get away from their assailant(s) and the situation? What did they do to make themselves feel more secure? To what place of safety did they go? It is a common belief that the assailant will come after them and try to assault them again. This belief can be immobilizing for many people.

Crisis and Disorientation. This stage is the initial period after escaping from the sexual assault. People who are sexually assaulted often report feeling helpless, out of control, fear, terror, anger, isolation, shame, confused, sad, and so on. Two more common styles of reacting are to appear (and often feel) completely out of control with crying and sobbing, or appearing more "in-control" by numbing out and not being in touch with any feelings at all. People who are victimized often seek out someone to receive support (who they may or may not disclose to). Many also feel a fear of being rejected or judged negatively for their choices, which hinders their willingness to disclose.

Outward Satisfactory Adjustment. The people who are assaulted have dealt with the immediate aftermath of the assault and the initial crises, and begin attempts to function "normally." They often attempt to go back to their pre-assault activities and behaviors. Some denial may be an attempt to regain a sense of control and reclaim a sense of life prior to the assault. Some specific behaviors may include forgetting or repressing, refusing to define the incident as a rape or sexual assault, minimizing the impact, forgetting some of the details, and so on.

The person may experience unexplained fears or anxiety, may change how they relate to others, and may experience nightmares. There is often a sense of frustration that they can't get their "old" life back.

This stage is often misinterpreted (by the victims themselves as well as by others) as resolution.

Reliving and Working Through. This phase is often triggered by a crisis. The person is unable to continue to deny or minimize the effects of the assault. The nightmares may become too intense, or the person may see someone who reminds them of the person(s) who assaulted them or the person who raped them. Or they may experience flashbacks, generalized anxiety, depression, and/or feelings of being out of control (much like they felt immediately after the assault). People who have been victimized often feel like they are "going crazy" because these feelings are recurring and they thought (largely based on denial and minimization) that they had gotten over it already. Friends and loved ones may also be confused and get frustrated during this period.

At some point, people who have been victimized may reenter counseling and continue the work of healing from the sexual assault.

Resolution, Integration, and Healing. In this period, people who have been sexually assaulted work to integrate the experience into their lives. They come to accept that the sexual assault happened; that it was a terrible, horrible thing that was done to them; but one that no longer controls them (thoughts, feelings, and/or behaviors).

Although described in stages in order to better understand and conceptualize it, the process is often much more cyclic in nature. Women or men who are raped may proceed through stage one and two, only to revert back to stage one as a court date arrives or on the anniversary of the assault(s). This means that the healing process can be extremely frustrating for the person who survived the attack as well as for loved ones. The anniversary of the attack, for example, may trigger increased feelings of tension, anxiety, anger, and more. People who have survived sexual victimization may get frustrated at re-experiencing these feelings after they have felt that they have already gone through those experiences.

Printed with permission from the Kentucky Association of Sexual Assault Programs, as adapted from Pam Remer, PhD.

The use of Rape Trauma Syndrome (RTS) and discussion of the impact of sexual assault is important not only in increasing men's understanding and thus their empathy with people who have been raped, but also is important in talking with men about how to respond to a loved one who has been sexually assaulted.

Educators can use RTS or the Stages of Coping with a Sexual Assault as a whole during a presentation, or they can use pieces. Furthermore, the better educators understand these processes, the better they can use the information and get that information across to men. Both RTS and the Stages of Coping provide relatively easy means to describe and understand that the healing from a sexual assault is a process.

Spend Time Busting the Myths

Every educational program needs to spend a substantial amount of time with myth-busting. This need not be the entire program, nor does it have to be a formal part of the presentation, but because of the number of myths and how strongly men appear to hold onto these myths, confronting myths needs to be integrated as a part of any presentation. This can be done in subtle ways. For example, during a conversation about the definition of rape, it is likely that several myths will emerge. Use this conversation to identify the beliefs that men have as myths and challenge them on it. Using the "Continuum—Make your Case" exercise in Appendix B is another good way to engage in conversations that challenge myths.

Address Sexism

Rape and sexual assault stem from sexism. Because this is true, educational programs need to be grounded in an analysis. Furthermore, educators need to address why men need to be concerned with sexism as a part of responding to rape or sexual assault. Confronting sexism is part of stopping rape. Confronting sexism is also a means by which men can better support their loved ones who are victimized.

Address the Sexual Assault of Men

While it is true that women are much more at risk for sexual victimization, men *are* raped and educational efforts *must* include information about male rape. This is true not only because the topic is likely to come up, but more importantly because male rape does happen. Any room that has men in it likely has men who have experienced some form of sexual assault. Just as is true with educating women, part of the job of educators is to reach out to these men, acknowledge what they may be going through, and encourage them to seek the services and support they deserve—in a way that doesn't draw attention to the men.

Roughly one in seven men is sexually assaulted in his lifetime, most often by other men. Men are more vulnerable as boys and younger men, although they do continue to be at some level of risk throughout their lives (unlike women who are at greatest risk for being sexually victimized between the ages of 16 and 25). Men who are or who are perceived as effeminate are at greater risk, as are gay or bisexual men or men *perceived* to be gay or bisexual.

The point of addressing male rape is that it happens, that it is wrong, that men can provide support to other men who are sexually victimized, and that men can work to stop the rape of men and women. In fact, working to stop rape, by definition, means working to stop the rape of *women* and *men*. Framing the discussion of male rape within a broader context of sexism and violence enables a more thorough understand male rape. Although men are targeted, the rape of men is still best understood as being motivated by power, control, and entitlement (not sex) and as an act of sexism.

Questions About Male Rape

When educating about rape or sexual assault, it is not uncommon for the question of the rape of men to arise. Very often, the person asking the question assumes that men are raped by women, and when educators respond by clarifying that men are indeed raped (although at a lower rate than women are) but by other men, there is often an uncomfortable response ranging from silence to laughter. A strong myth exists amongst men regarding male sexual assault, that myth being that a "real man" would die or kill before allowing himself to be sexually assaulted by another man. This feeling results directly from homophobia and the mistaken belief that the rape of men is sexually motivated. It is important when doing education about the sexual assault of men to challenge those myths and point out that, like women, men who are sexually assaulted do exactly what they need to do to survive.

The Term *Male Rape*

Although men are more likely to be raped by other men, and gay and bisexual men are at somewhat greater risk than heterosexual men of being sexually assaulted, the sexual assault of men is not and should not be referred to as *gay rape.* Referring to the rape of men as *gay rape* is a disservice to gay men and bisexuals. Homosexuality has nothing to do with violence, and there are about as many similarities between homosexual behavior and the rape of men by other men as there are between heterosexual behavior and the rape of women by men. To reiterate a point made several times, rape is *not* a sexual act. It is an act of violence using sexual parts.

Male Rape and Empathy for Women

It is utterly inappropriate to use the rape of men as a technique to develop men's empathy for women who have been raped. This will likely only encourage men's homophobia, and there is little evidence that recognizing their own vulnerability increases men's ability to empathize with women. Furthermore, men already have the ability to empathize with women who have been raped. There is no need to use emotionally manipulative techniques to get men to recognize what they already experience (although they may not be aware of). Male rape and the experiences of men who have been raped are deserving of attention in their own right.

Language and Male Rape

One way that clearly demonstrates how the rape of men, like the rape of women, is an act of sexism is through the words that rapists use when they rape. As part of the trauma in general, it is important to recognize (and offer when doing presentations) that rapists are not silent while they rape. They often say very cruel and hurtful things. What rapists say is cruel, hurtful, and also very gendered. Regardless of the gender of the person they rape, rapists often use language that can only be described as woman-hating, with phrases such as

- "How do you like this, you bitch?"
- "You nasty slut."
- "You're my woman tonight."

Men's and Women's Responses to Being Raped

Like women who are sexually victimized, men experience many of the experiences described by RTS. Some of the additional issues that men face include their own internalized homophobia and related feelings of their masculinity being threatened or damaged as a result of the sexual attack. Many men believe that it is feminine to be attacked, especially sexually. To rape is masculine; to be raped is feminine. For example, some say, "a real man would fight off a rapist...even to death." In fact, there have been men who have been raped who have responded "but men aren't supposed to be raped," which suggests that women *are*. In addition, this belief suggests that men who are sexually assaulted are more likely to redefine their experience as something other than a sexual assault and refuse to seek the assistance and support they need and deserve.

Added to the misconceptions discussed earlier is the traditional masculine training that teaches men to handle their problems by themselves. It is seen as feminine to ask for help. Masculinity requires that men "suck up and deal with it." This belief also acts as a barrier to men seeking support or assistance. So men who are raped are often in a Catch-22. They struggle with their own sense of themselves and their masculinity because they were raped as well as because they asked for help.

Address Consent

Almost inevitably, when an educator offers a presentation on rape and sexual assault, the issue of consent will arise. Because the issue of consent is so contentious and so poorly understood, it needs to be incorporated into most, if not all, presentations with men. Educating men about consent is most useful by providing an opportunity for them to examine what they think they mean by consent and engaging men in a process of stretching that definition. The "Is This Consent?" exercise in Appendix B is a very good exercise to use to dissect and explore these issues of consent. The more educators are able to involve men in the process of developing or defining the terms that educators are trying to get men to better understand, the more effectively men will begin to understand these terms.

The consent question arises when men struggle with whether a "Yes" means "Yes," or what a "No" means (as the exercise describes). When addressing the question, it is important to acknowledge that there may be times when truly knowing whether you have consent is indeed confusing. All people (though men are less likely to admit it) have times when they are somewhat ambiguous about having sex with someone, or how intimate they may want to get. People have the right to change their minds, both deciding to have sex when they initially thought they did not want to, and deciding not to when they initially thought that they did. For most men, Saying "No" appears to mean "Maybe" or "Try again later." Based on this information (which often arises from the "Is This Consent?" exercise), an educator could ask, "If saying 'Yes' means 'Yes' and saying 'No' means 'Try again,' what truly means 'No'?"

There is more to consent than just a yes or no. There are several elements to consent. One simple exercise to use that exemplifies this is to ask someone if you can touch him on the shoulder. If he says, "Yes," keep talking about consent, while continuing to tap the shoulder with your index finger. (If you want, you can vary this exercise: Ask if you can hold the person's folder, binder, briefcase, back pack and, after you have permission, begin rearranging the things in it). At some point, that person (and the rest of the audience) will challenge the behavior. The educator can use this exercise to illustrate that one of the elements of consent is that both people have the same understanding of what they are consenting to do. This is true regarding an educator tapping a person on the shoulder as well as for a woman agreeing to go up to someone else's room.

All the elements that are required to truly have consent are

- Both partners have the same understanding of what they are consenting to.
- Both partners are fully mentally capable of giving consent (in other words, one partner is not drunk, high, stoned, or otherwise incapacitated).
- Force or threats are not present.
- Both parties feel confident that if they change their mind, their decision will be fully respected and listened to.

Resources

Web

FaithTrust Institute (formerly the Center for the Prevention of Sexual and Domestic Violence). Specializes in developing materials and resources to work with communities of faith around issues of sexual and domestic violence. www.faithtrustinstitute.org

Mainly Men Against Violence and Sexism. A statewide effort mobilizing men in Maine to address sexism and violence. www.mmavs.org/

Men Against Sexual Violence (MASV). A project of the Pennsylvania Coalition Against Rape. Provides resources and activities to mobilize men against sexual assault. www.menagainstsexualviolence.org

Men Against Violence Webring. www.interactivetheatre.org/mav/

Men Can Stop Rape, Inc. A Washington, D.C.-based men's organization. www.mencanstoprape.org

Men Stopping Rape. A Madison, Wisconsin-based men's organization. www.men-stopping-rape.org/

Minnesota Center Against Violence and Abuse (MINCAVA). A wealth of resources and articles on all types of violence and abuse issues. www.mincava.umn.edu

National Alliance to End Sexual Violence. National coalitions working on public policy advocacy and grassroots organizing. www.naesv.org

National Center on Domestic and Sexual Violence. Provides training and technical assistance to local areas to increase the capacity to respond to and prevent domestic and sexual violence. www.ncdsv.org

National Organization Against the Sexual Victimization of Men. National network of providers who work with and on behalf of male survivors. www.malesurvivor.org

National Sexual Violence Resource Center. www.nsvrc.org

Rape Abuse and Incest National Network (RAINN). www.rainn.org

Violence Against Women Office. The office within the U.S. Department of Justice that addresses issues of violence against women. www.usdoj.gov/ovw/

Women of Color Resource Center. A valuable resource on issues of violence and others that impact on women of color. www.coloredgirls.org

Print

Anderson, L. A., & Shiston, S. C. (2005). Sexual assault education programs: Meta-analytic examination of their effectiveness. *Psychology of Women Quarterly, 29,* 374–388.

Beneki, T. (1982). *Men on rape: What they have to say about sexual violence.* New York: St. Martin's Press.

Berkowitz, A. D. (1994). *Men and rape: Theory, research and prevention programs in higher education.* San Francisco, CA: Jossey-Bass.

California Coalition Against Sexual Assault. (2001). *A vision to end sexual assault: The CALCASA strategic forum report.* Available from www.calcasa.org

Connell, N. & Wilson, C. (Eds.). (1974). *Rape: The first sourcebook for women.* (New York Radical Feminists). New York: New American Library.

Funk, R. E. (1993). *Stopping rape: A challenge for men.* Philadelphia, PA: New Society Publishers.

Funk, R. E. (1999). *What to do with men: A manual for rape crisis centers.* Available at www.rusfunk.com.

Funk, R. E. (1999). *A beginning of a beginning: Cross cultural competence for sexual assault workers.* Available at www.rusfunk.com.

Funk, R. E., & Mudd, A. (1999). *Partners in healing: Working with significant others.* Available at www.rusfunk.com.

Gager, N. & Schurr, C. (1976). *Sexual assault: Confronting rape in America.* New York: Grossett & Dunlap Publishing.

Robinson, L. S. (2003). *I will survive: The African-American guide to healing from sexual assault and abuse.* Emeryville, CA: Seal Press.

Russell, D. E. H. (1984). *The politics of rape: The victim's perspective.* New York: Stein and Day Publishers.

Scarce, M. (1997). *Male on male rape: The hidden toll of stigma and shame.* New York: Insight Books, Inc.

CHAPTER 5

Sexual, Gender, and Street Harassment

"So far as is known, men sexually harass women as often as they did before sexual harassment became illegal."

MACKINNON, 2004, P. 194

"Just to say 'fucking bitch,' to feel these obscenities on the tongue and in the mouth, and to hear oneself say them, socialized in men a hateful, violent, and righteous feeling of power over women."

HERNTON, 2001, P. 157

Sexual, gender, and street harassment are extremely common, often overlooked, and yet can be as damaging as other forms of sexist violence. All of these forms of harassment are related to each other, as well as to the other forms of violence and abuse described in this book. They all share the foundation in sexism, and they all share the experience and intent of defining space where women do not belong. These expressions of sexism are also distinct in important ways. In this chapter, each form of harassment is discussed with specific information about how to respond and address these issues when educating men.

Sexual Harassment

The statistics are sobering:

> 85 percent of girls (under 18) report some form of sexual harassment in school (Kopels and Dupper, 1999; AAUW, 2001).
>
> 78 percent of women (college age or older) are sexually harassed in the workplace or classroom (MacKinnon, 1979; Paludi, 1990).
>
> 10 to 20 percent of women who are harassed report the harassment to supervisors or someone in authority (Gutek, 1985; Gruber and Smith, 1995).

Sexual harassment is a range of sexualized behaviors that are experienced by the target as intimidating or uncomfortable. The law understands two forms of sexual harassment: quid pro quo and hostile environment.

- **Quid pro quo** harassment is offering a benefit in exchange for sexual activities, threatening some action unless sexual activity is provided, or implying or suggesting that sexual activity is a condition of education, employment, or advancement. Examples of quid pro quo harassment are the stereotypical "If you want this raise, you'll...," or "If you really want to pass this course, you'll..." Because of legislation and lawsuits, as well as the activism and education of feminists, much of this behavior is now understood to be inappropriate, and steps are taken in many places to curb this form of harassment.
- **Hostile environment** harassment is much more common, complicated, and difficult to address. It is creating or sustaining an environment that women (in most cases, although there are cases where men have successfully sued under the hostile environment framework) find intimidating, threatening, or uncomfortable due to the sexualized nature of the behavior or environment. In a hostile environment, the standard is that the atmosphere is so uncomfortable that a reasonable person would find working or studying offensive, intimidating, or threatening. Examples of a hostile environment include telling sexist jokes around the coffee station, making sexualized comments, displaying pornographic images in public space, and so on.

The other difference between these two forms of harassment has to do with who the perpetrators are. In general, the perpetrators of quid pro quo harassment are supervisors, teachers, and others in relative power over the person being harassed. The perpetrators of hostile environment harassment tend to be peers.

Educators need to understand these differences in part because it is likely that male audiences will have questions about the legal issues related to sexual harassment. Thus, educators need to be equipped to respond to these questions. In addition, and perhaps more importantly, this information is helpful in describing the myriad of ways that women (and some men) are harassed and can lead to a discussion of the impact of harassment.

EXAMPLES OF DIFFERENT FORMS OF HARASSMENT*

- "You're taking a job a man should have"
- "Women belong at home, not in the workplace"
- "Why don't you be a good woman and make us some coffee"
- "Nice legs" (or breasts or butt or comments on or about other body parts)
- Unwanted sexual attention

- Staring at breasts when talking to her
- Asking about her sex life
- Asking if she wants to "fool around"
- Rubbing hands up and down her back
- "Accidentally" brushing hands across her breasts
- Leering
- Blowing kisses
- Making cat calls
- Sexual derogation
- Rumor spreading
- Using offensive language to refer to women's body parts
- Placing pornographic pictures in hallways, coffee areas, lunch rooms, and so on
- Placing a "Woman Beaver Place" sign on the women's restroom door
- Open discussion of sexual exploits
- Solicitation with threat
- Coerced sex

**Based on Welsh, 2000*

The sidebar "Examples of Different Forms of Harassment" lists just some examples of what women experience from men in the workplace or classroom. These kinds of behaviors are harassing, as one can imagine by reading them, because they, first of all, have no place in a work or educational environment. Secondly, they are directed at women. They are harassment because they make women feel uncomfortable *because they are women*.

Some forms of harassment also combine sexist and racist dynamics so that the harassment targets a person because she is a woman and because she is a person of color. Furthermore, all these forms of harassment can be seen as possible rape threats. They remind women that men can choose to act in more extreme and violent ways.

As mentioned earlier, men are also sexually harassed, almost always by other men. Although the specific behaviors of sexual harassment may be somewhat different, the intent and reaction are the same. The intent is to make the person uncomfortable, and the reaction is one of feeling intimidated, threatened, or offended. Just as what happens when women are targeted, when men are targeted it is their sexuality that is the focus of the harassment. For example, men who do not act in ways that the other men in the workplace think they should—they don't act "manly" enough, they don't participate in the use of pornography, they don't engage in the sexist humor—often become targets for other men's harassing behaviors.

When educating men about sexual harassment, educators will undoubtedly hear the argument "Women do it too." This is certainly true. Women are just as likely as men to engage in some of these behaviors. However, the intent and certainly the impact is very different. This is true for several reasons. When women engage in these kinds of behaviors with men (for example, a group of women whistling or making comments at a man), men may report feeling embarrassed or humiliated; they often report also feeling somewhat flattered. But they never report feeling threatened, fearful, or worried that the behaviors may escalate. When men engage in these behaviors with women, on the other hand, women report feeling embarrassed, humiliated, possibly somewhat flattered, but often (if not always) feel some level of fear and threatened, and they worry that the behaviors could escalate.

One cannot separate sexual harassment from the larger context of other forms of men's violence. For many girls and women who are raised with the threat of various forms of men's violence, sexual harassment is a reminder of the possibility of this threat. Some men who rape use harassing behaviors as a means of "rape testing"—to see how a person is going to respond in order to decide whether to escalate to more aggressive behaviors. On some level, most women know this, and it is impossible to tell the difference between the man who harasses but is not going to escalate and the man who harasses who is.

Sexual harassment can and does have serious implications for women who are harassed. (The author is unaware of research that explores the health implications for men who are sexually harassed.) Harassment is more than just "unwanted attention." It has real health consequences for women. Some of the reactions of women who have been harassed include

- Changing jobs, schools, or residence
- Depression, anxiety, loss of self-esteem
- Headaches, nausea, weight loss or gain, insomnia, high blood pressure, gastrointestinal disorders
- Inability to concentrate
- Sleep disturbances
- Increased stress in interpersonal relationships

A close examination of this list exposes similarities to the symptoms of women who have been raped. Though the severity of the symptoms may not reach the level of Rape Trauma Syndrome, the symptoms themselves and the feelings that women report are quite similar.

Impact, Not Intent

One of the main points that needs to be stressed about sexual harassment is that the intent of the person who harasses is less important than the impact on the person who feels harassed. A person does not necessarily have to *intend* to create a hostile environment in order for another person to feel that she or he is unwelcome, unwanted, afraid, or intimidated. This focus on the impact, rather than intention, makes definition and enforcement much more difficult and complicated. People engage in many behaviors with the best of intentions that may, in fact, be harassment.

CASE STUDY

I am one of those people who uses touching to connect with others. I have always worked in settings that were mostly female. Several years ago, I worked at a youth and family-counseling center and was one of two men in a staff of ten. One evening, one of my female colleagues was working at the main computer and showing signs of physical distress (rubbing her shoulders, doing the "shoulder roll," and so on). I began giving her a shoulder massage. At about that moment, our state monitor came in and, without missing a beat, said to my colleague, "If you want to file a harassment suit, I will back you up."

My working relationship with my colleague was one in which giving each other shoulder massages was almost routine. She did not experience it as harassment in any way. My intent was not to harass, and there were no "sexualized" feeling in my actions. However, if she and I had had a different kind of relationship, or if we had been in a different kind of work environment, even if my intention had been exactly the same, that same behavior could very well have been harassment. If I had been her supervisor, if our work environment was one in which physical contact between co-workers was not the norm, if my colleague had experienced that behavior in any way as making her uncomfortable, then any of those dynamics could have made my behavior harassment, even though my intent was the same.

The point here, as with most forms of sexist violence, is not so much to define specifications or precise behaviors that are or are not sexual harassment. The point is that the experience of being harassed is contextualized in the relationship and the environment rather than in specific actions or behaviors.

A second point for broadening the definition of sexual harassment beyond specific behaviors is for men to notice how they and other men interact with women in the workplace and classroom. Some questions for educators to encourage men to ask themselves include

- What can we do to make sure that how we interact with women (and other men) is respectful?
- How do we make our relationships with women such that they feel that they can come talk to us when we do something that makes them feel uncomfortable?
- How do we respond appropriately when a colleague (be that student or worker) or supervisee (again, either student or co-worker) indicates that we are making them feel uncomfortable?

The goal of the work to eliminate sexual harassment is not to create work and study environments where women and men can't hug each other, rub each other's backs, and perhaps even flirt and date. The goal is for men to ensure that women and other men are treated with the respect and dignity they deserve.

The Target's Behavior

As will come up with just about any conversation about sexism and violence, men frequently ask, "Why doesn't she leave?" For many men, it seems obvious that if she does not like the way that she's being treated, she should just quit or change classes.

When men ask this question, educators can remind them how hard it can be to change jobs or classes. In talking about a classroom or job setting, ask the men how many of them have tried to change classes, work spaces, or departments. Ask them how many of them have tried to look for a new job.

The tone of the educator in these kinds of conversations is really important. It is crucial that educators ask questions such as "What would you do?" legitimately and from a curious position, without using a judgmental tone. In this way, educators can discuss some of the difficulties and barriers that women or men who are harassed face. Another question to ask in response to men's questioning why a women doesn't just leave is "Why should she have to?"

It is patently unfair for someone to feel that they have to leave a job or change classes in order to be treated with respect and dignity. They should be able to have any job or be in any class and still be treated well.

Sexual Harassment in School Settings

So far, most of this discussion has focused on sexual harassment generally, with a slight focus on the dynamics with regards to adult women. While the dynamics are very similar for adolescent and younger women, it is worthwhile to focus specifically on the issues of sexual harassment as they occur in school settings (specifically middle and high school).

"For adolescents who tend to be extremely self-conscious and very aware of how others think about them, having rumors spread can have devastating effects."

Sexual harassment in school settings is widespread. More than half of all female students, for example, report being afraid at least some of the time when they are going to school (AAUW, 2001). Sexual harassment in schools most often involves spreading sexual rumors, pulling on clothing, saying targets are gay or lesbian (as a derogatory comment), forcing them to do something sexual, or spying on them while dressing or showering (AAUW, 2001). These behaviors are somewhat different than those identified by adult women in workplace settings. For adolescents who tend to be extremely self-conscious and very aware of how others think about them, having rumors spread can have devastating effects. In addition, youth tend to be extremely conscious of their bodies (in part due to their typical self-consciousness). Having public or semi-public comments made about their bodies, or becoming aware that they are being watched when undressing or showering is a behavior that is much more harmful than it may appear at first.

When talking with adolescent boys, it is important to keep these differences in mind.* It's also crucial to remember that adolescents tend to be very concrete, and very gender-rigid, as in "Boys are this way, and girls are that way." When educating adolescent boys about sexual harassment, allowing plenty of time for the discussion around "why" is extremely important too. Even though the behaviors are the same, the intent and impact is different. This is not to say that it is okay for girls to engage in these behaviors and not okay for boys. It *is* to say that it means something different. Most boys and young men are able to understand this.

Gender Harassment

Much less understood or examined, especially by men, is gender harassment. Unlike sexual harassment, gender harassment rarely is sexualized. There isn't the same kind of behavior or atmosphere of referring to or relating to women as sexual objects. The lack of a sexualized tone does not make the harassment any less insidious. It only means that it is a different form.

Gender harassment is best understood as behavior that does not allow a woman to forget that she is a woman, and as such, does not "belong." As described in the sidebar "Examples of Different Forms of Harassment," it is assuming that a woman in a meeting will take the notes, make the coffee, prepare the room for a meeting, clean up afterwards, and so on. There is not the same kind of implied threat that occurs with sexual harassment, but there is an impact on women's performance and stress level in the workplace or classroom.

The dynamics of gender harassment are similar to sexual harassment. It is often men engaging in behaviors that have the impact of making a woman feel uncomfortable or out of place *because she is a woman.* As with sexual harassment, it is difficult to identify specific behaviors of gender harassment. The behaviors are contextualized in the relationship and the situation. In some cases, it may be perfectly fine to ask a women colleague to make the coffee. In other cases, it may be harassment.

**For a fuller discussion of talking specifically with male youth about sexual and gender harassment, contact the author at www.rusfunk.com.*

Street Harassment

"Systematically, street harassment can be understood as an element of a larger system of sexual terrorism."

Davis, 1983, p. 192

A whole other category of harassment that women face far too often is harassment on the street (Bowman, 1993). Street harassment can best be understood using the definition offered by feminist-anthropologist Micaela di Leonardo:

> *Street harassment occurs when one or more strange men accost one or more women...in a public place that is not the woman's/women's work site. Through looks, words, or gestures, the man asserts his right to intrude on the woman's attention, defining her as a sexual object and forcing her to interact with him. (1981, p. 51)*

As unseen as harassment is in general, street harassment is even more glaringly invisible. At least, and admittedly this is not much, sexual harassment has reached the public consciousness enough for there to be a language to describe it, texts written about it, laws defining it, and court cases that address it. Street harassment has had none of this. So the harm that women and men experience is a result not only of the abusiveness of the behaviors, but also is magnified as a result of having to experience this harm in silence.

One of the questions that men often raise during presentations on street harassment is the difference between street harassment and street flirting. While it seems that there *is* a significant difference in how one flirts on the street versus how one flirts in other situations, the difference between flirting and harassment is not as vague as this question suggests. The di Leonardo definition suggests that these key elements constitute street harassment:

- It is perpetrated by strangers.
- It occurs in a public place, not the woman's workplace (in other words, in the street, the quad, a public elevator, a parking garage, a park, and so on).
- There is some kind of behavior that positions her as solely a sexual object.
- He/they force an interaction.

While it is not necessary to have all these elements for a behavior to be harassing, examining all of them with men can help to define this behavior more concretely.

One critical way to challenge men when they struggle with the definition of street harassment is to ask, "Who are the men doing the behavior for?" In most cases, men are not doing the behavior in order to actually start a conversation with a woman. They engage in the behavior in order to make the woman uncomfortable and/or to "make points" with the other males. Engaging in a conversation by pointing this out (through a process of asking men in the room questions about the dynamics of harassing or "flirting" with women on the street) can help clarify some of these differences. Harassment is *much* more likely when men do things like this for each other's benefit.

What street harassment looks like in practice is men whistling, making comments, gesturing to or at, staring, making wolf noises (or other suggestive sounds), making kissing sounds, and so on as women walk down the street, across campus, into a parking lot, or any other public space. What it means when men do this, as di Leonardo describes above, is making an environment unsafe and threatening for women.

"The impact of street harassment is so strong that many women choose to avoid ever returning to the site of harassment if they can."

In response to street harassment, women report feeling embarrassed, humiliated, furious, helpless, vulnerable, and defenseless. Street harassment threatens women's self-esteem and increases self-consciousness. The impact is so strong that many women choose to avoid ever returning to that site if they can.

Ultimately, street harassment is the practice of men labeling women's identities as exclusively in their bodies, their "sex," and then claiming that identity, and thus, women's bodies as public space. Through street harassment, women lose the right to walk anonymously in public space. They become targets or potential targets. As Robin West (1987) states, "It is damaging to be pointed at, jeered at, and laughed at for one's sexuality, and it is infantilizing to know you have to take it." She goes on to describe the impact of street harassment this way,

> *It's not natural to smile when one is afraid or insulted. It's not natural to try and make oneself small or frozen. (p. 105).*

Yet this is exactly the kind of response that women who are harassed on the street are taught to have.

The impact of street harassment can be, and often is, broad and intense. In addition to these feelings, street harassment, even more than other forms of harassment, always carries a threat of more severe violence. Some men use street harassment as a method of "rape testing." They watch how women react to harassment to determine whether the women may be an easy target for rape. Some men who harass women on the street do escalate to the point of using violence if the women fail to respond the way men think they should.

While the incidence of men escalating to violence are relatively rare compared to the totality of street harassment, these occurrences do happen. Thus, street harassment can be akin to terrorist threats. No woman can know which man is hiding a knife, a fist, or a gun behind the catcalls, whistles, and comments:

> *I have lost the ability to discriminate between men who are being friendly and those who wish to do me harm. Now I view all gestures from men on the streets as potential threats. (Bernard, 1990)*

Responding to street harassment is extremely difficult for women. Research suggests that most women react with fear. They freeze or pretend to ignore what is being done to them (Bowman, 1993, p. 561). However, reacting with any of these strategies might lead to an escalation of violence. For example, it is not uncommon for a man who harasses a woman on the street to pursue a woman who ignores him with comments such as "Stuck-up bitch," "What's the matter, you fucking bitch? You're too good to talk to me?" and others, and/or to escalate with threatening gestures, yelling, and in some cases, physical violence.

However, if women do respond, they risk engaging men and having men interpret their response as an encouragement to continue. Men may (and reportedly often do) interpret women's responses as permission to continue the behavior, or in many cases, to escalate. Although not necessarily escalating with violence or abuse, the men may escalate with tenacity. When a woman answers the question "Where are you going in such a hurry?" some men may even take it as an invitation to join her and continue to converse.

Street harassment is a form of sexual harassment, but unlike sexual harassment that occurs in the workplace or classroom, in most jurisdictions, there is no legal recourse for women. As with other forms of men's sexist violence, the law was written with men in mind and fails to adequately protect the rights of women. Currently, the only recourse for individual women is self-protection, and, as a response to this common and systematic violation of women's rights, that just is not good enough. Street harassment, like all other forms of harassment, demands a public and coordinated response. It should not be up to individual women to figure out how to keep themselves safe in public spaces.

Strategies for Presenting on Harassment

When educating men about harassment, educators should focus on raising men's awareness about the issues and dynamics, about how harassing behaviors impact women and other men's lives, and about what men can do to confront these behaviors. Harassment can be somewhat more complicated and challenging because men tend to be even less well-educated about harassment than they are about rape, sexual assault, and domestic violence. (Men would be hard pressed not to have heard something about rape, sexual assault, and domestic violence.) Because of this lack of awareness and public discussion, educational programs for men about harassment will likely need to spend more time on defining the issues and attempting to raise men's general awareness.

Harassment is much less publicly debated or discussed than rape/sexual assault and domestic violence. With the notable exception of the Anita Hill testimony before the Clarence Thomas hearings in the early 1990s, there has been very little opportunity for men to be exposed to the issues of harassment. Therefore, educating men about the issues of harassment needs to begin with very basic information:

- Defining the issues
- Describing the incidence rates
- Examining the impact on women

It is only after men have some grasp of the issues that they can begin taking some personal ownership and can begin having conversations about what men can do to work to stop harassment.

SAMPLE EXERCISE: *Tracking Street Harassment*

This is a good exercise to use with male audiences to raise their awareness about the incidence of harassment. It was designed with men in mind, but it has been beneficial for women to do as well. (The italicized sections are those that are said to audiences.)

This exercise is designed for you to do with a female friend. Agree with her ahead of time about what you each are going to do and how each of you will behave.

Follow the female friend as she walks through a public setting (across the quad on campus, downtown, through a mall, and so on).

Count every time a man makes a comment at her, makes a comment about her, or looks at her the way men look at women they find attractive in public settings. Just notice the number of times, and, if you can hear them, the kinds of comments made.

What is your reaction?

How do you think the behavior of others affects her?

What did you learn from this experience?

What do you think your friend wants from you?

How will you find out?

Resources

Web

9 to 5. A national organization addressing the issues of working women. Sexual harassment is one of their main projects. www.9to5.org

American Association of University Women (AAUW). www.aauw.org

Street Harassment Project. Addresses issues of street harassment through direct action and advocacy. www.streetharassmentproject.org

Print

Hill, C., & Silva, E. (2005). *Drawing the line: Sexual harassment on campus*. Washington, DC: American Association of University Women.

Langelen, M. L. (1993). *Back off: How to confront and stop sexual harassment and harassers.* New York: Simon and Schuster.

CHAPTER 6

Stalking

"More than one in ten women are stalked during their lifetimes."

NATIONAL STALKING RESOURCE CENTER

Stalking is one of the more recent forms of sexist violence that has been labeled. As such, there is still much to learn about the dynamics and impact. What is known is that it, like the other forms of sexist violence, is extremely common, largely misunderstood, and vastly under-reported. There are still states, communities, and campuses that don't have laws or policies addressing stalking, and few educators seem prepared or comfortable addressing these issues, nor is stalking a regular part of most educational efforts.

Defining Stalking

Stalking is still largely misunderstood. Although a substantial amount of work has been done to address stalking, largely beginning in the early 1990s, there is still no clear or shared definition about what constitutes stalking. That being said, stalking can be understood as "unwanted pursuit" with an implied threat. It includes such behaviors as

- Following/surveillance
- Appearing at places that the person targeted frequents
- Unwanted contact (telephone calls, e-mails, faxes, letters, creating false Web pages, and so on)
- Threats (to the person or to family members, friends, or pets)
- Unwanted or threatening gifts
- Vandalizing property

Cyberstalking is a relatively new and increasingly common form of stalking. Cyberstalking, as the name suggests, involves using the Internet to pursue or harass another person. Increasingly common on college campuses, cyberstalking involves sending messages by e-mail, hacking into an e-mail account to identify messages or cull her address book, creating Web pages that disclose real or fantasized personal information, or engaging in other behaviors that constantly remind her that someone is present and watching. With the continuing development of Web-based technology and the increasing availability to access people (cell phones, text messaging, wireless connection, etc.), the forms of cyberstalking will likely increase. It is important, when educating men, to discuss the ways that these behaviors can be experienced as threatening, harassing, or frightening even if the innate behavior in and of itself does not appear to be anything more than annoying.

The preceding elements are frequently used in stalking. As such, the definition that arises from these behaviors and the pattern of behaviors that are used in a specific stalking situation mean that this definition is one that is victim- or survivor-centered. State and municipal laws regarding stalking vary even more widely than do state laws regarding rape or domestic violence. Some states define stalking more comprehensively, listing out specific behaviors that constitute stalking, while other states define stalking in much broader terms. As with other cases of sexism and violence, educators need to be well versed in both the above victim-centered definition, as well as the definition of their state or municipality. This includes, for those educators who operate on college campuses, knowing the campus definition of stalking as well.

Like domestic violence, stalking is best understood as a *pattern* of behavior. Although people can be stalked in a single incident, they are unlikely to even notice, much less will they find it threatening or intimidating. It is the *pattern* of behaviors that is problematic. This pattern consists of ongoing behaviors and usually a range of behaviors such as those described above. Like the other forms of sexist violence described in this manual, stalking does not have a precise definition. "Stalking is an extraordinary crime, given that it may often consist of no more than the targeted repetition of an ostensibly ordinary or routine behavior...many stalkers do not overtly threaten, instead using behavior that is ostensibly routine and harmless." (Sheridan, Blaauw, & Davies, 2003, p. 150).

Furthermore, this pattern of behavior must, in some way, be threatening or frightening to the person who is the target of these behaviors. It is not enough, for example, to simply give unwanted gifts to another person. While this may well be annoying, frustrating, and disempowering, it is not considered stalking until it crosses the line of being done in a way that is threatening or frightening. According to most state laws, the way they identify this is whether or not a "reasonable person" would feel threatened or frightened by such behavior.

This "reasonable person" standard often proves to be a challenging standard for both advocates and educators. For advocates, the challenge is often defining what kind of person is the standard from which "reasonable" comes. As has been described throughout this book, because of sexism and violence, women tend to have a very different standard of what constitutes threatening or frightening behavior than do men. If the "reasonable person" standard does not take this into account (in effect, becoming a "reasonable *woman*" standard), than many of the behaviors that women may "reasonably" find threatening or frightening may not be considered stalking by law.

A similar difficulty can arise when educating men about stalking. Although perfectly able to understand that a pattern of behavior such as those listed previously can be annoying and bothersome, men may have a harder time understanding why that pattern of behavior may be experienced as threatening by a woman. Providing a context of sexism helps to bridge this gap of understanding and help men to empathize with how women may experience these behaviors differently from men.

Overview of Stalking

Although both women and men are stalked, women are at substantially greater risk. Furthermore, although both women and men stalk, men make up the vast majority of stalkers. Thus, stalking is a gendered crime. The National Violence Against Women Survey found that women are more than three times more likely than men to be stalked. More than one in ten women is stalked during her lifetime, with approximately 6 million women stalked every year. Based on these findings, women are more likely to be stalked than they are to be raped. Most stalkers (87%), of both women and men, are male. Stalkers are also usually European American and are generally between the ages of 18 and 29 (National Stalking Resource Center, 2003).

It's About Power, Control, and Entitlement

Stalking, like the other forms of violence and abuse discussed in this manual, is primarily motivated by power and control, and has the effect of making the person stalked feel powerless and out of control. In addition to the power and control dynamics, the person who stalks feels entitled to the attention of the person he stalks: a response, some form of communication, and so on. Men who stalk act on these feelings of entitlement in ways that limit the ability of the person they are stalking to set limits on how other people interact with them. For example, most people trust that if they tell another person to stop calling them or sending e-mail messages, the other person will do so. In stalking, the person may chose to ignore the request to stop their behavior, shift to new behaviors, or escalate to more threatening or violent behaviors.

Stalking is a form of violence because of the limits it places on the lives of those who are stalked and the implied and very real threat that is inherent within the stalking dynamics.

To explain how stalking is motivated by a sense of entitlement, it is important to understand how most stalking happens. Stalking is most frequently an extension of a dating or marital relationship, with women being stalked most frequently towards the end of relationships and after relationships have ended. There is often a history of domestic violence or dating abuse in these relationships, and the threat that these stalkers pose is very real. While men are also stalked, they are stalked much less frequently than women and are more likely to be stalked by strangers or acquaintances (whereas women are more likely to be stalked by intimates, former intimates, or acquaintances). Women are also more likely than men to be harmed as a result of stalking.

Stalking is a behavior that is inherently threatening, even if no overt threats are made. A man who stalks can engage in the behavior on an ongoing basis, or may stalk the person "only episodically." Stalking may include constantly being outside the classroom, dorm, apartment, or place of work, or it may be showing up periodically. Regardless of the specifics of the behavior, the people who are stalked begin to feel that they are always under surveillance. They may or may not know why they are being followed, whether the person stalking them poses a threat of violence, and whether the behaviors are escalating. These unknown factors increase the fear, which fuels the power of men who stalk.

CASE STUDY

After ten years of being abused by her husband, Barbara (not her real name) finally left. Because her roots were in the same community, she decided to stay in the same community. After leaving the battered women's shelter, she began volunteering. After a couple of years, she got a job there. As she continued in her development and growth, she continued to move up in the organization. She continued employment at the shelter for more than 12 years—14 years after leaving her husband. During the entire time that she worked there, once a month, she would receive a dozen white roses (what had been her favorite and had been part of her wedding bouquet). Although her ex-husband had stopped including any note or even any identification that he was sending them, she, and everyone else around her, knew that they came from him.

There are a number of interpretations to this behavior—although the fact that he kept it going for more than 12 years makes it more difficult to explain away. One possible explanation was that he felt really sorry for his behavior and simply was trying to apologize and make amends. After all, he knew that white roses were her favorite. This case example provides an excellent example of the challenge of the "reasonable person" standard. Without understanding the context of sexism and the history of domestic violence, there is absolutely nothing threatening or frightening about this behavior—annoying, creepy, weird, a bit obsessive, yes; but threatening, probably not. Even understanding the context of sexism and history of domestic violence, it may be difficult for her to file stalking charges against him (in fact, in most states, she would not be able to get legal relief from this behavior).

An educator can use this case example to point out how subtle stalking can be, and how damaging, traumatic, frightening, or abusive stalking can be even though it may be subtle. This case example is also effective as an educational tool with men about stalking. It has proven particularly effective in mixed-gender presentations when the educator describes the story and asks for feedback from the audience. Men, in general, have little to say other than her husband is "creepy." Women, in general, are much more able to identify the threat (as opposed to the "creepiness") that is inherent in this behavior within its context.

As described in the case study, stalking is generally associated with domestic violence or dating abuse. Less is understood about stalking that is related to other forms of sexism and violence, but it clearly also has a relationship with rape and sexual assault. Some men who stalk use stalking as a means to test their target's reactions and attempt to determine how easy they may be to rape. Rape and sexual assault may also be the end result of stalking, or some sexually assaultive behaviors may be associated with and incorporated into the stalking dynamic.

The Impact of Stalking

Like most forms of sexist violence, defining the impact of stalking is a challenging task. While there appears to be a clear set of typical reactions to stalking, there is a great deal of variance depending on multiple factors: length of time that the stalking occurred, the kinds of behaviors used in the stalking, the relationship between the stalker and the person they stalk, the support systems for the person who is being stalked, the coping skills of the person being stalked, etc.

That being said, there does appear to be a number of impacts that stalking generally has on people who are stalked. These impacts can be divided into several categories: economic, social, and psychological.

The economic impact of stalking includes

- Loss of job or work/school performance due to the stalking behaviors or anxiety about the stalking
- Spending money on increased security measures
- Spending money on stolen or broken property

The social impact of stalking includes

- Changing jobs or school
- Changing phone number (sometimes repeatedly)
- Changing e-mail addresses
- Moving
- Avoiding social activities
- Going underground (i.e., "disappearing" from their normal life or relocating without any forwarding information)

The psychological impact of stalking includes

- Decreased trust
- Paranoia
- Fear

- Chronic sleep disturbances
- Weight loss
- Anger or aggression
- Depression
- Frequent headaches
- Persistent nausea
- Difficulty concentrating

In some studies, more than half of women who have been stalked reported symptoms consistent with Post Traumatic Stress Response (see Pathe and Mullen, 1997).

Many of these symptoms have long-term consequences for the person who is stalked.

Perhaps most frightening, arrests, convictions, and restraining orders do not appear to be effective in stopping stalkers. The most effective means for women or men to stop men from stalking them is to move to an undisclosed location with an unlisted phone number, something that is inherently unfair to ask someone of who is being victimized. Because of the difficulties in defining stalking and the challenges around the legal definitions described at the beginning of this chapter, many women who report stalking to the police find the legal process to be incredibly frustrating and unhelpful. Depending on how that jurisdiction defines stalking, many of the behaviors may not fit into that definition. In addition, there has to be enough behaviors to identify a pattern and enough of a threat that a "reasonable person" would find the behaviors threatening.

Strategies for Presenting on Stalking

Educating men about stalking poses challenges for the educator that are similar to the challenges around domestic violence. Discussing definitions, motivations, and the target's experience are effective strategies for educating men on stalking.

Explore the Definition of Stalking

An important part of a conversation with men is exploring the definition of, and the difficulty in defining, stalking. Men likely have a wide range in their understanding of what stalking is, mostly based on lack of or misinformation. Men are rarely taught that there is a line between pursuing and stalking.

Address the Question of Why Men Stalk

In order to effectively combat stalking, it seems essential that efforts be developed to address the reasons or justifications for stalking. Much of this behavior stems from the same reasons as the other forms of sexism and violence: a sense of entitlement, a sense of ownership or of being owed, and a rejection (even violent rejection) of any attempts to control him—whether it be by the woman setting limits, the law imposing limits, and so on.

As in the case of domestic violence, many men who stalk do not necessarily intend to stalk. Rather, they are doing that they think they have the right to do. There are plenty of images available in music, movies, and books of men who continued to pursue love interests after initially being told "No" only to have their love interests fall in love with them in part (we are led to believe) as a consequence of their persistence. This imagery, and the countless ways that these messages get reinforced, teach men that it is not only acceptable, but that they *should* pursue past an initial rejection. This is not to say that men who stalk are not fully responsible for their behavior and all of the consequences of their behavior. Just because they don't know that they've crossed the line between pursuing and stalking doesn't mean that they're not still responsible for their behavior and the fear or intimidation that a woman may experience as a result of their behavior.

Talking with men about stalking requires a clear conversation addressing why men stalk and critically examining where men get the notion that it is okay to continue to pursue someone who has clearly indicated that she or he wants to be left alone. This kind of critical dialogue can occur in ways that engage men in the conversation. For example, simply asking a male audience under what circumstances is it okay to continue to pursue someone that he is interested in after she or he has said no, can open the door for a fruitful conversation.

Discuss the Target's Experience of Stalking

Imbedded in any conversation such as this is how women may experience those behaviors differently from men. Build upon men's inherent empathy by having them describe what they believe the impact of stalking may be. Clearly, this comes later on in the conversation, after some discussion about the definition and the forms of stalking. Any conversation with men needs to include how they might respond to a friend who is being stalked, how to challenge a friend who may be engaging in stalking behaviors, and what resources are available in their community.

Resources

Web

Anti-Stalking Web Site. www.antistalking.com/

Stalking Resource Center of the National Center for Victims of Crime. www.ncvc.org/src/

Stalking Victims Resource Site. A comprehensive Web site of resources for people who have been victimized by stalking. www.stalkingvictims.com/

Print

Gross, L. (2000). *Surviving a stalker: Everything you need to know to keep yourself safe.* New York: Marlow and Company Publishers.

CHAPTER 7

Domestic Violence and Dating Abuse

"The four main sources of conflict leading to violent attacks are men's possessiveness and jealousy, men's expectations concerning women's domestic work, men's sense of the right to punish 'their' women for perceived wrongdoing, and the importance to men of maintaining or exercising their position of authority."

DOBASH, R.E., AND DOBASH, R.P., 1992, P. 4

Domestic violence and dating abuse are long-term and extremely challenging issues. All evidence suggests that domestic violence and dating abuse have been relatively consistent for as long as they have been identified. With as much work and awareness that has been done over the past couple of decades, there is still more that isn't known than what is known.

Understanding the Issues Related to Domestic Violence and Dating Abuse

Coming to understand, rather than just know about it, is a further complication. As challenging at this is, it is important for educators to be able to begin to understand some of the more complicated issues related to domestic violence and dating abuse before being able to effectively educate men.

These points are all true, and can be effectively used as "attention getters" for male audiences.

- The most dangerous place for a woman is her own home.
- The leading cause of women's visits to the emergency room is domestic violence—causing more visits than rapes, muggings, and car accidents combined.
- One in three women is hit or raped by a date or husband in her lifetime.
- One in five young women between the ages of 15–21 is hit or raped by a dating partner.

Domestic and dating violence, in many ways, have been even harder to capture statistically than other forms of men's sexist violence. A 2001 study in Massachusetts, however, found that one in five teenage women experience physical or sexual violence by a dating partner (Silverman et al., 2001). Although women in their high school and college years (roughly ages 15–25) are at the highest risk for these kinds of violence by men, women continue to be at risk at any age for abuse by their boyfriends or husbands. One of the key problems of domestic violence and dating abuse, and one that is crucial in truly understanding (and educating about) the dynamics of domestic violence, is that the violence, abuse, threats, and intimidation may not end just because the woman leaves the relationship.

A Note About Language

There is an increasing tendency to refer to domestic violence/dating abuse as "abusive relationships," "violent relationships," "relationship violence," or some similar descriptions. Advocates need to guard against this tendency. Relationships are not abusive—people are. Relationships can be unhealthy or addictive or problematic, but *relationships* are not and cannot be abusive.

"Relationships are not abusive—people are."

This language places the responsibility for the abuse on the relationship, not on the person who is being abusive. It is a person who chooses to act in abusive ways in a relationship. Using language such as "abusive relationships" suggests that any violence or abuse that occurs within relationships is shared responsibility. This colludes with the abuser and blames the person victimized because it suggests that the abuse occurs relatively equally and that the abuse is a part of the relationship dynamic, not the sole responsibility of one partner. Men and women are not equally likely to commit acts of violence or abuse. Men are the majority of perpetrators of abuse and violence within relationships, and suggesting that it is common or equitable only furthers women's victimization. When talking generically about abuse within relationships, it is more appropriate to use language such as "abuse within a relationship," or "in a relationship with someone who is abusive."

Towards a Definition of Domestic Violence and Dating Abuse

Domestic violence and dating abuse can best be understood as a *pattern* of behavior designed to maintain power and control in a relationship. Most legal definitions and most of the public focus on domestic violence by focusing on specific incidents or actions such as a hit, a punch, a kick. While these behaviors are certainly problematic when they occur within a relationship, and while these behaviors are certainly violent, these behaviors in and of themselves do not necessarily indicate domestic violence. First of all, there are times when people engage in these kinds of behaviors in self-defense, and defending oneself by using violence does not make that person a perpetrator of domestic violence. Secondly, it is important to try to get at the pattern because it is the pattern of behaviors that cause the damage and destruction.

Domestic Violence/Dating Abuse as Gendered

The evidence is unequivocal: domestic violence and dating abuse are almost always acts perpetrated by men against their female dating or life-partners (Kimmel, 2001). When men are victimized in domestic violence, it is almost always by their male partners, and when women perpetrate domestic violence, it is almost always against their female partners.

While it may be true that women engage in some violent behaviors as often as men, they overwhelmingly do not operate from a pattern of power and control. It is during conversations about the alleged gender parity of domestic violence that the definition stated above becomes so crucial. As defined above, domestic violence is a *pattern* of behaviors using a variety of tactics in order to maintain power and control within a relationship. Engaging in certain behaviors does not by itself indicate the presence of a pattern. To further confuse this, research techniques have not been developed fully enough as yet to truly capture patterns. Research tends to focus on what is easiest to identify—namely, the specific acts or behaviors and the most common used. The research suggests that women and men use physical violence (slapping, hitting, pushing, throwing things at, and so on) almost at the same levels. When the research measures sexual violence within relationships, there is a clear gender difference (men perpetrate sexual violence).

Just counting the incidents of physical violence, however, is misleading. One must take into account the reasons for using physical violence, the context of the violence, and the implications of using violence (Kimmel, 2001). When asking these questions, it becomes clear that women most often use violence in self-defense, in the context of having been abused, and their use of physical violence rarely results in serious injuries to men. Men, on the other hand, use physical violence to maintain control in the relationship and the results are often serious physical injuries to women.

The Impact of the Violence

Imagine for a moment that you love someone enough to live with him or her. Now imagine that this person is, for all intents and purposes, holding you captive. You must report where you go and why you are going there. You are limited in the number of friends that you have and the amount of contact you have with your family. You are forced to ask for anything that you need, and often must justify and explain why you need it. In addition, you are subject to threats, name-calling, put-downs, and episodic physical violence. Oh yeah, and you must be available for sex on demand, including immediately after being beaten.

This is what domestic violence looks like. It is extremely damaging to a woman's self-esteem. Domestic violence is a traumatic and complicated situation into which people are forced, both interpersonally and socially, that make it extremely difficult for women to even know what is best for them, much less make any movement towards new goals. In addition, the dynamics of domestic violence in the context of sexism (and in many cases, racism and homophobia as well), add to the barriers that women face, and the distrust they likely feel about being supported in the ways they need and deserve.

Tools to Use with Domestic Violence Education

Two powerful tools to use when educating about domestic violence that graphically illustrate key points are the Power and Control Wheel and the Cycle of Violence. Males and females understand the messages behind both these tools.

The Power and Control Wheel

When people think of domestic violence/dating abuse, they generally think of the most dramatic forms, such as a hit, punch, kick, slap, or the use of a weapon. However, understanding domestic violence and dating abuse as *patterns* of behaviors shifts the focus from examining particular violent actions to looking at patterns of power and control, with physical or sexual violence being the most extreme forms. The Power and Control Wheel (on the next page) is the best description of the variety of tactics used to maintain power and control within a relationship and how these tactics are used in concert. As the Power and Control Wheel describes in Figure 7.1, actual violence is only one tactic used to maintain a position of dominance in the relationship. In most relationships, physical and sexual violence are the last tactics used. In most cases, before a man hits or slaps his partner, he has already established a pattern of power and control in the relationship using other tactics.

For example, a man may call a woman names and belittle what she does, be the one who decides when they go out and where they go, isolate her from her friends and family, try to control what clothing or how much make-up she wears, and so on long before ever using physical violence. These tactics are used to establish his dominance in the relationship and define a relationship in which he is being abusive.

Some examples of the tactics of power and control that are used in relationships are

- **Physical violence.** Pushing, hitting, slapping, choking, shoving, shaking, biting, pulling hair, burning with cigarettes, hitting with objects, stabbing, shooting, and so on.
- **Emotional abuse.** Put-downs, name-calling, belittling, "mind games," emotional withdrawal, making another think she or he is crazy, and so on.

Figure 7.1

- **Economic abuse.** Making the other ask for money, keeping tight controls of household funds, taking her money, sabotaging her work, and so on.
- **Sexual assault/rape.** Making the partner do things sexually she or he doesn't want to do, forcing her or him to watch pornography, forcing her or him to perform acts he has seen in pornographic images, raping, physically attacking the person's sexual parts, spreading sexual rumors, and so on.
- **Using children.** Making the other feel guilty about the children, using children to send messages, making the children hit or otherwise abuse his partner, threatening to hurt the children or to take them, and so on.
- **Using pets.** Threatening or actually harming animals, refusing to provide care for the animals, and so on.
- **Threats or intimidation.** Making threats to hurt the person or someone she or he knows/loves; placing a partner in fear through the use of looks, actions, gestures, a loud voice; smashing things; hitting walls; displaying or cleaning weapons at strategic times; and so on.
- **Isolation.** Limiting who the other person sees (who, how often, when, and so on), not allowing her or him to call family or friends, controlling where she or he goes, limiting funds to go out with, and so on.
- **Limiting independence.** Limiting the kinds of clothes or make-up she or he wears, telling her how to wear her hair, deciding for her what kinds of birth

control she uses, checking in repeatedly on a cell phone or pager, driving her or him to and from work, and so on.

- **Violating personal boundaries.** Reading personal notes, mail, or e-mail; listening in on phone calls; going through her purse or locker; and so on.
- **Degrading/humiliating her.** Calling her names in front of others, putting down her religion or extracurricular activities, going out with other girls/women after agreeing to be exclusive, touching her inappropriately in public, talking about her private business with others, and so on.
- **Using male privilege.** Making all the "big" decisions, treating her like a servant, acting like the "king of the castle," demanding sex, expecting things to be "a certain way," and so on.
- **Minimizing, denying, and blaming.** Making light of the abuse, blaming her for being abused ("If you didn't make me so angry" for example), saying that it was not abuse or that the abuse did not happen, shifting responsibility for the abuse, and so on.

The Power and Control Wheel demonstrates how men who are abusive use a variety of tactics in a complex dynamic to maintain power and control. One important factor to reemphasize is how domestic violence is a pattern of control and dominance, not necessarily an individual act.

The Cycle of Violence

A model that has been developed to explain the dynamics of abuse within a relationship is the Cycle of Violence (L. Walker, 1979). According to that model, a relationship has three stages of violence and abuse: the tension-building stage, the acute battering stage, and the reconciliation stage (also sometimes referred to as the "honeymoon" or "hearts and flowers" stage).

The process of domestic or dating violence begins with the tension building, i.e., increased anger, blaming, arguing, increased name-calling, and so on. After a period of time, this tension often leads to the acute battering, i.e., the attack itself. As soon as the acute battering occurs, the reconciliation stage begins, during which the man who acted abusively apologizes, offers gifts, and makes promises such as "it won't happen again" or "I'll be better." He may cry or beg for forgiveness, and so on. The nature of the reconciliation stage is that it ends as the tension begins to build again. This process is shown in Figure 7.2.

Frequently, domestic violence is used to describe specific violent and overtly abusive incidents, and legal definitions will tend to take this perspective. However, when violent and abusive behaviors happen within a relationship, the effects of those behaviors continue after these overt incidents are over. Advocates and counselors will refer to domestic violence as a pattern of behaviors, including those listed above.

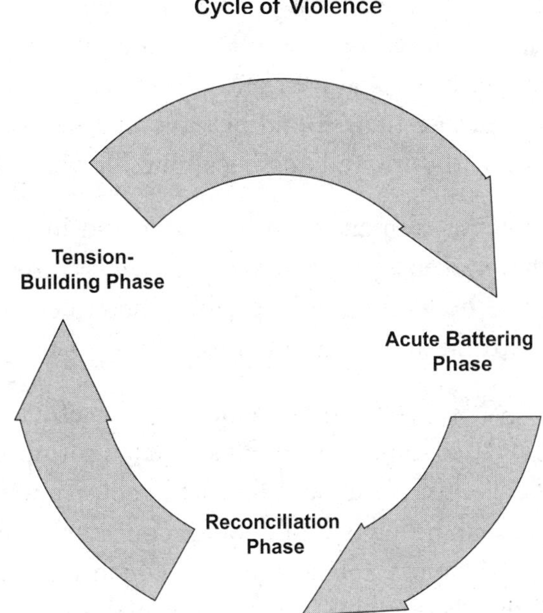

Figure 7.2

It is important to point out that the acute battering phase generally lasts between 2 to 48 hours. People often assume that the acute battering is an individual incident such as a slap, punch, or shove. Most people make sense out of the Cycle of Violence by reflecting on when they have experienced a tension-building phase followed by a blow-up. This is something, undoubtedly, most people can relate to. In relationships in which violence is being used, however, the battering often continues over a prolonged period, often with a variety of tactics used during this phase: verbal abuse, extreme name calling, physical violence, threats (to her, her family, the children, or pets), destruction of property, minimizing, blaming, and rape—and it goes on and on and on. It is important, when educating, to convey the level of hell that women who are battered endure during this period. It is extensive, exhausting, and seemingly endless.

"The reconciliation stage is not the absence of abusiveness but is rather a shift in abusive tactics."

It is important to note, too, that the reconciliation stage is not the absence of abusiveness but is rather a shift in abusive tactics. This part of the cycle is complicated because men who have been abusive *are* often sorry. The intention was to maintain their power or control in the relationship, not necessarily to hurt their partner. However, these behaviors—being loving and attentive, making promises or apologies, offering gifts, and so on—are best understood as additional tactics used to maintain power and control.

One of the effects of the Cycle of Violence as a whole is to keep the partner in the relationship and, thus, more vulnerable to the power and control tactics. The reconciliation stage provides yet another opportunity for that. In addition, there is no real acceptance of responsibility of his abusiveness. During this period, his blaming and minimization is often most severe. For example, he may apologize profusely, make promises, get himself into counseling, and do a number of behaviors that suggest he's sorry, but will also suggest or outright state that "if only she hadn't..." These kinds of statements expose that he still believes that she is responsible (by making him mad, disagreeing with him, "talking back," etc.) for his abusiveness.

The cycle tends to increase in frequency and intensity over time. The cycle that may initially have taken a year to develop may, over time, be reduced to a period of only several weeks. The level of violence also tends to escalate in severity over time, resulting in more extreme and severe injuries.

The Cycle of Violence is one model that is useful to understand the dynamics of abuse within a relationship. Not all abusive relationship demonstrate the cycle. Some men who abuse are just plain mean and act in abusive ways all the time. However, the Cycle of Violence can be a powerful tool for educators to use to help explain the dynamics of some, perhaps most, relationships in which one partner chooses to use violence. In addition, the cycle can be valuable in explaining how a man who batters uses a variety of tactics to get his partner to stay.

The Questions Domestic Violence and Dating Abuse Trigger

When a report of continuing domestic violence or dating abuse arise, it often is met with two questions: Why does he hit?, and the more common one: Why does she stay? The following sections look at the reasons someone stays with someone who is abusive and what motivates the person who abuses.

Why Does She Stay?

The question of why someone stays when they're being abused is perhaps the most common question faced by domestic violence educators and advocates. Many people assume that it is easy to leave relationships and, that, if she really wants to, all someone has to do is walk out the door. Even with, and indeed sometimes as a result of, the increase in the numbers of shelters and other services to assist battered women, there is a common misunderstanding of the complexity of the feelings that battered partners experience and of the barriers to leaving. There is also inherent blaming that is a part of this question—suggesting that because someone chooses to stay with a person who is abusing them, they somehow share in the blame for being abused.

There are several responses to the question of why she stays and there are many reasons why women or men stay in relationships with people who abuse them. This is often a frustrating question for educators. The frustration generally stems from the blaming tone that is inherent in the question. As frustrating as the question is, and as tempted as educators may be to dismiss the question outright, there is some legitimacy in asking why women or men stay in relationships with men who abuse them. Women stay for a variety of reasons.

Fear for Safety

Perhaps the major reason why someone stays is fear. A man who abuses uses a variety of threats in order to keep his partner in the relationship. He has followed through on some of his previous threats; others he has not. If he has escalated to using physical violence, he has probably threatened to hurt her (or her family or children) more severely, or even kill, if she leaves. People who are being abused have ample reason to believe that he will follow through on these threats, just as he has on others. The terror this creates is very real. The most dangerous time for a woman is when she leaves; most murders of the women who are killed by their partners occur when the women are trying to escape (it is unclear if these last statistics hold true for men who are abused).

While fear for their safety may be the main reason that people who are being abused may stay with the person who's abusing them, there are other fears as well.

Fears for the Children or Pets

A woman who has children face yet another series of barriers. She may fear being able to take care of the children on her own. The man likely has threatened to take the children if she leaves. She likely feels ambivalent about the degree of involvement she wants him to have with the children, and continuing to have access to the children increases his access to her (and thus his ability to abuse her). In addition, courts and child protection systems, not only tend to fail to recognize the degree of harm caused by fathers who batter, but also often continue to enforce his rights to access to his children. To the degree that they recognize the harms to children of being exposed to domestic violence, they as often as not consider battered mothers as responsible as the fathers who batter for the harm done to children. Thus, the very systems that should be available to support and protect battered mothers *and* their children often act as additional barriers that prevent women from being able to escape safely. Finally, a mother's presence may, and often is, a protective factor for the children. Her staying with him keeps him from abusing the children (or lessens the severity of his abuse of the kids). She may stay because she knows that if she leaves, he'll hurt the children worse.

For people who have pets, they may stay in order to protect their pets. Anyone who has a pet knows how important pets can be. People often love their pets as much as they love their children. Sometimes people who are being abused by their partner stay because they fear (rightly so) that if they leave, he (the person abusing them) will take it out on the pets.

Fear of Being Alone

Another reason that people stay in relationships where they are abused is because, like many people, they fear being alone. This rather normal fear is compounded for women or men who are abused by the person they are dating or to whom they're married because of the dynamics of abuse, in particular the verbal abuse. Men who abuse very often "pound" their partners with emotional messages designed to make her or him feel unworthy of even the love of the person abusing them, much less the love and respect from others. The emotional damage of being in a relationship in which one is abused cannot be overestimated.

Commitment to the Relationship

In addition to the fear, women or men who are abused stay for some of the same reasons that we all stay in bad or unhealthy relationships, which is not to say that being abused is "just a bad relationship." A person may stay in a relationship because of a commitment to the relationship.

Almost anyone who has ever dated has at some point dated someone who was bad for him or her, not necessarily abusive, but who for various reasons was not a good partner. When people are in love, they stay in the relationships and put up with some bad times because of the good times. In good relationships, the good far outweighs the bad. In the midst of a relationship, a person can find it very difficult to know when the bad begins outweighing the good. This is a judgment call that may be easy to make from the outside looking in, but not from within a relationship. The reason people stay is because they love the person and are committed to the relationship.

Even in relationships where there is violence, there is still good; most men who choose to abuse also have good behaviors and loving attitudes. There is more to a relationship than the bad, there is more to a battered woman or man than being battered, and there is more to a man who batters than his battering. The dynamics are *much* more complicated than the simple fact that he is abusive.

Feelings of Failure

Women stay in relationships where they are being abused in part because, like most people, they do not want to feel like failures. It is common to feel like a failure when a relationship ends. Most people have learned to talk themselves out of those feelings, but the feelings are still present:

- "Maybe I could have tried harder."
- "Was that wasted time?"
- "What could I have done differently?"
- "I should have seen that coming."

These are all common thoughts when relationships end, even the bad ones. It is nearly universal to experience these murmurs in the background after breaking up with someone. In addition to this, however, society puts a great deal more pressure and responsibility on women to keep relationships going, so for women, there is often an even higher sense of failure than for men. For battered women, the dynamics used by men who batter collude with this larger context and place all the responsibility for the violence and the failure of the relationship on her: "It is her fault that the relationship is failing—just like it is her fault that she is being hit." This misplaced responsibility is very difficult for a woman to overcome on her own, and so she may stay in a relationship because of this pressure.

Restrictions and Isolation

The various forms of power and control used by men who batter add another series of barriers to women's escaping. If a man controls all or most of the money, if he undermines the woman's ability to get or keep a job, if she does not have transportation, and if she has become isolated from her family and friends, leaving the relationship becomes very difficult. All these tactics commonly used by men who abuse make it much more difficult for women to escape.

Immigrant women also face additional barriers. A man may control a woman's green card or passport and may (probably does) threaten to report her to the federal authorities if she leaves. Because immigration law is extremely complicated, a woman may fear her partner's ability to have her deported or jailed if she does not stay with him.

Low Self-Esteem

Low self-esteem can also play a role in some women choosing to stay. A woman who is victimized by domestic violence often suffers from low self-esteem. There are those who argue that women's low self-esteem causes them to get into relationships with men who abuse them. However, it seems safe to assume that being abused by the person whom one loves would have a detrimental effect on anyone's self-esteem. When one loves a person who responds to that love with belittling, name-calling, threats, and violence (which reinforce the belittling), there will undoubtedly be a negative impact on self-esteem. So the question becomes, "Does women's low self-esteem cause them to get into relationships with men who batter, or does men's abusiveness cause battered women's low self-esteem?" Additionally, people who have lowered self-esteem or who are depressed tend to have more difficulty making decisions, making life-altering plans, and putting those plans into action. These may be some of the indications why women with low self-esteem stay with abusive partners.

Lack of Resources and Support

So far, the explanations offered for why people stay have focused primarily on the internal reasons. But there are also external barriers to escaping domestic violence. Women or men may stay because there are too few resources and supports to help them escape. In most cases, women who are under the age of 18 cannot get a

EFFECTIVE STRATEGY

When discussing all the reasons that women or men may stay with someone who is abusing them, it is helpful to turn the question back onto the participants. Ask them "how many of us, in our dating histories, have dated someone that, when we look back now, we wonder why we ever dated that person?" (have them raise their hands along with you). "How many of us, while dating that person, had periodic questions about why we're dating this person?" (again, have them raise their hands, and keep yours up). "Why did we stay?" Through this conversation, listing all the reasons that relatively healthy people continue to date people that they know are not good for them, men can begin to loose some of the judgment and blame for battered women or men. The point is that most people stay for many of the same reasons that battered women stay—except battered women have additional barriers that make it much harder for them to escape.

protective order (P.O.) on their own—and often can't get one at all. In many states, people who are dating (regardless of their age) cannot get a protective order. Even if a person does secure a P.O., there is no guarantee it will be enforced by the local police. In most jurisdictions, there is a lack of available social supports to assist her as she tries to escape. Most domestic violence shelters, which generally do an incredible job with the resources they have, do not have enough to support *all* the women in need (especially those women who are in special circumstances—teenage women, recently immigrated women, lesbians, women who are physically challenged, and so on). In addition, most shelters frequently have more people than they are designed to hold and do not have enough room for all the people who seek shelter.

In addition to these barriers, working through the legal process is terrifying and daunting for most people, and without adequate legal support/advocacy services (which are still quite rare), women may find this process too daunting to continue.

These are just some of the reasons that women stay. There are countless others. Even with a thorough conversation about why people stay, it is not uncommon for men to continue to argue that "some women" like it, or that they are still to blame. It is a firmly held myth that is very challenging to break in one presentation.

The exercise described to the left also exposes that ending a relationship or leaving a dating partner is extremely hard to do and is a process, or a series of processes. There is a process for deciding to break up (or leave), there is a process for deciding how to break up (or leave) and there is the process of actually doing it. This is a difficult enough process for people in relatively healthy relationships. It is much more challenging and dangerous in the context of dating abuse or domestic violence.

The following table lists some of the main reasons women stay when they have been abused.

WHY SHE STAYS...*

Internal Reasons	***External Barriers***
Fear (of being alone, of his threats, of being judged, and so on)	No real protection
Self-Blame	Lack of access to protective orders
Anger	Lack of shelter
Depression	No transportation (to escape)
Lowered self-esteem	Lack of child care
Want the relationship to succeed	Fear for pets
For love	Lack of health care (for her or her children)
Self-doubt	No affordable housing
Belief/hope that he'll change	Lack of transportation (to get around once she's left)
	Lack of language accessible services

**This table offers only a few examples and is not an exhaustive description of all the barriers that women face. Asking male participants in a workshop to list the barriers in a blank table like this is an effective way of increasing understanding.*

Why Does He Hit?

A much more salient question than "why does she stay?" is "why does he hit?" When offering presentations, it is helpful to respond to the question "Why does she stay?" by answering the question with the information available, as given in the preceding sections, and then reminding the audience that a much more salient question is, "Why does he choose to abuse his partner?" To reiterate, asking why she stays suggests that there is no reason for her to stay, and that she shares in some of the responsibility for being abused. Shifting the question to why he hits not only shifts the subtle undertones of blame by placing the responsibility squarely where it belongs, but also raises the underlying question of where does any man learn to believe that it is okay to act in abusive ways to the person he is dating, married to, or supposedly loves. After all, this is the real question.

"A much more salient question than 'why does she stay?' is 'why does he hit?'"

There are as many reasons why men choose to abuse as there are men who are abusive: personality, psychological state, family background, and so on. There is some evidence, for example, that men who choose to hit are somewhat more likely to have grown up in homes where they witnessed domestic violence. This rather elementary linkage must be read with caution. Although there may be a link between witnessing domestic violence and choosing to act in abusive ways, it is not causal, and there are more questions raised by this evidence than the answers it offers:

- Why, for example, is it that only barely a majority of the men who abuse have witnessed abuse?
- Why are there so many men who grew up witnessing domestic violence who are not abusive?
- Why is it that women who are exposed to domestic violence are not abusive?

EFFECTIVE STRATEGY

When offering presentations, it is helpful to respond to the question "Why does she stay?" by reminding the audience that a much more salient question is, "Why does he choose to abuse his partner?"

Excuses 1 and 2: Mental Illness or Drug Abuse

Two common excuses given to explain men's abusiveness are that men who abuse are mentally ill, or that they are drunks or addicts. While this may be true for some small portion of men who batter, the vast majority are no different (in terms of mental illness or substance abuse) than any other category of men. In other words, men who batter are no more likely than the general population of men to have a mental illness or to abuse alcohol or drugs.

One way to assess the relationship is to examine the degree to which men act violently towards others. There are forms of mental illness that cause men to act out violently. Those men for whom mental illness is truly related to their domestic violence are violent and abusive in other relationships and towards other people.

Similarly, there are indeed mean drunks. If a man has a substance abuse issue and abuses or is violent to people indiscriminately, then his violence may be related to his substance abuse. In both cases, however, these dynamics do not reflect the nature of domestic violence. For that portion of men who batter who have a mental illness or addiction, the vast majority still choose to perpetrate their violence against only their wife, girlfriend, or partner. This suggests strongly that their mental illness or substance abuse are separate issues from the domestic violence.

Excuse 3: Peer Pressure

For some men, there is also the role that their peers play in their choosing to act abusively. It is not uncommon for men to pressure their male friends to assert control in their relationships. Consider how common it is for men to accuse other men of being "whipped" if they don't control the decisions in the relationship. Peers exert considerable pressure on men to be masculine, to devalue women, and even to the level of being abusive (DeKeserdery, 1990; Myers, 1995; Silverman & Williamson, 1997; Price & Byers, 1999; LaViolette & Barnett, 2000).

Excuse 4: History of Child Abuse or Witnessing Domestic Violence

There is some evidence that indicates that witnessing domestic violence may make it easier for some men to choose to be abusive. It is also commonly believed that being abused as a child may lead some men to be abusive to their partners (although there is no evidence to support this claim). While it may be true that some men who are abusive may have been abused as a child or witnessed domestic violence, there are far too many men who were abused or witnessed domestic violence and are *not* abusive for this to be interpreted as a causal link. Furthermore, there are far too many men who are abusive to their partners who did not witness domestic violence and were not abused as a child.

Excuse 5: Low Self-Esteem

Many people erroneously believe that men who batter must have low self-esteem. While it is certainly true that some men who batter do have a low self-esteem, there is no evidence that men who batter have higher rate of low self-esteem than any other group of men. Men who batter may, like any other person, suffer from periodic low self-esteem, but as an overall theme in their lives, this simply does not appear to be the case. Furthermore, low self-esteem is not a reason to be abusive. There are many people who have low self-esteem, much more than those who are abusive.

Social Forces That Support Domestic Violence

"Our culture permits and encourages male aggression" (LaViolette & Barnett, p. 16), especially against women.

More important than the preceding Why questions, which attempt to place domestic violence/dating abuse solely as issues of individual psychopathology, are the social forces. Domestic violence is far too common to be a matter of an individual's pathology. It stretches the limits of common sense (or any other kind of sense) that one in four men are pathological. One in four men are not pathological, yet it seems that one in four men are abusive in their relationships. Clearly, there are reasons that men choose to abuse other than individual pathology or experience.

Men choose to abuse for a number of socially enforced reasons:

- Abusing works (to maintain power and control in the relationships).

  Men who feel that they are entitled to be in power and have control in a relationship (and thus of their partner) find that abusive behaviors work. It is effective in providing the illusion of power and control.
- The men feel entitled to use abuse.
- There are few sanctions (legal, social, or interpersonal).

The laws that do exist around domestic violence only focus on physical violence and are not consistently enforced. Men who are abusive also rarely face any consequences for their behavior.

- They are rarely held accountable when they choose to abuse.

  Although technically against the law, men are rarely held accountable in any real way for their abusiveness. It's not terribly different than why most people who drive speed: they are unlikely to get caught, and if they are, they're willing to pay the consequences. Men who batter are not much different.

- Women are systematically undervalued and de-valued in our culture.

  In a society in which women don't matter as much as men, and one in which men are taught that they should have the "upper hand" with regards to their relationship (often under the guise of "protecting" "their" women) the option to use violence or abuse as a means to maintain that upper hand becomes legitimized.

"Regardless of the reasons or background or culture or any other reason, the main point is that men abuse because they *choose* to do so."

Regardless of the reasons or background or culture or any other reason, the main point is that men abuse because they *choose* to do so. Abuse is not caused by mental illness or addictions (there are far too many men who are mentally ill or addicts that not abusive for this to be an explanation), anger management issues (most men who batter are very adept at managing their anger with everyone else: co-workers, secretaries, neighbors, friends, family members, and so on), or any other reason. These factors may, for some men who choose to abuse, have some impact on their choices, but whether to hit, or belittle, or control one's partner is an active choice.

Furthermore, from a social movement perspective, one has little control, ultimately, on the personal decisions of individuals. Individuals, however, do have some control over the social environment in which people make those choices and the kinds of choices that they see as open to them. If men did not learn that they have a viable choice to be abusive, and that they are likely to be sanctioned if they do abuse, then fewer men would choose to abuse.

Strategies for Presenting on Domestic Violence or Dating Abuse

Educating men about domestic violence or dating abuse best begins by examining how common these forms of abuse are. Men frequently blame women, on some level, for being abused and will often ask questions relative to the blame of women for being abused, such as "What do you do when you just get so mad that you can't help yourself?" Acknowledging that people have the right to be angry (in most cases) and that people in dating relationships can act in unhealthy ways and do something just to make the other person angry can be a good way to bring men further into the conversation.

That being said, people never have the right to put their hands on others, call them names, or make them feel bad about themselves. Being angry is one thing; how people choose to express their anger is solely their responsibility.

Focus on the Impact on the Victim

EFFECTIVE STRATEGY

To keep men engaged, encourage them to focus on how they would feel if they were abused by a partner.

Throughout an educational program with men, encourage them to re-focus on the impact of the behaviors on the person being abused. This is an important tactic to continue to keep them engaged, but it also can help them access their empathy. Men can grasp how they would feel if they were abused within a relationship. Helping them stay in touch with that empathy for the battered partner is an important part of educating men.

Focus on Men's Choice to Use Abuse or Violence

Throughout the process, it is important to shift the focus to the fact that men *choose* to use abuse or violence and the social-cultural context that tolerates men's use of abuse and violence. Bringing the connection between domestic and dating abuse back to the sexism from which they come is one part of educating men. Helping men to see how the systematic devaluing of women is related to some men choosing to hit women not only helps men to grasp the dynamics better, but can also open the door for men's engagement in working to end sexism and domestic violence/dating abuse.

Resources

Web

Alianza: National Latino Alliance For the Elimination of Domestic Violence. www.dvalianza.org

Asian and Pacific Islander Institute on Domestic Violence. www.apiahf.org

Battered Women's Justice Project. A national organization that addresses legal and justice advocacy for battered women. www.bwjp.org

Break the Cycle. A national organization addressing teen dating violence. www.breakthecycle.org

FaithTrust Institute. (Formerly the Center for the Prevention of Sexual and Domestic Violence) Specializes in developing materials and resources to work with communities of faith around issues of sexual and domestic violence. www.faithtrustinstitute.org

Family Violence Prevention Fund. National information and resource center on domestic violence. http://endabuse.org/

Institute on Domestic Violence in the African American Community. www.dvinstitute.org

Mending the Sacred Hoop. Addresses domestic violence as it relates to Native American women and communities. www.msh-ta.org

Minnesota Center Against Violence and Abuse. (MINCAVA) A wealth of resources and articles on all types of violence and abuse issues. www.mincava.umn.edu

National Center on Domestic and Sexual Violence. Provides training and technical assistance to local areas to increase the capacity to respond to and prevent domestic and sexual violence. www.ncdsv.org

National Coalition Against Domestic Violence. National organization advocating for battered women and their children. www.ncadv.org

National Domestic Violence Resource Center. (c/o the Pennsylvania Coalition Against Domestic Violence) www.pcadv.org

National Network to End Domestic Violence. Works on federal policy advocacy and support of local advocacy efforts. www.nnedv.org

Sakhi: For South Asian Women. National organization addressing violence against women and children, focusing on south Asian women and communities. www.sakhi.com

Sheila Wellstone Institute. Resource center and training institute addressing domestic violence. www.wellstoneaction.org

Violence Against Women Office. The office within the U.S. Department of Justice that addresses issues of violence against women. www.usdoj.gov/ovw/

Women of Color Resource Center. A valuable resource on issues of violence and others that impact on women of color. www.coloredgirls.org

Emerge. A Boston-based program working with men who batter and working to educate men about domestic violence. www.emergedv.com

Men's Initiative of Jane Doe. A project of the Jane Doe Coalition in Massachusetts—working within the state to mobilize and organize men to address domestic violence. www.mijd.org

Men Overcoming Violence. San Francisco-based men's organization. 1385 Mission Street, Suite 300, San Francisco, CA 94103 (415) 626-6683.

Men Stopping Violence. Atlanta-based men's organization. www.menstoppingviolence.org

Mentors on Violence Prevention. Works with men, primarily targeting athletes and college campuses, on ending violence against women. www.sportsinsociety.org

Nonviolence Alliance. Domestic violence training project focused on working with men who batter. www.endingviolence.com

Print

Barnett, A. W., Miller-Perrin, C. L., & Perrin, R. D. (1997). *Family violence across the lifespan: An introduction.* Thousand Oaks, CA: Sage Publications

Greig, A. (Ed.). (2002). *Partners in change: Working with men to end gender-based violence.* United Nations International Research and Training Institute for the Advancement of Women. Santo Domingo, Dominican Republic. (Available from www.un-instraw.org)

Island, D. and Letellier, P. (1991). *Men who beat the men who love them: Battered gay men and domestic violence.* Harrington Park, NY: Harrington Park Press.

New York State Department of Health AIDS Institute. (2001). *Domestic violence in lesbian, gay, transgender and bisexual communities: Trainer's manual.* Available from www.health.state.ny.us/nysdoh.

West, C. M. (2002). *Violence in the lives of black women: Battered black and blue.* New York, NY: Haworth Press.

White, E. C. (1994). *Chain chain change: For black women in abusive relationships.* Seattle, WA: Seal Press.

Office of the Attorney General. (2002). *Toolkit to end violence against women.* Washington, DC. http://toolkit.ncjrs.org

Ramos, M. D. (1999). *Cultural consideration in domestic violence cases.* San Francisco, CA: The Family Violence Prevention Fund.

Renzetti, C. M., & Miley, C. H. (Eds.). (1996). *Violence in gay and lesbian domestic partnerships.* Harrington Park, NY: Harrington Park Press.

Richie, B. E. (1996). *Compelled to crime: The gender entrapment of battered black women.* New York: Routledge Press.

CHAPTER 8

Pornography and Prostitution

"...pornography is a discriminatory practice based on sex that denies women the right to participate equally in society. It maintains sex as a basis for subordination, fostering bigotry and contempt sexually along gender lines and, in so doing, ensures that inequality remains society's central dynamic."

KENDALL, 2004, P. 8

"...pornography—like prostitution more generally—does not ultimately exist because of women's choices. Rather it exists because men, as a class, demand that there be a sub-class of women (and children, and men, and transgender people—but mostly women) who are available for their unconditional sexual service."

WHISNANT AND STARK, 2004, P. 25

Pornography and prostitution are rarely considered violent or abusive. The harm that is perpetrated within both pornography and prostitution is ignored or re-defined as something else. These two issues, related but distinct, are typically understood and described in ways that distinguish them from the violence and abuse that is inherent in them. The prevailing attitude about pornography and prostitution is based on the viewpoint of the men and women who make the profit and the perspective that pornography and prostitution are things that men use or have the right to use. Examining pornography and prostitution from the perspective of those who make the profit (which includes the spokespeople that they choose) provides a skewed view. Of course the profiteers are going to minimize the harm that is caused and done in pornography and prostitution. Of course they are going to use their resources to identify and support people who are used in pornography or prostitution who advance their perspective. And of course they are going to use their considerable wealth and other resources to systematically silence those who disagree with them. This is a long-standing business practice. Any business or industry is known for finding ways to promote the good it does and silence the people who disagree with their efforts.

Pornography is typically defined as a free-speech issue and often dismissed as "dirty pictures" (stories, films, Web sites) that have little impact on anyone. Prostitution is most commonly understood as a "victimless crime" (if it is seen as a crime at all).

Linking these separate but related issues under one heading may seem somewhat confusing. The reason this linking is made is that there is a clear connection between pornography and prostitution (and trafficking for that matter, but trafficking is beyond the scope of this manual). From a conceptual purpose, if prostitution is understood as paying money for sex, and pornography is taking pictures (usually paying a small amount of money) for sex, then what truly is the difference between these two? From a "front line" perspective, women and men who are used in pornography are often also used in prostitution. It is also not uncommon for women or men who are prostituted to have pictures taken of them (either by a trick, a john, or a pimp/"manager") that is then distributed on the Internet or sold (often without the woman or man's permission or even knowledge) to a pornographic magazine. Pornography and prostitution are linked in this manual because they are so linked in real life.

Why Pornography and Prostitution Exist

Pornography and prostitution exist for two primary reasons: the subjugation of women and men's entitlement to sex. There are certainly many other reasons, but at the core, pornography and prostitution exist because men believe that they have the right to sexual interaction and release whenever they want it; and because we live in a society that views women as lesser than men. As such, women become deemed as the appropriate targets for men's sexual release on demand.

The Subjugation of Women

Pornography and prostitution encourage and maintain a view of women as subordinate to men. This subjugation is taught as normal, acceptable, and, through pornography and prostitution, is sexualized. While it is true that these lessons are prevalent throughout our society in multiple ways (as suggested throughout this book), the link made by pornography and prostitution is exaggerated. Thus, not only do men learn that they are entitled to be dominant over women, but they also learn to eroticize this dominance. This, ultimately, has disastrous implications for the efforts to obtain gender, racial, or sexual justice between and amongst women and men.

Men's Entitlement to Sex

Another lesson that is reinforced by pornography and prostitution is that men are entitled to sex. Like the subjugation of women, the lessons of men's entitlement to sex are found in many ways throughout our society. But pornography and prostitution reinforce and exaggerate these lessons. If men don't receive "adequate" sexual release or involvement from their partners, men have the "right" to use other women or men to meet these sexual desires. This idea that men are entitled to sex is taught to men in many ways, but pornography and prostitution, and the access that men have to both, reinforces this message in ways that add layers of additional danger and potential harm to women and other men.

Some Challenges to Critiquing Pornography and Prostitution

When doing presentations that critique pornography or prostitution, there are a number of arguments that educators can expect to face. Three of the most common arguments are that people "choose" to get involved and, therefore, there really isn't any harm; that pornography (in particular, but this also relates to prostitution) is a free speech issue; and that using pornography or prostitution reflect a person's morality. What follows below are some ways to address these arguments when they come up in presentations.

People "Choose" to Be Involved

The vast majority of people believe that involvement in pornography and prostitution are choices made by the people who are used therein. Women or men displayed in pornography are seen as "models" who are "comfortable with their bodies" and who "freely choose" to have pictures or movies taken of them. Women or men who are prostituted are more generally pitied, but still seen as choosing to be involved. When defined as a choice, any harm that someone experiences or abuse that a person is subject to is coincidental. Furthermore, when seen as a choice, and thus as protected by the right to privacy, pornography and prostitution are defended by apologists for the following reasons:

- Women have the right to freely choose whether to be involved.
- Pornography and prostitution do not hurt anyone.
- People have the right to do what they want in the privacy of their own homes.

The women and men (in the case of gay male pornography) who are used to produce the pornography are ignored or forgotten. The violence, abuse, and harm that is inherent in pornography and prostitution is not recognized or is actively denied. Both pornography and prostitution are staunchly defended, any harm that results is excused and dismissed, and the people who challenge pornography and prostitution are subject to accusations of being "pro-censorship" and anti-sex.

In this manual, the harm that women and men experience in pornography and prostitution are forefront and considered as significant as any other form of sexism and violence. While these other factors may confuse the issue more than in the other forms of sexist violence (some women and men may indeed freely choose to be involved in pornography and/or prostitution) the crucial questions are: Is anyone harmed? Who? And how? The acceptance of pornography and prostitution is dangerous in and of itself because it disguises, minimizes, and ignores the harm that is caused. In addition, that acceptance of pornography and prostitution is also symbolic of the acceptance of other forms of sexism and violence. Understanding the links, even if not addressing pornography and prostitution directly, is important so that the women and men who are harmed can be heard and these forms of violence can begin to be addressed.

The Issue of Free Speech

Perhaps the core difficulty in defining and understanding pornography and prostitution is due to the traditional understanding of these issues as being primarily about free speech and expression. For most people, pornography and prostitution are considered private acts (from the perspective of the people, mostly men, who use pornography and prostituted people). As private acts, engaging in pornography or buying women or men through prostitution is rigidly defended as "free speech," and as such, something that must be protected. Once defined as a free-speech issue, pornography and prostitution, it seems, are seen as right and, therefore, cannot be limited or criticized in any way. Although it is common knowledge that men use pornography and access prostituted women, these acts are understood as something that men do "behind closed doors" and as something private, something that should not be politicized.

The Issue of Personal Morals

Another difficulty in critiquing pornography and prostitution is that the main perspective most of us have heard critiquing pornography and prostitution has been from a particular moral perspective, a morality that is not based on how women and men are treated, but on opinions about sex and sexuality. People who have a different moral compass have not been given a language to oppose pornography and prostitution.

The accepted definition of pornography is based on obscenity and provides little opportunity to explore the issue of harm. What is wrong with pornography, according to the obscenity-based analysis, is not the harm it causes, but rather the violation of a community standard. For example, to say that one is opposed to pornography suggests that one's critique is due to an opposition to nudity and sexual expression.

"There is a position that is not anti-sex, anti-nudity, and anti-sexuality but that also does not ignore the harm that is inherent in pornography and prostitution or the silencing of those who are victimized."

Similarly, the loudest voices against prostitution and all forms of sexploitation-type "work" are those who come from a particular moral position who oppose prostitution, not so much because of the harm that it causes the women or men who are used, but to the harm done to moral standards. To be opposed to pornography and prostitution on the one hand and pro-sex on the other seems like a contradiction, according to the parameters of the current pornography discussion. There is a position that is not anti-sex, anti-nudity, and anti-sexuality but that also does not ignore the harm that is inherent in pornography and prostitution, or the silencing of those who are victimized. It is this position that is the foundation in this manual (see also, Kendall, 2004; Whisnant and Stark, 2004; and Farley, 2003).

"*How do you define pornography*?" is a common question that stems directly from the obscenity framework. Pornography and prostitution are difficult topics to include in an analysis of sexism and violence because there are few organizations that address these issues and the women or men who are harmed. Without a network of services and resources, it becomes a challenge to figure out how to respond to questions or to know where to refer people who have more questions. Without a network of organizations that address these issues, there is little opportunity to develop clear analyses.

The goal of including these topics in the broader discussion of sexism and violence is to provide educators with the tools to offer a presentation to men about these issues as forms of men's sexist violence. They are forms of sexist violence and should be included in the work to educate, mobilize, and organize men. An additional goal is to explain how pornography and prostitution are connected to other forms of sexism and violence, and to encourage educators to include pornography and prostitution in their analysis and in their educational efforts.

Pornography

"Pornography is 'the construction of sexuality that reduces sex to a thing and woman to an object....'"

BARRY, 1995

"The effect of pornographic material is to reinforce male-female stereotypes to the detriment of both sexes. It attempts to make degradation, humiliation, victimization, and violence in human relationships appear normal and acceptable."

WOMEN'S LEGAL EDUCATION AND ACTION FUND, 1992

Several definitions are used to lay a foundation for discussing pornography. All the definitions offer different perspectives but are based on similar foundations, namely, the sexualized depiction of harm. Diana E. H. Russell, a sociologist and long-time anti-pornography feminist activist, defines pornography as "...material that combines sex and/or exposure of genitals with abuse or degradation in a manner that appears to condone or encourage such behavior" (Russell, 1993-b, p. 3).

"Pornography is '...material that combines sex and/or exposure of genitals with abuse or degradation in a manner that appears to condone or encourage such behavior.'"

According to this definition, it is the combination of "sexualized content" with abuse or degradation that makes a form of expression pornographic. It is worth noting that in Russell's definition, material need not be sexually explicit in order for it to be pornographic. There is plenty of sexualized material that is not explicit but which is combined with abuse or degradation. Thus, many pictorial spreads in advertising could be defined as pornographic.

Author/activist Andrea Dworkin and activist/lawyer Catherine MacKinnon defined pornography in a much more detailed way as part of a model civil rights ordinance they wrote in the early 1980s (which Minneapolis and Indianapolis both passed). This civil rights ordinance allows women or men, when harmed by pornography, to sue the publisher, and/or the distributor, as well as the person who harmed them for damages based on the harm that they experienced. Dworkin and MacKinnon's definition of pornography is

> *The graphic sexually explicit subordination of women through pictures and/or words that also includes one of the following: (i) women are presented dehumanized as sexual objects, things or commodities; or (ii) women are presented as sexual objects who enjoy pain or humiliation; or (iii) women are presented as sexual objects who experience sexual pleasure in being raped; or (iv) women are presented as sexual objects tied up or cut up or mutilated or bruised or physically hurt; or (v) women are presented in postures or positions of sexual submission, servility or display; or (vi) women's body parts—including but not limited to vaginas, breasts, or buttocks—are exhibited such that women are reduced to those parts; or (vii) women are presented as whores by nature; or (viii) women are presented being penetrated by objects or animals; or (ix) women are presented in scenarios of degradation, injury, torture, shown as filthy or inferior, bleeding, bruised, or hurt in a context that makes these conditions sexual. (1988, p. 36)*

In short, pornography is the sexually explicit depiction of sexualized harm. The Dworkin-MacKinnon definition also delineates the forms of harm that women experience and the activities that can be found as damaging under this ordinance. The main purposes of the ordinance are to define and identify some of the harms caused by pornography and to provide the women or men who have been harmed a means for civil recourse.

For the purposes of educating men, the Dworkin-MacKinnon definition is probably much more detailed than would ever be needed. It is helpful to be aware of and comfortable with this definition as a way to better understand the specific harms of pornography. The definition also provides a framework to understand pornography in a way other than the obscenity framework. (For more detailed information on the civil rights ordinance, as well as the harm caused by pornography, see *In Harm's Way: The Pornography Civil Rights Hearing*, edited by A. Dworkin and C. MacKinnon.)

Both of these definitions shift the focus away from the contentious issue of obscenity and refocuses it squarely on the question of harm. Obscenity is not only difficult, if not impossible, to define, but it also keeps the discussion away from the harm that pornography does. Focusing on obscenity keeps the argument away from how men treat women and other men in pornography, and how men treat women because of pornography. Shifting the definition of pornography onto a harm standard, as the Dworkin-MacKinnon definition does, forces one to acknowledge that pornography results in harm and demands that there be remedies and protections.

These definitions also, perhaps most importantly, remove pornography from the conceptual (as it is when defined as obscenity) and make it real. Pornography is, of course, real. What is shown in pornography is not acted nor is it fantasy. It is depictions of *real* behaviors, exploitation and harm, that is done to *real* people (mostly women and children) by other *real* people (mostly men) for the pleasure and enjoyment of others (mostly men). In the construct of pornography, "Slapping and kicking thus become foreplay, degradation and rape become consensual, cuts and bruises become signs of pleasure, and tears of pain become tears of sexual ecstasy" (Kendall and Funk, 2003, p. 100).

The Impact of Pornography

Pornography is a huge industry. One measure of its size is by annual sales. In 1997, the estimated amount of money spent on pornography was $4.2 billion a year, as of 2000, the revenue of the U.S. pornography industry was estimated at $12 billion (Whisnant, 2003). This is more money than the annual sales of baseball, movies, and music combined. It is estimated that there are well over a million so-called sex sites on the Internet, with as many as 10,000 being added every week (Baker, 1999). With the explosion of pornography over the past several years, these are the most recent figures that could be found, and are from 1997, meaning that they are likely outdated and probably severely underestimate the current figure.

The impact of pornography is not just identified by its sheer volume as measured by the number of Web sites, strip clubs, and video stores or by how much money is made by exploiting others. These numbers do not represent the amount of harm. The real harm of pornography is in what it does to the women and men who are used in its production and to women in general. The harm is also in what pornography says to men, what it says to women, what it says about women (especially women's sexuality), and what it tells men to do to women (Funk, 2004).

The Freedom (or Lack Thereof) of the Actors

The pictures, movies, stories, and people on stages are not fictionalized accounts, and the people involved are not "acting." Women and men (in gay male pornography) who have been used in pornography report being humiliated, traumatized, and abused in the process of making the pornography. They also state that they have little choice in what is done to them that is then photographed or videotaped (Kendall, 2004; Russell, 1993-b; Dworkin and MacKinnon, 1997; and Marchiano, 1980). Once caught on camera and labeled "pornography," these behaviors, these acts of victimization, are redefined as entertainment and erotica. This redefinition hides the harm to the women who are victimized. The acts become defined as speech and as such are seen as protected by the First Amendment. This "free speech" then becomes better protected than the women or men who are harmed in the production of the material itself. It is also better protected than those who are forced to watch pornography and then have done to them what was depicted in the pornography images.

Women and Men of Color

African American, Latino, Native American, and Asian women and men are subject to even greater levels of violence and abuse and appear to have even less voice than do European American women and men. African American, Latino, Native American, and Asian women and men are also used in pornography in ways that sexualize racist stereotypes and violence. It is more common that the photo spreads that show women having sex with animals, with multiple partners, or that include the use of violence or force use women of color than white women. As Vednita Carter describes, "Everything about African American women is sexualized in pornography, even our efforts to win civil rights for our people" (Carter, 2004, p. 86).

The Subjugation of Women

There are two levels of harm to consider when addressing pornography. The first is the harm done to the women (and men in gay male pornography). This level of harm is addressed above. The second level of harm is the harm to women generally.

> *When reduced to their sexual parts and seen in terms of how they can be sexually used, women are forced to live in a social climate of disrespect, denigration and comparative deprivation of human regards. Women's opportunities for autonomy and self-determination are undermined...(Women's Legal Education and Action Fund, 1992).*

Pornography both endorses women as second-class citizens and requires that women be seen as second-class citizens. Women, in pornography, become sexual objects that not only deserve but also desire the kinds of things that men do to them in pornography. Experience and research consistently demonstrate that men who use pornography on a regular basis have less empathy for rape victims/survivors, are more hostile to feminism, and hold women in general in less esteem than do men who don't use pornography. (Malamuth and Donnerstein, 1984; Linz and Bryant, 1984; Zillman and Bryant, 1989; Dworkin and MacKinnon, 1997; Russell, 1993-a). Men who use pornography look at women as a class differently. They tend to see women, as a class, the way that women are portrayed in pornography.

The Warped View of Sex and Sexuality

An additional harm caused by pornography is the harm that it causes men, particularly men's views of sex and sexuality. For many men, pornography is their first sexual experience (for far too many, it is also their primary source of sex education). The messages that pornography send to men begin with the message that sex is only about physical sensation (touching, kissing, stroking, and so on) that is genitally focused. Men, while using pornography, disengage from their own emotions, feelings, and thoughts to focus on the genital stimulation while also learning to ignore the feelings, thoughts, and desires of a sexual partner. As Peter Baker convincingly states, "...when men masturbate while using pornography, they are able to treat themselves to sexual pleasure, which is free of all responsibility to another person" (Baker, 1999, p. 135).

Pornography is boringly redundant with constant themes reemerging throughout the different venues. Most of these themes are based on overcoming women's initial hesitations or unwillingness to participate in the sexual acts that the men in the scene want to do—to the ultimate ecstasy of the women (or man in the case of gay male pornography). One of the lessons of pornography is that men should overcome the hesitations or resistance of their sexual partners. This is a lesson that is consistent in mainstream media as well. The film, *Gone with the Wind,* for example, has a famous scene in which Rhett Butler rapes Scarlet—and she awakes to a glorious new day in utter love with him. This message is replicated constantly throughout pornography: Rape, force, exploitation, manipulation, and coercion do not exist. It's all foreplay and women or men simply need to relax. For men who use pornography before or as they begin dating, the possible dangers for their young dating partners should be self-evident.

In pornography, sex is something that men do *to*, as opposed to *with*, other people. The point of the sex is men's orgasms/ejaculations (which pornography defines as being the same thing). In pornography, and with men's use of pornography, sex loses all emotional or spiritual connection. Sexual activity becomes only about the physical act. Pornography rarely depicts people actually kissing, being affectionate or kind, or engaging in any kind of mutual caressing (other than of the genital areas). There is little patience or communication depicted in pornography. Rather, it is about "getting down to it" as quickly as possible. The typical communication that occurs is the man (or men) telling the woman what he wants her to do. Sex is depicted exclusively as stroking the penis to the point of ejaculation, and any body part is available to be used in the stroking.

In and of themselves, these lessons are disconcerting, but placed in the context as one of the primary forms of "sex education" for most men, these lessons become even more alarming. If an adolescent or pre-adolescent boy's first lessons about sex are that it is solely genitally focused and based on his physical sensation and pleasure that revolve around his turning of a page, what are the implications when he becomes engaged in sexual activity with a real girl or boy his own age? It would not seem too big a stretch to imagine that he probably is not in touch with his own emotions at the time and all but completely disengaged with what his partner may say, feel, or want. When this lesson is combined with the other main theme in pornography—overcoming a woman or man's initial hesitation or revulsion— it seems clear that the possibility for rape increases.

"Pornography teaches nothing about mutuality, sharing, compassion, or caring."

Through the way that pornography constructs sex, the only point of sex is for him to have a huge and satisfying orgasm. If his partner also gets enjoyment, this is an added bonus, although in pornography's construction of sexual enjoyment, his partner's enjoyment is based on satisfying his desires. If his partner does get enjoyment from the experience, pornography teaches that he can take credit for bringing her to orgasm, which continues to keep him at the center of the sexual experience. Pornography teaches nothing about mutuality, sharing, compassion, or caring.

The Misconception of the Partner's Desires

Pornography also teaches men lessons about what sexual acts women and men (in the case of gay male pornography) prefer. The mythology surrounding and inherent in pornography is that women *like* to be treated in the ways that they are portrayed in pornography. For some men, this lesson is interpreted to mean that "some women" (or men) like to be treated in the ways that women are portrayed in pornography. This interpretation, however, leaves it up to the man to determine how he decides which women are the women who like to be treated like that. What criteria distinguishes the people who like to be used in those ways from the women who don't?

The mythology created by pornography is that women like being used in sexual ways. Part of the confusion about pornography is that most people *do* like to be sexual. Pornography suggests that, for women, being sexual and being sexually used are the same thing.

Even in so-called soft-core pornography, the illusion created (and reinforced) is that women like for people to look at them. Women who are used in pornography know that their roles are to be masturbation tools for men and that their pictures are going to be ejaculated on. They are physically positioned as if they are ready to be used in a sexual way, often smiling and enticing, suggesting that they enjoy it. The message is that they want to be the fantasy that men who look at pornography make of them.

In hard-core pornography, women are depicted as liking whatever it is that the men are doing to them: being entered from different positions, being thrust into harder and harder, being insulted and verbally debased, having multiple partners, being ejaculated upon, and so on. One question that must be asked is that if heterosexual men learn these lessons too well, what are the ramifications for the women or men with whom they engage sexually?

Harm to Other Women

Experience and research consistently demonstrate that men who use pornography often try to get their sexual partners to do exactly what they saw in pornography (Kimmel, 1990; Russell, 1993-a and 1993-b; Dworkin and MacKinnon, 1997). Many men view pornography, either alone or with their partners, and then want to try what they saw done in pornography with their partners. Given the inherent lessons of pornography and the minimizing of threats or coercion, it would seem safe to assume that at least some of the time, men who try to engage their partners to do what they saw in pornography may also use threats, coercion, or manipulation. This is not to say that sexual experimentation between couples is bad. It is to say that any kind of sexual experimentation should be truly and fully mutual. The use of pornography draws into question how fully mutual any experimentation can be.

A similar message is learned by gay or bisexual men when looking at gay male pornography. Like with heterosexual pornography, the lessons offered by gay male pornography are that partners should always be ready for whatever the initiator wants, that the aim is orgasm or ejaculation, that partners like being denigrated, and so on.

Strategies for Presenting on Pornography

It is assumed that most presentations addressing pornography will be with heterosexual audiences and, therefore, referring to heterosexual pornography. The suggestions that follow will, therefore, focus on educating about heterosexual pornography. These suggestions, however, can be used just as well with gay, bisexual, or transgendered men to address gay male pornography.

A question that will likely arise in a presentation on pornography (which may also be true for some of the readers of this manual), is what about lesbian pornography? It is true that there has been a dramatic growth in lesbian pornography corresponding to the relatively recent growth in heterosexual and gay male pornography. That being the case, the point of this book, and the presentations that this book advocates, is with men. Why have a critical conversation with men about lesbian pornography? Given that many more men are active users of heterosexual or gay male pornography, it seems appropriate to focus on those forms of pornography. Furthermore, men discussing and critiquing lesbian pornography keeps the issues at the conceptual level. When educating men about pornography, as is true with any form of sexist violence, engaging in a conceptual or theoretical conversation is not an effective means to engage men.

Begin by Asking Questions About the Women or Men

One way to reach men about pornography is to encourage them to think about the real women and men who are used in pornography. Encourage men to consider the women or men depicted in pornography by asking some questions about what the experience might be like for women.* The questions that follow are designed for men to examine more thoroughly their relationship to pornography and the ways that pornography impacts on how they look at women, sex, men, and power. These questions are also a very good way to humanize the women who are presented in pornographic imagery. The women are more than depictions. They are real human beings, and these questions help readers to remember that. The readers of this manual are urged to read these questions and process what comes up as a result. By definition, and as a warning, the questions that follow are quite graphic.

**Thanks to Robert Jensen who helped to develop some of these questions.*

DOING YOUR WORK: *Humanizing the Women*

Does the woman in the pornography really like that?

Does she really like being penetrated by all those different objects? Does she like having objects inserted into her vagina or rectum?

Does she really like having sex in all those different positions?

Does she really like being ejaculated upon, probably several times? Does she really like double or triple penetration?

Does she really like being placed in those positions and told to "spread it wider" for the camera?

Does she really like knowing that hundreds and perhaps thousands of men will ejaculate onto her image?

Does she like the names that the men in pornography call her?

Would she want her sister or daughter doing the same thing?

Would they (the male audience members) want their sister, mother, daughter, or girlfriend to be in the pornography that they watch?

As an educator proceeds through these questions with men, some of the men in the audience will undoubtedly answer these questions with a resounding "Yes." They may believe that some women truly like to be treated in these ways, or may say yes only to cause a reaction in the educator. The point of engaging men in these questions and the conversation that follows is not necessarily to convince them but rather to encourage them to begin thinking critically about something they likely have never thought critically about. When some men do answer yes to some or all of these questions, educators are encouraged to engage the other men in the room and facilitate a conversation amongst the men who disagree with each other. This not only takes the onus off the educator, but encourages the critical thinking that is the point of this kind of conversation.

Ask Questions About What Brought Women to the Industry

In addition to these questions, it is also worth asking, "How did she get here?" There is a story behind how each woman used in pornography got there, and it is worth examining what the rest of their stories might be. Research shows that women who are used in pornography tend to have been sexually abused as children. If this is so, what opportunities have they been given to heal from the abuse, and what is the connection between their being abused as children and their involvement in pornography?

Ask About the Motives and Behaviors of the Men in the Industry

Another way to reach men is to encourage them to think critically about the men in pornography, and the relationship between the men and the women in heterosexual pornography (and the relationships between the men in gay male pornography). What about the men behind the camera? Is she threatened by them? Does her partner, perhaps one of the producers, abuse her? Can she say "No" to any or all parts of the video or camera shoot? Those few women (and even fewer men) who have spoken out about their experiences in pornography suggest that threats and violence are very real in pornography. These courageous stories suggest that the actors have very little say in what they will and will not do or have done to them in pornography.

The following series of questions has to do with the men in pornography.

DOING YOUR WORK: ***Recognizing the Males' Roles***

How do the men in pornography view the women in pornography?

Do they like their "co-stars"?

Do the men in pornography (the stars, the producers, the distributors, and so on) respect the women in pornography?

How do they feel about women in general?

Do they really mean what they say when they call women in pornography those names, or is that "just acting"?

Would they (the male actors, producers, editors, etc.) want their sisters or daughters being used in pornography the way that they are using women?

The Criticism of Censorship

One criticism that is very likely to arise at some point when doing a presentation on pornography is that the educator is advocating censorship. This criticism arises regardless of whether or not an educator makes any reference to censorship or any kind of legislative response to the harms caused by pornography. Just being critical of pornography, it seems, is seen as advocating for censorship. However, these questions are questions of empathy and compassion, *not* of censorship. Only governments have the authority and power to censor. An individual asking questions, even pointed and critical questions, does not constitute censorship. These questions are designed to encourage people, readers of this manual and the men to whom educators offer presentations, to explore the ways that they have allowed themselves to not see the women and men in pornography as human beings—as women and men. There is much more to pornography than the imagery that is depicted. These questions are designed to explore the underlying assumptions and myths that surround pornography. These questions help move the dialogue from a conceptual or theoretical level (pornography as obscene) to pornography as real, with real consequences. Ultimately these are questions of justice.

Discuss the Correlation Between Domestic Violence and Pornography

The research is quite clear: Not only does watching pornography decrease men's empathy for rape victims, but it also increases men's willingness to use force in their sexual acts. There is ample anecdotal evidence from battered women's shelters of how men view pornography and then force their women to perform the acts that men have seen in the pornography (Websdale, 1998; Kennedy-Bergen, 1999; DeKeseredy et al, 2003). It seems unlikely that only men who are abusive to their partners use pornography as "training" for what they want to do with their sexual partners.

Personalize the Issue

A third way to reach men is to make pornography personal for men. Viewing pornography causes a reaction and influence's one's thinking and behavior. Most men never question their pornography use and are hardly aware (if they're aware at all) of how pornography influences them. Asking questions that encourage men to critically consider how viewing pornography impacts them can have a profound effect. Beyond discussing any kind of causal or correlational relationship, it is probably most telling for men to ask themselves the following questions:

DOING YOUR WORK: *Recognizing the Harm*

What is the impact of my viewing pornography?

How do I look at my girlfriend and at women in general after viewing pornography?

How do I look at sex after viewing pornography?

Exactly what is it about watching pornography that is such a turn on for me?

- Is it the graphic depictions of sexuality?
- Is it that the women are doing and depicted as enjoying exactly what I want them to be doing and enjoying?
- Is it because I am in control (of the images I choose, the speed of the action, the kind of women I'm looking at when masturbating, the view of the woman, and so on)?

How do I feel about myself after watching or looking at pornography?

How would I feel if I opened one of my pornographic magazines or turned on a video and saw my sister, mother, daughter, girlfriend, or wife there?

Men's answers to these questions can tell us something about the harm done using pornography. These questions also challenge the notion that using pornography is free of harm. Most men's true experiences of using pornography have elements imbedded that expose the harm of using pornography. There are many reasons why men deny or are not aware of these elements, but through educational efforts, it is possible to help men recognize the harm and realize what they already know.

Address Questions About the Definition

Men, and sometimes women, will frequently attempt to shift the topic to definitional issues. They either will disagree with the definition that the educator offers or will express frustration at the lack of a clear definition (the "I'll know it when I see it" argument). These are attempts at trying to keep the conversation at the conceptual or theoretical level. These arguments also suggest a level of discomfort that men may be having with the content. Rather than engaging the debate about what is or is not pornography, it is helpful to remind men that people are comfortable in lots of situations with varying definitions. For example, the law has one definition of rape, activists have another, and the men in the room probably have yet others. The same can be said for any other issue, including pornography.

Address Free Speech Arguments Head On

In responding to the freedom of speech argument, remind people that only governments can censor. Critiquing pornography, even critiquing pornography harshly, is not censorship. This behavior, in fact, is honoring freedom of speech. Furthermore, there have been more efforts to silence the voices of feminists who are critical of pornography, and the people who have been victimized in pornography, than there have been efforts by feminists or activists to shut down pornography.

"Freedom of speech also comes with responsibility."

Moreover, freedom of speech also comes with responsibility. People have the right to say whatever they want to say, but every person is also responsible for the harm that may be caused by what they say (or do)—or don't say or do. We have a full array of laws that limit what people can and cannot say, as well as laws that hold people responsible for what they do say (slander or libel laws, for example). One response to the challenge of "free speech" is to answer with "to use freedom of speech to suggest that people used in pornography are not harmed, or that if they are harmed, than no one is responsible, is outrageous and completely misinterprets what freedom of speech really means."

Another response to the free speech argument is to respond to the underlying allegation that by critiquing pornography, advocates are asking for more or stronger laws. The point of speaking against pornography is not necessarily to encourage more laws against pornography; laws will not stop men from using pornography. The point of educating about pornography is to redefine the debate so that it focuses on the harm that is done to women, as well as the harm done to our experience of sex and to men.

The solution may be to change or stiffen laws. The solution may well include other actions altogether or in addition to changing laws.

There are times when these kinds of answers are necessary in a discussion, but as stated above, as quickly as possible, move the conversation back to the harms and impact of pornography.

Stay Focused on the Harm Done to Persons

When educating men about pornography, it is important to stay focused on the damage done to persons. While it may be tempting to engage in conversations about defining obscenity, or freedom of speech, or what *exactly* is the definition of pornography, these discussions continue to keep the issue of pornography at the conceptual level, and away from the real impact on the people who are most victimized and at risk. Maintaining the focus on the harm that using pornography causes forces educators and their audiences to be more honest and directly address the pain and victimization and how it is sexist.

Reframe the Issue to Focus on Harm Rather than Obscenity

Another important factor to remind men of is that the legal definition of what constitutes pornography is based on the obscenity model and does not reflect the harm done or experienced. The point of current pornography law is not to protect women from harm or even to define the harm that women experience. Rather, the point of pornography laws is to protect community standards.

It is not necessarily the responsibility of educators to come up with what will work to resolve the issues that they raise. The responsibility of educators is to educate about various forms of sexism and violence, encourage men's critical thinking, and hopefully engage men to take action. Regardless of one's perspective on pornography, the point of an educational program about pornography is to educate and sensitize men to the harm inherent in pornography.

Jeffrey Cullen has developed an excellent resource for educating men about pornography and the harms thereof. It is available at www.jist.com as well as www.rusfunk.com.

The following sample outline is a brief overview of how to begin a conversation with men about pornography. It is a very basic outline and does not go into much depth, but in an introductory conversation, an educator is unlikely to get into much depth with men anyway.

SAMPLE OUTLINE: ***Defining Pornography***

I. Addressing Obscenity
   A. Feminist Definitions
      1. Dworkin-MacKinnon
      2. Dines, et al
      3. Russell
   B. Lack of a Single Definition (as is true in most cases, e.g., rape)
   C. Heterosexual and Gay Male Pornography
II. Defining the Harm
   A. The Harm of Production
      1. Women forced to participate
      2. The message to women of pornography
      3. The message to men about women in pornography
      4. Re-enforcing male entitlement
   B. The Harm of Consumption
   C. The Harm of Witnessing
   D. The Harm of Using Pornography as a Guide
III. What's to Be Done
   A. Social Action Against Pornography
   B. Using the First Amendment as a Weapon to Combat Pornography
   C. Civil Cause of Action

Prostitution

"In prostitution, she is depersonalized; her name and identity disappear. She shuts down her feelings to protect herself. She becomes 'something for him to empty himself into, acting as a kind of human toilet.'"

FARLEY, 2003, P. XIII, QUOTING HOIGARD AND FINSTAD, 1986

Although pornography and prostitution are closely related, there are some important distinctions between the two that warrant separate conversations with men. In many ways, prostitution may be an even more difficult conversation to have with men than pornography. As guarded and defensive as men are about their use of pornography, they tend to be much more secretive about their use of prostituted women and their perceived right to use prostituted women.

A Note About Language

Readers will note that the women or men involved in prostitution are not referred to here as "prostitutes." This is a gross misnomer. Instead, the term "prostituted women" or "prostituted men" is used. This language more accurately reflects that most women or men are generally engaged and kept in prostitution as a result of coercion, deception, violence, or abuse.

Towards a Definition

Prostitution is much harder to define than pornography. It is, in essence, the buying of a human being for sex. While the most commonly thought of forms of prostitution (i.e., "street walking") are illegal in most parts of the country, the use of prostituted women is extremely common, often referred to as "the world's oldest profession." For the purposes of this manual, prostitution includes escort services, phone-sex, real-time Internet workers, strippers, dancers, and lap dancers—all those activities that involve buying women or men for sexual satisfaction.

The Impact of Prostitution

Rarely is prostitution looked at in terms of the harm done to the women or men who are used in it. If discussed at all, the conversation tends to revolve around the right of women to choose to engage in prostitution, the right of men to buy women or other women to use sexually, or the characteristics (usually in a judgmental way) of the women or men who are prostituted. However, prostitution is indeed harmful to the women and men who are used in it. Additionally, like the other forms of violence and abuse discussed in this manual, prostitution is decidedly gendered. Although there are some men who are used in prostitution, women make up the vast majority of those who are prostituted in this country and around the world. As such, it requires just as thorough examination as does any form of men's sexist violence.

Prostitution—A Form of Slavery

At its core, prostitution is a form of men's violence, just as, at its core, slavery is a form of white violence. There are those who suggest that prostitution evolved out of slavery, that men's access to women's bodies was imbedded in slavery and, when slavery ended, men created ways to continue to have access to women's bodies. Regardless of the possible historic connections between the two, there are clear similarities between them. In the cases of prostitution and slavery, it rarely matters how kind, considerate, or caring a john or pimp is (in the case of prostituted women) or a master or overseer is (in the case of slavery). Both are inherently violent. Like slavery, prostitution maintains and sustains broader forms of oppression, namely, sexism and homophobia. Prostitution harms individual women and men who are used in it, and it harms women as a class. Thus it is a form of sexist violence.

The harms to prostituted women and men are numerous. One can broadly categorize the harms of prostitution as

- The harms to prostituted women and men
- The harms to men's perceptions of women
- The harms to women generally
- The harms to notions of sex and sexuality

It is within the context of overt male domination and control that prostitution is created and it is within the context of male supremacy that sustains men's demand for women and men through prostitution. In prostitution, a woman is not considered a human being but is rather the property of some man: the pimp or manager, the john or customer, or even random men on the street. As property, a woman is seen as available and accessible to be used by men as the men choose. Prostituted women can rarely set limits on what is done to them or how it is done. If they try to set limits, they are subject to violence and abuse by the john. This is, in fact, why women and men in prostitution refer to customers as "tricks," because of the common practice of men attempting to "trick" prostituted women or men into doing what they want them to do. Prostituted people also face an increased chance of being robbed (for instance, a john agrees to pay a certain amount but afterwards refuses to pay that amount or to pay at all). They may also be subject to any kind of abuse or violence that the john may choose to inflict.

Loss of Personal Identity

In most cases, prostituted women adopt a male-imposed identity (even to the point of a different name) that is used to further control her (in some cases, she takes on a different name and different identity in order to protect herself from what is done to her). This identity can be imposed on her by the john, her pimp, or men on the street. She has little recourse but to go along with the identities that are given to her. As Melissa Farley describes, "She constructs a self that conforms to the masturbatory fantasies of johns, a self that smilingly accommodates verbal abuse, sexual harassment, rape and torture. Over time...she is disappeared" (Farley, 2003, p. xiii).

CASE STUDY

A prostituted woman, named Sarah, created a street name Sheila and a persona. For her, it was almost a form of split personality. Now she steps into a prescribed role whenever she takes on the new name and dresses for her part.

There are also endless examples of women or men who are told by the men who buy them what name they will be called or what role they will fulfill for the period that he has paid for them. A prostituted woman may have to play the role of the john's niece, for example. The woman's true identity, her true self, is of no consideration for the john. All she is, is a sexualized body that he can do whatever he wants.

Physical Abuse

In addition to the abuse perpetrated upon prostituted women and men within prostitution itself, prostituted women (or those women who are assumed to be prostituted) are subject to severe forms of street harassment and assaults just by being on the street. This harassing and propositioning of women on the street because they are assumed to be prostituted women suggests that men feel entitled to women's bodies (at least for comments). The harassing also assumes a connection between men's ownership of women's bodies as constructed in prostitution and the real women who happen to be walking down the street. Figure 8.1, based on the work of Laura J. Lederer in The Protection Project, clearly illustrates the multitude of harms and threats posed to women as a result of prostitution:

Consequences of Commercial Sexual Exploitation—
The Harms of Trafficking and Prostitution

Trafficking Prostitution
Child Prostitution
Pornography
Child Pornography

HEALTH HAZARDS	PHYSICAL HAZARDS	PSYCHOLOGICAL HAZARDS	SOCIAL PROBLEMS
AIDS/HIV VD STDs Infertility	Physical violence Battery Assault Rape Forced drugging Unwanted pregnancy Drug addiction	Mind/Body/Separation Disembodiment Hatred of Men Distrust Emotional Impairment Loss of Childhood Depression Suicidal Thoughts Self-Mutilation	Discrimination Alienation Marginality Ostracism

Figure 8.1: This figure was created by Laura Lederer and is an excellent graphic of the kinds of harms that result from prostitution.

As this diagram depicts, the harms that threaten prostituted women are multiple and layered. Dr. Lederer's research, as well as that of most others who have examined these issues, demonstrates that these kinds of injuries and others are common amongst prostituted women and men (Farley et al, 2003; Kendall, 2004; Ross et al, 2003).

The majority of women in the United States (even more so internationally) who are used in prostitution or in any aspect of the so-called sex industry, are controlled by pimps or managers (Farley, 2003). Those who are not controlled by pimps are generally European American and from more privileged backgrounds (in other words, they are in their mid-twenties, have other access to income, are U.S. citizens, and are "prettier" by U.S. standards). Because pimps or managers control most women who are prostituted, the women have fewer choices about what is done to them and with whom they do it. They are generally required to bring in a certain amount of money every night, the majority of which belongs to the pimp. If women fail to comply, they are subject to violence and abuse.

Prostituted women are also subject to the whims and choices of the men who buy them. One cannot truly consent unless one knows that she or he has the right and freedom to refuse. As Melissa Farley (2003) states, "The line between coercion and consent is deliberately blurred in prostitution…" (p. 2). Prostitution purposefully makes coercion look like consent; the allusion of consent provides a level of legitimacy to prostitution and provides another layer of cover over the harm committed.

Hernandez, as quoted in Farley, (2003, p. 2), explains that "in prostitution, the conditions which make genuine consent possible are absent: physical safety, equal power with customers, and real alternatives." Prostituted women rarely have that choice in regards to either their pimps or to the johns. If the women try to say no, they do so at grave risk to themselves, for physical violence is a common response by both pimps and johns to women who try to say no or try to negotiate during the act (for example, asking the john to wear a condom). Seventy percent of prostituted women suffer rape, 65 percent are physically assaulted by johns, and 66 percent are physically assaulted by pimps (Silbert and Pines, 1981 and 1982).

In addition to these assaults, prostituted women (which includes those who lap-dance, strip, dance, and so on) report being touched, groped, pinched, fingered, verbally abused, grabbed on their breasts and buttocks, bitten, slapped, spit on, and penetrated vaginally and anally (Lewis, 1998; Holsopple, 1998). These assaults generally go unreported as prostituted women have no recourse, have no one to report to, will likely lose the only source of income they have, and may face increased violence (by the pimp as well as by the police) if they do report the assaults. Furthermore, because prostitution is illegal in most areas, the woman may also face being arrested if she reports violence.

Because of the myths that still surround prostituted women and men, few social service agencies (rape crisis centers, battered women's shelters, victim's advocacy organizations) have developed specific services or resources for them. Lacking specific services, agencies are unlikely to be seen by prostituted women as a place they can go for support and advocacy. As a result, not only does the victimization of prostituted women go unreported to the police, but it often also goes unreported to local advocacy or service organizations. Thus, prostituted women and men who are victimized are generally left to their own devices to deal with and heal from the victimization they experience.

The Connection of Prostitution to Trafficking

As if these dynamics are not problematic enough, any discussion of prostitution is incomplete without also examining trafficking. The connection between prostitution and trafficking is well established. The trafficking of human beings, almost exclusively women and children, is between the second and third most common form of illegal trafficking and is the fastest growing form (the other two common forms of trafficking are weapons and drugs).

There is no clear tracking of the occurrence of trafficking within the United States, but it is estimated that as many as 50,000 women are trafficked into the United States every year, and between 2 and 4 million women are trafficked throughout the world annually. According to a 2003 report from the U.S. Department of State, the U.S. is the second most frequent entry point for trafficked women and children, following Germany. If not sold outright, women and children are commonly tricked into leaving their home countries with promises of the opportunities to make better livings or to improve their own conditions or those of their families. Once caught in the dynamics of trafficking, people who are trafficked often lose access to their passports, which are frequently controlled by the pimp, and are held in deplorable conditions in what amounts to an indentured status until they pay back the money loaned to them to get them to the new country. As with most indentured situations, the person in control often steals and lies to keep people who are trafficked in a status of having to continue to work to pay off the so-called "debt."

EFFECTIVE STRATEGY

One of the points to make when educating men is that using prostituted women or men in whatever form is not only participating in sexism and violence against that person, but is also supporting the trafficking trade.

The experience of trafficking does not stop at international borders. Women who are brought into this country, and women who are brought into prostitution or pornography, are also trafficked within the nation's boundaries. For example, a woman may enter the U.S. in Atlanta, but be sent up the east coast (with several stops along the way for "sexual exchanges") through North Carolina, to Washington, DC, to New York, to Boston. Or a woman or man who is coerced into prostitution or pornography in New York may be sent to New Jersey or Philadelphia, based on the "needs" or whims of her pimp. It is worth examining how this dynamic mirrors the isolating dynamics of domestic violence. By continuing to move the prostituted from place to place, pimps prevent the women or men from developing support networks, which in turn makes it increasingly difficult for them to escape.

Educating men about prostitution is not terribly different than educating men about pornography. As discussed above, the biggest misconception is going to be the view that prostituted women and men choose to be prostituted. By talking about the experiences of real women and men who have been prostituted, educators can make progress in moving men to understand the prostitution and the harms inherent in this industry. Like with pornography, it is unlikely that educators will effectively convince men about the harms of prostitution in one presentation, but they should be able to engage men in a critical dialogue that encourages their empathic understanding of the impact of prostitution on the women in it and on women generally.

The Lessons of Pornography and Prostitution

More than just the women and men who are used in pornography and prostitution are harmed as a result; there is a "ripple effect." Women who are not involved in either pornography or prostitution are also directly harmed as a result of these industries—for example, the women who walk down a street that has pornography shops or strip clubs or where prostituted women are known to be present. Women in general report not only higher rates of street harassment, but also more extreme and violent forms of street harassment, up to and including physical assaults (Barry, 1995).

Perhaps at their roots, pornography and prostitution create a message that men's sexual pleasure (or sexualized power) is more important than women's human rights. The pleasure that men experience is of greater value to men and to society (given the protections provided for men's continued sexual pleasure as compared to the protections provided for women who are harmed as a result) than are women's basic human rights to be free from harm, to be protected from harm, to be offered services and support when they are harmed, and more to the point, the basic human rights of personal autonomy and bodily integrity.

This premise is not an argument against sexual pleasure—men's or anyone's. It is a call to recognize that men's sexual pleasure happens in the context of sexism and to encourage educators, advocates, activists, and others to consider how to balance sexual pleasure with the human rights of women.

Resources

Web

Coalition Against Trafficking of Women. An international organization with local networks that works against trafficking of women and children and sexual exploitation. www.catwinternational.org

Project Prosper. A grassroots advocacy and organizing organization that works to support prostituted and formerly prostituted women and to eliminate prostitution. www.escapeprostitution.com

Prostitution Research and Education. An education and advocacy organization that addresses the harms caused by prostitution. www.prostitutionresearch.com

The Protection Project. An international organization that addresses issues of prostitution and trafficking of women and children. www.protectionproject.org

The Storm Project. Provides training, advocacy, and resources to assist women in escaping pornography and prostitution. www.thestormproject.com

Print

Dworkin, A. (1979). *Pornography: Men possessing women.* New York: Perigree Books.

Russell, D. E. H. (1998). *Dangerous relationships: Pornography, misogyny and rape.* Thousand Oaks CA: Sage Publications.

CHAPTER 9

Racism, Homophobia, Sexism, and Men's Violence

This manual would be woefully incomplete indeed if it did not examine the intersections of racism and men's violence, and homophobia and men's violence. Racism and homophobia work in concert with sexism in ways that have varied and complex impacts on both women and men. Not all women have the same access to services or receive the same quality of care when they are victimized and men are not treated the same when they are accused or convicted of abuse or violence.

"While sexist violence is clearly a weapon of sexism, it is also a weapon of both racism and homophobia."

While sexist violence is clearly a weapon of sexism, it is also a weapon of both racism and homophobia. Educating men requires that these connections be exposed and interrogated. For men (regardless of sexual orientation or race) to understand the issues, to be better able to support their loved ones who are victimized, and/or to work effectively as allies in the movement, they must understand how racism and homophobia intersect with sexism to maintain a system in which men's violence continues. Racism and homophobia are powerful weapons that tend to keep men away from each other and are impediments to men's working together to respond to and address sexism and violence. By examining these connections, educators can offer means for men to understand racism, homophobia, and sexism better and enable them to improve their relationships with other men.

This does not mean that educators need to incorporate racism and homophobia into every presentation on sexism and violence. Depending on the topic, the dynamics of the presentation, the audience, and numerous other factors, this may not make sense. However, educators *do* need to have an analysis of sexism and violence that includes how racism and homophobia intersect. Being aware of and conversant in these connections means that educators will be better prepared to address these issues when they arise, as well as be more able to address the connections more frequently. Ultimately, it means educators will be able to be more effective with a broader range of male audiences.

Racism and Sexist Violence

The vast majority of sexist violence is perpetrated intra-culturally; that is, women are most likely to be victimized by men within their cultural group (European American women are victimized by European American men, African American women are victimized by African American men, Latinas are victimized by Latinos, and so on). When victimization crosses these cultural lines, it is almost always women of color being victimized by European American men.

Myths Men of Color Face

There are two inter-related myths related to African American, Latino, Asian, and Native American men. The first is that they are more likely to perpetrate sexism and violence than are European American men. The second myth is that these men pose a greater threat to European American women. Both of these myths are just plain false (Bernard, 1990; Davis, 1983; hooks, 1981; Jaimes, 1992; King, 1992). Although a myth, it has an amazing ability to continue and thrive even against all available evidence. Men of color are still often seen and defined by European Americans and the general public as more scary, threatening, and intimidating than are European American men, in spite of the evidence that European American men are as likely (if not more so) to commit violent crimes (especially sexism and violence as discussed in this manual) as are men of color.

These myths were created in the founding stages of this country. To some degree, there are regional variations of these myths, but there is a certain degree of consistency amongst these regional variations. European American men defined men of color as a threat to European American women as a means of dominating both segments of society. European American men used the alleged threat that men of color pose to European American women to justify harsh treatment of men of color, as well as restrictive policies and practices towards European American women. For example, the lynchings of most of the men of color were the result of accusations of rape or violence perpetrated against European American women. European American Christian men (there were examples of Jewish men who were also lynched after falsely being accused of victimizing non-Jewish European American women) who were similarly charged or arrested were not lynched. Nor were men of color lynched for accusations of sexist violence against women of color.

Simultaneous and integrated into this myth, is the myth that African American, Latino, Asian, and Native American men are more sexist or violent than European American men. This myth has been used to justify some of these same behaviors.

Risks Women of Color Face

African American, Latina, Asian, and Native American women are not only at risk of being victimized by men of color, but are also at risk of being victimized by European

American men. This dynamic has its roots in the history of colonization and slavery when European American men assumed the "right" to force sexual relations with enslaved women, Native American women, Latinas, and Asian women. African American women who were enslaved by European American men (or who were indentured servants) were defined as the property of those men. As property, women of color had no right to refuse their treatment. Thus, European American men claimed the right to use their "property" as they chose to—including access to their sexuality. Although the direct link between these assumed property rights and European American men's sexist and racist violence is most clear in terms of African American women (who were, in fact, enslaved), the mindset that supports this behavior was held for all women of color. This mindset also has implications for the interactions between African American, Latina, Native American, and Asian women, and European American men, even to today.

"Trivializing the harms perpetrated against women of color makes them at increased risk for victimization and less likely to have access to services or to have an appropriate and supportive response if they report the violence."

One way this mindset gets played out is the discrepancy between how European American women who are recognized as "victims" are treated compared with how women of color who are recognized as "victims"* are treated. One modern example of this discrepancy is related to the Central Park gang rape of the late 1980s. This case, which came back into the news in mid 2004, allegedly involved a gang of male youth of color—mostly African American—who brutally attacked, beat, and gang-raped a white female jogger. This story received national news, was heard all across the country, and was met with moral indignation and outrage. Within one week, an African American woman was similarly attacked, gang-raped, and thrown out of a three-story window by a gang of European American male youth. In contrast to the Central Park case, this story received only minimal coverage, even in the local New York press, and none nationally. The moral indignation and outrage offered the African American woman was deafening in its silence, made even more deafening when compared to the response given to the European American woman. This is not to suggest that the moral indignation and outrage about the Central Park rape was not deserved, but rather to point out the difference in who has access to this kind of attention and whose victimization is seen as deserving of moral indignation and outrage.

Trivializing the harms perpetrated against women of color makes them at increased risk for victimization and less likely to have access to services or to have an appropriate and supportive response if they report the violence.

** I say "recognized as 'victims'" here to reinforce how rare it is for any women to have their victimization experiences recognized as such.*

African American, Asian, Native American, and Latina women, based on racist myths, are seen as more deserving of violence, are typically blamed more strongly for being victimized, or are seen as strong and, therefore, not needing the support and assistance made available to European American women. This point will be discussed in more detail later in chapter.

Racism in the Conviction of and Penalties for Crimes

Racism also impacts on how men who perpetrate violence are treated. As noted previously, the myth of the "Black Rapist" (or any man of color rapist) as a greater threat to European American women was generated and is maintained to preserve white supremacy. It is perhaps most well known with respect to African American men, but wherever there are large populations of men of color, those particular men are defined as greater threats. As a result of this myth, African American, Asian, Native American, and Latino men are much more likely to be convicted and to serve more severe penalties than are European American men charged with similar crimes. Perhaps the most notable recent example is the difference in the outcomes of the allegations of rape against William Kennedy Smith and Mike Tyson. Both William Kennedy Smith and Mike Tyson were accused of strikingly similar cases of rape: inviting a woman to their homes, plying them with alcohol, and forcing sex on them. William Kennedy Smith, a European American physician and nephew of a senator, was acquitted; Mike Tyson, a large African American whose profession is beating people up, was convicted. While there are certainly many who would argue for multiple different possible explanations for these differences, this example highlights the fact that as a society, we are much more likely to believe that a large black man raped a woman than we are that a medium built white man did.

Racism in the Quality of Support Offered Women of Color

The results of these two dynamics are that African American, Asian, Native American, and Latina women are more at risk for being victimized by a larger array of men, and when they are victimized, they are less likely to receive the kinds of supportive legal and healing services they deserve. African American, Asian, Native American, and Latina women are seen as more deserving of men's violence, and are more often defined as stronger and, therefore, more self-sufficient. As a result, they tend to be less likely to be taken seriously when they do report being victimized.

These dynamics are not unknown in communities of color. These issues raise a level of distrust and wariness that are part of any conversation about sexist violence. Men of color know that they and the women in their lives are treated differently than European Americans and that the larger movements against sexism and violence are predominately European American, which suggests to people and communities of color that their issues and concerns will not be heard, respected, or even understood by educators. Therefore, educators need to understand these dynamics and research how racism intersects with sexism and violence within their local communities.

Homophobia and Sexist Violence

As with the link between racism and sexist violence, there is also a strong connection between homophobia and sexist violence. Homophobia not only plays a role in the incidence and dynamics of the violence, but it also plays a role in keeping men from listening to presentations and becoming engaged.

The Increased Risk for Lesbian, Bisexual, and Transgendered Women Victimization

Lesbian, bisexual, and transgendered (LBT) women are at somewhat increased risk for victimization—not only because they are women, but also because they are gay. The result is not only increased amounts of harassment and abuse, but also often increased intensity of the violence. It is not uncommon, for example, for LBT women who have been sexually assaulted to report (based on the verbal violence of the perpetrator) that the rape was perpetrated as a form of "punishment" for her sexuality. As described throughout this book, women are at increased risk for all of these forms of violence than are men. LBT women are at risk for not only men's generalized sexist violence, but are also at risk for men's homophobic violence, which often intersects with sexist violence. In other words, LBT women are at risk for being bashed because they are lesbian, bisexual, or transgendered. A part of the bashing that they experience often includes sexualized and sexist comments and violence.

Once assaulted or victimized, LBT women are then forced into positions of having to either come out as lesbian, bisexual, or transgender (and possibly confront the hostility and hatred that some people have for lesbians or bisexual women) or choose to stay closeted and hide parts of the truth. As with women of color, lesbian, bisexual, and transsexual women are seen as deviant by some and, as such, as somehow more deserving of violence and less deserving of support and advocacy than heterosexual women.

The Myth of Gay, Bisexual, and Transgendered Men as Perpetrators

Gay, bisexual, and transgendered (GBT) men have been labeled as potential perpetrators that may sexually abuse children and to rape other men. This is patently false. All available evidence suggests that most adults who sexually abuse children (male or female) are heterosexual men, and the majority of men who are sexually assaulted are raped by heterosexual men. These homophobic myths continue despite contrary evidence and are used to reinforce hatred against gay and bisexual men and to fuel discriminatory practices.

The implications of this mythology for educating GBT men about sexism and violence can be profound—especially when combined with the increased risk that GBT men have of being victimized by these very same forms of violence. Educators need to find ways to incorporate some myth-busting statements into their presentations to indicate to GBT men who may be in the audience that the educators are aware that these are myths, and at the same time, educating heterosexual men that these ideas are false.

The Legally Hostile Environment

Gay or bisexual men who are arrested and charged with some form of sexist violence face a more hostile environment and stiffer penalties than their heterosexual counterparts. Although there is scant research available, experience suggests that gay or bisexual men (like men of color) are more likely to be convicted and more likely to receive harsher penalties when they are convicted than are heterosexual men.

The Victimization of Gay, Bisexual, and Transgendered Men

Gay, bisexual, and transgendered (GBT) men are also victimized by sexist violence. They are sexually victimized (during hate-attacks, by heterosexual men in other situations, as well as by other gay men), experience domestic and dating violence, are harassed, and are used in pornography and prostitution. As with the experiences of LBT women, when GBT men are victimized, they are much less likely to find the supportive services and advocacy that they deserve. Social services that are available to other GBT men or other people who have been victimized have had more difficulty in providing adequate services to GBT men who are abused (Funk, 2006). Law enforcement can often be openly hostile in investigating the victimization of an out GBT man. And the law itself rarely recognizes or offers adequate supports for GBT men.

The Plight of the LGBT People

As Suzanne Pharr suggests, the attacks on gay men, lesbians, bisexual, and transgendered (GLBT) people have a base in sexism (Pharr, 1988). Homophobia is both fueled and maintained by sexism, and the violence and abuse that GLBT people face can be seen as another form of sexist violence. Part of the experience of GLBT people is to be subject to the same forms of sexism and violence as heterosexual women, but as with people of color, GLBT people are subject to additional forms of sexist violence. GLBT people are also at increased risk for increased levels of violence when they are assaulted. And, again, GLBT people who are victimized face legal and social service systems that may be openly hostile, that blame them for their victimization, or that require that they remain closeted in order to receive services.

The Impact of Racism and Homophobia on Sexist Violence

After they are victimized, women of color and LBT women often receive different responses from both legal and social services. Because of the legacy of racism and the American justice ("Just-Us") system, women of color are often more hesitant to call on formal institutions than are European American women. If African American women do call on formal institutions, they are less likely to have their complaints taken seriously and to have charges filed against the abusers, especially if the abusers are European American men. Lesbians and bisexual women are often also hesitant to use the legal system and often cannot "come out" as lesbian or bisexual, which means they cannot describe the full details of the attack. When they fail to disclose all the details, the legal system is more likely to drop the case.

Social services that have been developed to respond to sexist violence are often located in sections of town that make them less accessible for African American, Latina, Asian, or Native American women. In addition, social services addressing victimization are often perceived to be closely connected with the legal system and institutions. Because of the legacy of racism within the U.S. legal system, some people of color may be hesitant to access social services that are believed to be connected to the legal system.

Lesbian, gay male, bisexual, or transgendered women may feel intimidated about seeking services from what has been seen as an exclusively heterosexual environment. An environment that is far too often not safe enough for people to "come out" in is an environment that is not conducive to people healing from the trauma. If it is not safe for GLBT to be open about their sexuality or gender identity, then it becomes difficult to openly discuss the implications of their victimization (and thus their healing) and as such, their healing is hindered.

The point is that sexism and violence do not have one set of implications nor one series of results on all communities. It is important to examine the issues of sexist violence and the ways that it intersects with racist, homophobic, and other forms of bias, violence, and abuse while working to eliminate it all. Just as it is highly unlikely that activists will successfully eradicate rape without also eradicating domestic violence, it is unrealistic to believe that there will be an end to sexist violence without also ending racist, homophobic, and other biased violence. Educating men of different communities means being able to make these connections explicit, and expanding definitions and understandings of justice so that men are encouraged to move beyond mobilizing for justice out of self-interest and into becoming committed to justice holistically.

Strategies for Presenting on Racism, Homophobia, and Sexist Violence

Given the intersections of racism and homophobia with sexism and violence, it is crucial to incorporate these issues when educating men. This is not to say that every presentation needs to include all this information. But educators do need to be prepared to address issues of racism and homophobia as they may arise during presentations. In addition, depending upon the makeup of the audience, these topics may be more salient and essential in terms of being able to effectively reach the male audience members. What follows are some brief suggestions about how to incorporate this information in presentations with men.

Acknowledge Racism

The implications for doing educational programs for African American, Latino, Asian, and Native American men should be immediately obvious. In order to do effective educational work with men of color, some effort must be made to identify and label the racism of the U.S. legal system and support services, and the increased likelihood that men of color may be targeted by that legal system. For European American educators, this becomes a crucial responsibility. European American educators have the obligation to provide a framework through which to connect with African American, Latino, Asian, or Native American men, and to acknowledge the existence of the discrepancies described above even while talking about the ways in which women are harmed by men and men's violence.

Mention Men of Color Who Have Worked to End Sexism

To effectively provide a framework for male audiences to connect racism, sexism, and men's violence, educators need to describe how working to combat sexist violence is also working against racism and racist violence. One way to do this is to highlight the men of color who have worked to end sexist violence (for example, Frederick Douglass, W.E.B. DuBois, and James Baldwin. A fuller list is provided in Chapter 10, "Social Change Efforts to End Sexism and Violence." Another way to describe how working to end sexism and violence is inherently anti-racist work is to describe the ways that sexist violence has been used to maintain and sustain racism.

Examine the Impact of Racist Policies on Women of Color

Another way to provide a framework for examining the interconnections among racism, sexism, and violence is to describe the experience of women of color who have been victimized. Discussing, with male audience, some of the information that was outlined above, or using some of the resources offered to develop a more detailed examination of the experience of Latina women, for example, challenges men to see how racism and sexism intersect.

Furthermore, challenge male audiences to work to support *all* of the women in their communities. Doing so will probably elicit empathy and action from the African American, Latino, Asian, or Native American men who are in the audience.

SAMPLE OUTLINE: ***Rape and Racism***

I. Introduction

Hi, I'm_____________and I am from the_____________organization and I'm here to talk with you a bit about rape and racism.

Rape and racism have a long linked but often hidden history.

II. Definitions

A. Define rape

B. Discuss consent. Consent is a, perhaps *the*, key element of sexual activity—the absence of consent is sexual assault.

In order to have true consent, sexual partners must be more or less equal.

III. Dynamics

A. Historically, slavery, which can be understood as one quintessential form of racism, provided white men who were slave owners with unlimited sexual access to the bodies of enslaved women. Due to the extreme lack of equality, a truly consensual relationship was impossible between slave owner and enslaved person.

B. Currently, rape and racism continue to be linked. Most rapes are *intra*racial, that is, most men who rape do so against women of their own racial or ethnic class (white men tend to rape white women, African American men tend to rape Africa American women, Asian American men tend to rape Asian American women, and so on). Most *inter*racial rapes are perpetrated by white or European American men against women of color.

C. Overall, rapes rarely make it to trial, much less to a conviction. Women of color, however, are even less likely to get a conviction if they are sexually assaulted than are white or European American women.

D. Men of color, on the other hand, are much more likely to be convicted of sexual crimes, and white or European American men are more likely to be acquitted (or not even arrested for).

E. In addition, men of color have long been subject to allegations of rape or sexual assault (although more by European American men than by European American women) and perceived and reacted to as a threat.

F. Combating either rape or racism means working to combat both.

Analyze, Understand, and Present the Dynamics of Homophobia and Sexist Violence

As with racism, the implications of homophobia should be immediately apparent when considering doing educational programs with gay, bisexual, or transgendered (GBT) men. In order to develop effective educational programs for GBT men, educators and advocates need to understand the dynamics of homophobia (in its many and varied forms) and how homophobia uses sexism and violence as weapons against GBT men. As described above, the impact is both in terms of GBT men who are victimized, as well as the myth of the threat that GBT men pose to victimize children or other men. Addressing these issues directly is a way to engage GBT men into the conversation.

From this analysis, and the framework of how homophobia, sexism, and violence intersect, educators can explore how addressing sexist violence is, by definition, confronting and resisting homophobia. Furthermore, because there will be GBT men in any audience in which educators are presenting, some level of this information should be incorporated in nearly all presentations to men.

The Full Impact of Men's Sexism and Violence

The full impact of men's sexism and violence cannot be measured by statistics alone. The statistics, as scary as they are, disguise the real impact on the real human beings.

The impact of sexist violence often mirrors the impact of combat on soldiers, prisoners of war, and people who have been held hostage for prolonged periods of time. Post Traumatic Stress Disorder (PTSD), a psychological diagnosis, was first defined to address Vietnam combat veterans who had come home, yet were harmed and troubled by the experience of being in a combat situation. PTSD has become understood to also apply to women who have been victimized by domestic violence, to women or men who are raped, to women or men who are prostituted (Farley, et al, 2003), and with men or women who are harassed or stalked. PTSD begins with an understanding of trauma as being a crisis situation that overwhelms a person and disrupts the ability to cope.

Even looking at the physical traumas that women or men who are victimized experience does not fully address the impact, for the *threat* of sexist violence affects every woman, regardless of whether or not she has been victimized or directly knows anyone who has been victimized. In *The Female Fear*, Margaret Gordon and Stephanie Riger examined how the threat of rape impacts women's lives and choices, resulting in these statistics:

- 25% of women don't walk alone in their own neighborhoods after dark; 3% of men don't.
- 68% of women don't go to bars/clubs alone after dark; 5% of men don't.
- 49% of women don't use public transportation alone after dark; 23% of men don't.
- 52% of women don't go to parks alone after dark; 10% of men don't.
- 48% of women say they don't go downtown alone after dark; 7% of men don't.

These findings suggest that women are much more hesitant than men to go places alone after dark. In other words, women's freedoms are much more restricted than men's. Through no fault of their own, women restrict their behavior, limit their lives, and constrict their choices (to the degree that they are able), all under the guise of making themselves more safe.

The sad reality is that these behaviors are not likely to increase women's safety. Women may *feel* safer, and this feeling of safety cannot be discounted, but they are not likely to *be* any safer even if they do follow all these restrictions and the myriad of others that they are told they should follow. Men do not have to limit themselves in these kinds of ways and are rarely even aware that women limit themselves.

Male partners know the threat of male violence and often reinforce these limits in an attempt to "protect" the women they love. If men did have to face the kinds of restrictions that women face due to the threat of men's violence, there would be much stronger institutional and societal responses to remove the threats and make men feel and *be* safer in the world.

It is important to note that Gordon and Riger examined only the impact of the threat of rape on women's behavior and choices. If one were to add the threats of other forms of men's violence, the impact would undoubtedly be more dramatic. There are two key pieces that these findings alone fail to address. First, this research only looks at women who have the luxury of choosing whether they engage in these behaviors. Many women *must* use public transportation or walk in their own neighborhood after dark because they have to. If they work late shifts, public transportation may be their only option. These women may still fear men's violence and likely engage in other self-restricting behaviors as a result, but this behavior is not reflected in these statistics.

The second area that Gordon and Riger don't explore is *why* people restrict their behaviors or choices. Their research suggests that both women and men restrict their behaviors and limit their own choices in significant ways. For women, one of the key reasons is the fear of violence. For men, there is likely a wide variety of reasons (not wanting to, being bored, not seeing the point, and so on). To the degree that men restrict their behavior due to their fear of violence, it is not *women's* violence that they fear. If men restrict their behaviors out of fear, it is probably a result of the fear of other men's violence. The point is that fear of men and men's violence places restrictions on women's lives. Fear of men and men's violence place much less significant restrictions on men's lives.

"Women choose to live their lives differently as a result of a well-founded fear of men's violence and restrict themselves from engaging in what, by all rights, they should be able to do at least as freely as men."

What is clear, then, is that men's violence, both the actual occurrence of and the threat of, has a direct and profound impact on all women. Women choose to live their lives differently as a result of a well-founded fear of men's violence and restrict themselves from engaging in what, by all rights, they should be able to do at least as freely as men. Being free to walk in one's own neighborhood or to a local park is a basic right. Women restrict themselves, and they restrict themselves as a result of men's behavior, as a result of the threat that men pose.

Therefore, men's sexist violence is not only traumatizing for the women or men who are victimized and not only a horror for the friends and loved ones of those who are harmed, but it also disproportionately poses restrictions on women's choices and women's lives generally. Thus, men's sexist violence is gendered. It has a different impact on women than it does on men.

Even when men are victimized, their experiences of victimization are different than the experiences of women. This is not to say that men are any less traumatized or harmed. It is to say that when men are victimized by sexist violence, the context in which that victimization occurs is different. This means that the experience of being a victim is different. As an example, the state of Maryland still allows local police jurisdictions to require that a rape "victim" take a polygraph exam before they proceed with the criminal investigation. This means that women, who have been raped and have the courage to report it, may be subject to being doubted by the police and forced to undergo a procedure that is so flawed that it is not admissible in court. Those jurisdictions that use this practice force only women who report rape to take the polygraph exam, not men. This suggests a view that women are more likely to lie about being raped than are men.

The case of the Maryland state law and the way that it is being used demonstrates the context in which women and men are victimized. Though the experience of being raped may be similar for individual women or men, the social context in which women are more often sexualized and more often blamed for their own victimization results in a very different meaning of the experience. The context of systemic and widespread sexism means that men who are victimized are shielded from some of the harms that women experience routinely. It also means that the systemic responses are different as is the support for moving through the process of healing.

Resources

Web

Alianza: National Latino Alliance For the Elimination of Domestic Violence. www.dvalianza.org

Asian and Pacific Islander Institute on Domestic Violence. www.apiahf.org

Mending the Sacred Hoop. Addresses domestic violence as it relates to Native American women and communities. www.msh-ta.org

Sacred Circle: National Resource Center to End Violence Against Native Women. 877-733-7623

Sakhi: For South Asian Women. National organization addressing violence against women and children, focusing on south Asian women and communities. www.sakhi.com

Print

Hadhubuti, H. R. (1990). *Black men: Obsolete, single, dangerous: Afrikan American Families in Transition: Essays in discovery, solution and hope.* Chicago: Third World Press.

Island, D., & Letellier, P. (1991). *Men who beat the men who love them: Battered gay men and domestic violence.* Harrington Park, NY: Harrington Park Press.

New York State Department of Health AIDS Institute. (2001). *Domestic violence in lesbian, gay, transgender and bisexual communities: Trainers manual.* Available from www.health.state.ny.us/nysdoh.

Renzetti, C. M., & Miley, C. H. (Eds.). (1996). *Violence in gay and lesbian domestic partnerships.* Harrington Park, NY: Harrington Park Press.

Richie, B. E. (1996). Compelled to crime: The gender entrapment of battered black women. New York: Routledge Press.

West, C. M. (2002). Violence in the lives of black women: Battered black and blue. New York, NY: Haworth Press.

White, E. C. (1994). Chain chain change: For black women in abusive relationships. Seattle, WA: Seal Press.

PART 3
Educating for Change

The last part includes three chapters that examine social change efforts, educating men to take action, and sustainability. All of this work, educating men about sexism and violence, is both part of a long-standing social change movement and has a goal of changing our society. Creating a world where sexism and violence do not exist requires social change. Chapter 10 looks at how this work is a form of social change and provides a brief sketch of the social change history that we are all a part of. Specifically, Chapter 10 looks at both the "herstory" of the feminist movement against sexism and violence and the history of the men's movement to support these feminist efforts.

Chapter 11 speaks specifically to educating men to take action. One of the beginning conversations to have with any man about taking action against sexism and violence is what it means to be an ally. So this chapter begins with a conversation about being an ally and the kinds of behaviors that are expected from allies. From here, this chapter explores the kinds of things that men can do, have done, and are doing (both individually and collectively) to address sexism and violence.

Part 3 ends with Chapter 12, which looks at sustainability. The first part of this conversation about sustainability is accountability. This chapter examines who educators are accountable to while educating men, and offers some suggestions for ways that they can be accountable to these various groups in the process of educating men. But educating men to take action also involves educating men about what they need to think about in terms of being accountable. This chapter includes some key points about men being accountable. Educating men about sexism and violence is draining, challenging work that takes a toll on those who do it. So the last part of the conversation about sustainability is how educators can take care of themselves (and each other) in order to sustain these efforts.

CHAPTER 10

Social Change Efforts to End Sexism and Violence

"I am concerned about the issue of women's rights because I understand that women's rights is a political issue, and I am a political person. I understand that the oppression and exploitation of women is an integral aspect of every reactionary social system that ever existed, and I am struggling to be a progressive. I understand that women, like the land, are primary to life, and I am a living being."

YA SALAAM, 1980, P. 113.

Sexism and violence are important to address on both the individual and social levels. So far, this book has explored educating men on both levels about men's violence. In this chapter, the attention turns slightly to focus more directly on the social levels. This chapter provides a brief sketch of the rich herstory of feminist efforts to combat sexism and violence, the history of men's work to end sexism and violence, an overview of the socio-political context of sexism and violence, and some strategies, in addition to education, that can be used to combat sexism and violence.

"Herstory" of the Movement Against Sexism and Violence

As has been described throughout this book, addressing sexism and violence is best understood as a social movement. The efforts of educators are not just isolated activities of individuals or groups. These efforts are connected to other efforts that are occurring across the country and around the world. These efforts to end sexism and violence are also connected to the efforts that have gone on in the past. Understanding these efforts to end sexism and violence within a historical context diminishes the sense of isolation and minimizes the frustration that can occur. This knowledge then becomes a means to prevent burnout.

All educators should have some knowledge about the history of the social change movement of which they are a part (including the local history of where each educator works). This section provides a brief overview of the rich and vibrant history of women's activism against sexist violence. Although this section focuses on the history of the U.S. feminist struggles, what happens in the U.S. is part of an international effort. Every culture has similar and additional forms of sexism and violence that are simultaneously condoned and in response to which there are organized efforts to resist.

Each form of sexist violence has slightly different roots. All of the efforts to combat sexism and violence have their foundation in the feminist movement—women have a long history of organized resistance against every form of sexist violence. Beyond these common roots, there are some variations in terms of how these efforts gained ground. The pages that follow offer a brief overview of each of these movements in their historical context.

The Roots of the Anti-Domestic Violence Movement

The anti-domestic violence movement has deep roots in this country. Women have organized together since the mid-1800s to resist domestic violence. After the explosion of the feminist movement in the 1970s, the battered women's movement found renewed energy and experienced tremendous growth.

The temperance movement was one of the first mass efforts to organize women and mobilize our nation to combat domestic violence. The leadership recognized a connection between men's drinking and the violence perpetrated on women and children, and organized against alcohol in an attempt to relieve women from the violence and abuse they suffered. (It has also been argued that the temperance movement was the first time women took public space to organize and advocate for social change. See Mattingly, 1998). By mobilizing to stop men's use of alcohol, these women pioneers were also attempting to stop men's abuse of women. Another early highlight of the organized efforts to combat domestic violence include the founding of the first shelter for battered women by Elizabeth Cady Stanton in 1852 (in her own home).

The Roots of the Other Feminist Anti-Violence Efforts

The roots of the battered women's movement is much better documented than the roots of the other feminist efforts to resist sexism and violence. What has been uncovered is more sporadic and it appears less fluid—particularly the efforts against pornography, prostitution, and trafficking. That being said, it is important to realize the depth of the roots that do exist.*

**Because the herstory of the rape, sexual harassment, and pornography movements are somewhat less documented than is the herstory of the domestic violence movement, my overview of this heritage is not complete. If I miss events or organizations, please contact me directly at www.rusfunk.com.*

The first recorded effort of women to resist sexual violence occurred in 1866, when a group of African American women testified before Congress about the rapes they experienced during the Memphis Riots (Lerner, 1972). This reference not only suggests the depths of the efforts to combat rape and sexual assault, but it also reinforces the discussion made in Chapter 9 on the intersections between racism and sexism. African American, Latina, Asian, and Native American women have always been integrally involved in all of these efforts—ending sexism and men's violence is *not* just a white woman's movement. At the time of the testimony, the rape of black women was not considered a crime.

The first efforts against prostitution and trafficking were efforts to end "white slavery" (which, by definition, focused only on European American women who were prostituted) and were launched in the U.S. and Northern Europe in the mid-19th century.

The Recent Feminist Movement

The recent women's movements against sexism violence developed as a result of consciousness raising groups of women and feminists in the early 1970s. As women began listening to each other, they began recognizing how common men's violence against them was and started to recognize the connection between men's violence and institutionalized sexism. As a result, they began to organize. This consciousness raising was occurring at the same time that other community organizing and social change efforts were common, many of which had women in their leadership. Women started using this knowledge and skills and began applying it to sexism and violence.

The initial organizing efforts focused on offering direct support and services for women who had been victimized. The first hotlines were often the home phones of women providing leadership in their communities, and the first shelters for battered women were safe houses that women offered each other as they attempted to flee from abusive men. This section is a brief overview of the history of each movement against sexist violence.

The first U.S. battered women's shelter in the recent battered women's movement was opened in St. Paul in 1973. Erin Prizzey, from England, wrote the first book about domestic violence, *Scream Silently or the Neighbors Will Hear,* in England, in 1973, followed in 1976 by Del Martin, who published the first book about domestic violence in the U.S. Martin's book, *Battered Wives,* is still available from Volcano Press. The National Coalition Against Domestic Violence, a coalition of domestic violence programs and services for battered women, was founded in 1978.

The New York Radical Feminists organized the first Rape Speak-Out in 1971, reportedly the first time in the U.S. that women spoke out publicly about rape and their experiences. The first rape crisis centers were opened in Washington, DC and California in 1973. Later that same year, they organized a conference on rape and sexual assault, and in 1974, released *Rape: The First Sourcebook for Women.* Andrea Medea and Kathleen Thompson co-wrote *Against Rape,* also in 1974. Susan Brownmiller wrote what has become one of the classics in feminist anti-rape literature in 1975, *Against Our Will: Men, Women and Rape*. Nancy Gager and Cathleen Schuur wrote *Sexual Assault: Confronting Rape in America* in 1976, and the National Coalition Against Sexual Assault was organized in 1978.

Women Against Pornography was organized in 1979 in New York as a speak-out against pornography and violence against women. Andrea Dworkin wrote the groundbreaking *Pornography: Men Possessing Women* in 1979, and Laura Lerderer edited *Take Back the Night: Women on Pornography* in 1980. In 1983, Andrea Dworkin and Catherine MacKinnon drafted a local anti-pornography ordinance in Minneapolis, based on a civil rights analysis (rather than an obscenity analysis). Their efforts, along with the tireless efforts of local organizers, resulted in three days of hearings on the impact of and harm caused by pornography. The City Council of Minneapolis voted to pass the ordinance as did the city of Indianapolis (which was ultimately struck down by the U.S. Supreme Court).

During the late 1970s and early 1980s, women engaged in major organizing around sexual harassment. The Alliance Against Sexual Coercion (AASC) was organized in Boston in the mid-1970s and was the first community-based group to provide services to women who were sexually harassed in the workplace. AASC published *Fighting Sexual Harassment* in 1979, which is believed to be the first book on sexual harassment of any kind and certainly the first written from a feminist perspective that used the voices of women who had been sexually harassed. On the national level, 9to5, the National Association of Working Women, was organized in 1973 with the initial focus being to address sexual harassment. This organization has since grown to address other issues faced by working women. Women began filing sexual harassment lawsuits in the mid 1970s, with the first court case filed by a Latina in 1971. Women's organizing, agitation, and court cases resulted in the Equal Employment Opportunity Commission (EEOC) finally issuing guidelines forbidding sexual harassment in 1980, and the U.S. Supreme Court finally recognized sexual harassment as a violation of federal law in 1986. It is worth noting that the majority of the court cases defining sexual harassment were brought by African American, Latina, Asian, or Native American women.

There have also been heroic (or *she*roic) efforts on the grassroots level of organizations to help women get out of prostitution. WHISPER (Women Hurt in Systems of Prostitution Engaged in Revolt) was organized in the mid 1980s in Minneapolis-St. Paul, and other cities have followed with similar grassroots organizations. Susan Kay Hunter founded the Council for Prostitution Alternatives in Portland in the early 1980s as the first agency to offer long-term services for prostituted and formerly prostituted women. Breaking Free, a self-help and advocacy organization for women escaping prostitution, was formed in 1987 in Minneapolis, and Kathleen Barry wrote *Female Sexual Slavery*, the first book addressing the issues of prostitution from a feminist perspective, in 1979.

Aegis, the first magazine devoted to ending violence against women, began publishing in 1978. *Aegis* addressed all forms of violence against women in its pages and helped to develop and expand the feminist movement against violence against women. The magazine had a very grassroots feel and focused not only on consciousness-raising, but also on concrete skills-building articles that addressed organizing and advocacy issues. It stopped publication in the late 1980s.

Fight Back: Feminist Resistance to Male Violence (edited by Delacoste and Newman) was published in 1981. *Fight Back* was written as a manual for community organizing and direct action for feminists addressing all forms of male violence. It is, unfortunately, no longer in print.

The value of the efforts that this herstory describes goes far beyond this list of accomplishments, as vital as they have been. To fully understand the scope of what women did, it is necessary to contextualize these efforts within what was going on socially and politically at the time. The magnitude of the work that women did and the impact of this work cannot be overstated. The silence that surrounded these issues in the 1970s and 1980s, when most of this organizing and activism occurred, was immense. This silence, coupled with the low status offered to women in general and the outright hostility directed at feminists, meant that the efforts by these women to even get heard were truly Herculean. Most of the early centers and programs working to address these issues began out of women's homes or basements and were completely unfunded. The laws were utterly draconian. Publishers laughed them out of their offices when women proposed books; the women had to organize publishing houses to publish many of the first books. The media refused to pay attention to these issues (except for the rare titillating or dramatic case). It was in this context that these women organized, wrote, fought, advocated, and, perhaps more importantly, in which they provided services to women in pain.

Educating for Social Change

Educating the public has always been an integral part of feminist efforts to combat sexist violence. Although providing immediate services and support to women in crisis was the primary focus of most of these initial efforts (especially rape and domestic violence programs), advocating for better laws, organizing the community, and educating the public were also understood as core activities. The educational efforts were provided to achieve three primary and interrelated goals:

- To raise awareness about sexist violence
- To demonstrate how ordinary people can support their loved ones when they are victimized
- To lay the foundation for radical social change to stop all forms of men's abuse and violence against women

Feminists recognize that men's abusiveness stems from cultural attitudes and norms that overvalue men and men's lives while simultaneously undervaluing women and women's lives. This cultural environment is the context that allows men to think that it is okay to hit their wives, not listen when a woman says "No," buy a woman on the street, or hit on a woman at work, in the classroom, or on the street. This feminist analysis recognizes that sexist violence is much more complicated than individual men perpetrating individual acts of violence against individual women, children, or other men. Sexist violence involves individual men choosing to act violently in a context of a society that sanctions the view that women are less important than men. A feminist analysis sees sexist violence as being part of a continuum of sexist behavior.

"Sexist violence involves individual men choosing to act violently in a context of a society that sanctions the view that women are less important than men."

Educational efforts are needed to raise awareness about the context of sexism in which men's violence occurs, and to change these cultural norms, while simultaneously addressing the specific issues of these various forms of sexist violence. Educational efforts to stop men's violence against women are recognized as forms of social change. Because men choose to be violent towards women in a society that systematically overvalues masculinity while simultaneously undervaluing femininity, educational efforts must be dually focused: They must address

- Why individual men choose to use violence
- How the social context allows those choices to be seen as viable options

Education can become a tool to motivate the public to challenge the systems that enforce women's devaluation.

Stemming from this analysis, the early educational efforts of the first agencies that addressed sexist violence focused on exposing and destroying the myths that were (and to a large degree still are) prevalent. For example, the anti-rape movement significantly educated to counter the myth that sexual assaults are sexual acts. These early efforts redefined sexual violence as violence that is perpetrated by a sexual means. The belief that men perpetrate sexual violence because they are turned on is still quite common and is grounded in the false understanding of sexual violence as sexually motivated.

Feminists were the first to recognize and identify sexual violence as being motivated by power and control acted out in sexualized ways. As discussed, for some men who perpetrate sexual violence, power and control itself is sexualized, but the underlying motivation is not sexual release, but power release. In fact, given our societal norms about sex, power, and control, it seems fairly normative for all men to in some ways confuse and merge these concepts. Admittedly, this notion is confusing, especially when discussing the everyday forms of men's sexual coercion and manipulation. The motivation may appear to be for men to "get some" by any means necessary, but underneath that motivation is a sense of entitlement and power. Examples of this kind of conflation can be seen in the media nearly every day. The idea that men can seduce women is, in part, based on the belief that men can (and should try to) overpower women's initial hesitation.

Early educational efforts of the movements to address men's violence had two main foci:

- Empowering women who might be experiencing abuse
- Educating the general public about the issues

The public education efforts focused on confronting the myths that surrounded the various forms of violence and their connection to sexism. For example, the frequency of woman abuse (dispelling the myth that domestic violence is rare), describing how "woman battering" was (and still is) sanctioned by law and custom, and explaining how domestic violence is related to the undervaluing of women's lives in our society. The goal was to raise women's and the general public's awareness about the issues and their impact on women, while at the same time address the issues of sexism and misogyny in the broader society that were seen as the foundation upon which men's violence occurred. The issue addressed by the early feminist leaders was not only the fact that individual men acted violently towards wives or girlfriends, but that the choice to act violently was sanctioned by a sexist society. Thus, educating people about the issues of men's violence included information about social and systematic sexism.

The public education efforts about the issues of sexual harassment, stalking, and pornography and prostitution had similar histories and the same dual focus. Empowering women has always been seen as one of the core reasons for these movements and the priority of empowering women was included in the educational design and efforts. At the same time, feminists understood that the general public needed to

- Be better educated about the issues
- Be more sensitized to the harms that women face
- Have their myths challenged

The goal of empowering women resulted in the early efforts (and many of the current ones) focusing on three main areas: defining the violence, both legally and from a feminist or "victim-centered" perspective; exposing the threats of sexist violence (thus empowering women to avoid sexist violence); and identifying the remedies and resources available to women if they are victimized. Although distinct, these goals were inter-related. By combining these three goals, the efforts focused on using this information to empower *all* women to stand up against a sexist and misogynist culture. Assisting women to see that every woman is at risk for sexist violence, and how those risk factors are based within institutional sexism, provides a means to further educate women about ways to reduce their risk—by reducing sexism.

A secondary goal of these educational efforts has been to educate the general public about the realities of men's violence against women and about ways that the public can join the effort to better support women or men who are victimized. These educational efforts have been expanded and deepened over the years.

As feminists developed their skills and knowledge about educating, they began developing more specific and specialized educational programs. They also began expanding the educational foci to include other kinds of issues such as addressing the impact of violence on lesbian and bisexual women, developing educational expertise about the experiences of immigrant women, examining the barriers women of color face, exploring men who are victimized, and so on.

It has only been relatively recently that some programs have initiated efforts to educate men as a specific target. Still, most programs, organizations, agencies, and groups that provide educational efforts tend to focus on educating women and the general public. Educating men specifically is only beginning to be recognized as an important component of the work, and as the expertise is growing, so too is the understanding that educating men about these issues is different than educating women, requiring different kinds of skills, different arguments, and using somewhat different tactics. Even still, with limited resources to provide education, the priority continues to be on educating women.

Take Back the Night

One of the most dramatic and still controversial forms of activism in the feminist movement to end men's sexist violence was the development of Take Back the Night (TBTN) marches and actions. In the U.S., Take Back the Night began in New York and San Francisco in the late 1970s as public actions against snuff films, pornographic films that depicted the sexualized murder of women as the climax of the movie. By tying together the issues of pornography, the systematic devaluing of women's lives and pain, and the threat of sexual violence that all women live with, TBTN events became powerful symbolic actions. The focus of Take Back the Night was initially to challenge the silence about men's violence against women by publicly taking the night, the night being used to symbolize the silence, secrecy, and shame that surround sexual assaults. By symbolically taking back the night, women declared their resistance to living in fear, silence, and shame.

These events are generally locally organized and, as such, have the local flavor. Although not always containing a march, they frequently do. The marching takes on symbolic meaning in the context of taking back the night. When walking to reclaim the streets that have been taken from them as a result of the threat that men pose, women demonstrate their power to walk collectively to protect each other from men's threats. Marching sends a powerful message to the public in addition to being a very empowering action for the women who participate.

The role of men in TBTN events is often debated. On one hand, it is argued that men should fully participate along with women to demonstrate their solidarity with women and to show that women are not making this walk alone. On the other hand, it is argued that TBTN is historically about women's empowerment and *women* taking back the night. Thus, women should be allowed and encouraged to walk alone while men do support work separately. There are, of course, variations of this debate, and the solutions that local communities come to as a result run the gamut. Some events do not have male speakers or performers and ask that men do not march at all. Others ask men to march behind women (thus signifying men "following" women's leadership), while others include men's participation fully in every aspect including speaking, marching, and participating at any post-TBTN events.

It is worth noting that this debate almost always occurs in the context of women doing the actual organizing. Men have never taken the initiative to organize a TBTN event.

"The best and greatest impact of the men's work is not on behalf of women, or with women, or even for women; men's best work is with men."

It is my view that while it is important for men to show solidarity with women during a Take Back the Night event, there are valuable and more important ways for men to show their solidarity than by marching alongside or even behind women. Although it is crucial that women and men work together in this movement, women and men have different work to do. The best and greatest impact of the men's work is not on behalf of women, or with women, or even for women; men's best work is with men. Malcolm X stated the best work that white folks could do on behalf of ending racism was to work with white folks. The parallel argument can be made about men in regards to ending sexist violence.

MY EXPERIENCE OF TBTN

My view, of course, is shaped by my experience. Although I have participated in many TBTN events and do love them (as an activist, there is something particularly moving about marching or "taking the streets"), Take Back the Night is also somewhat lacking. The message and the purpose of TBTN, by definition and necessity, is the empowerment of women. As such, the speeches and chants are often focused on what women can do to empower themselves. There is little discourse on what men can do. As a result, after the march is over, women are empowered to act and men are left waiting for the next action—undoubtedly organized by women. It seems that, if men are going to be present, they need to be directly spoken to about what they can do the days, weeks, and months after a TBTN event. I think that organizers should consider holding men's forums during the march itself so that men are given chances to discuss what they can do to work to end sexist violence.

The first time I tried this, in Washington, DC, the men who stayed back received an unexpected bonus. When the women returned from their march, the men offered them a standing ovation. *That* show of support and solidarity was as moving for the men who were involved (and by all reports, for the women as well) as any amount of marching alongside the women that the men could have done.

Take Back the Night actions will continue to be (hopefully) somewhat controversial, and the role of men in TBTN events will not be settled here. There are a variety of ways that men can act in solidarity with women to end sexist violence, and men's participation in Take Back the Night actions symbolically reflects these various forms of men's support.

Other Forms of Activism

Take Back the Night is not the only form of activism that women have organized to address the issues of men's sexist violence. As a result of women's organizing, the following awareness events are recognized nationally:

Calendar Period	***Event***
January	Stalking Awareness Month
February 14th	V-Day (Calling for a day of activism against men's violence. In many communities, *The Vagina Monologues*, by Eve Ensler, is produced as an awareness and fundraiser.
April	Sexual Assault Awareness Month (SAAM)
October	Domestic Violence Awareness Month (DVAM)
A Specific Day in October	Day of No Prostitution

Internationally, the end of November and early December have been identified as the "16 days of Activism" against violence against women, during which time local efforts in communities around the globe are organized to draw attention to the local issues of sexist violence and what can be done in response. In many local jurisdictions, a host of activities and events organized during these months raise awareness about the issues and generate more public support. TBTN events, vigils, speak-outs, forums, public campaigns, marches, petition drives, summit, conferences, debates, round-tables, and other forms of activism are common.

Educators need to be aware of various forms of activism and the awareness months in which they occur. Educators can and should find ways to tie education to whatever activism may be going on. In addition, most activist events can be understood as forms of public education.

"It should not be up to men to give to women what is rightfully theirs."

FREDERICK DOUGLASS

Although Frederick Douglass was referring to women's right to vote, it reverberates strongly with the men's movement to end sexism and violence. Being able to sleep in one's own bed without fear and danger, to live in one's own house without violence and abuse, to walk down a street without insults and threats—these are rights that women ought to just have. It should not be up to men to give women these rights; these rights are (or should be) inherent. These rights have been taken from women, but it is not up to men to give them back.

"The work of men in being allies with women to end sexist violence is as much about liberating men from the constraints of masculinity as it is about rescuing women."

The foundation of men's work to end men's violence can be drawn from the Frederick Douglass quote. Men who work to end men's violence are not acting as heroes in order to save defenseless women. Rather, the men act from a place of understanding that living free from sexism and violence is a basic human right and that joining with women to remove the barriers to their achieving these rights is essential. The work of men in being allies with women to end sexist violence is as much about liberating men from the constraints of masculinity as it is about rescuing women.

The Work of Men Who Endorsed Feminism

The history of men's work to support women and feminists is long, though not nearly as deep, as the history of a women's or feminist movement. Some of the examples include the following:

- **John Adams.** As a result of the advocacy of his wife Abigail, John Adams argued that the Declaration of Independence be broadened to include women. (He later caved in to the pressures of his male colleagues, abandoning his wife's advocacy to ensure that gender equality was part of the foundation of the new nation.)
- **John Stuart Mill.** In 1859, Mill wrote *On the Subjugation of Women*—a brilliant and scathing indictment of the attempts to maintain women's subordination.
- **Frederick Douglass.** Douglass was a strong advocate for women's right to vote. Until the efforts of the white male legislators to drive a wedge between the women and black suffrage activists, there was a strong and vibrant coalition between the two.
- **William Lloyd Garrison.** Garrison supported and was actively involved in the struggle to gain women's right to vote. Other men who were part of this feminist struggle include Theodore Parker, Wendell Phillips, Henry Parker, and Parker Pillsbury.
- **W.E.B. DuBois.** DuBois wrote eloquently of the need for men to support women's rights and worked to end men's domination of women (see *The Damnation of Women*). He was also one of the first authors to expose the sexual abuse of African American men during lynchings and other violence to which they were subjected.
- **Alexander Crummell.** In the 1800s, Crummel wrote on and was active in the support of women's rights (see his speech "The Black Woman of the South: Her Neglects and Needs").

- **James Baldwin.** In the 1950s, Baldwin wrote and spoken on issues of men's support of women's rights (see his article "Here Be Dragons," reprinted in Byrd and Guy-Sheftall, 2001, pp. 207–218).
- **Bayard Rustin.** In addition to being a forceful voice for nonviolence and civil rights for all, Rustin was also a supporter for women's rights (see "Feminism and Equality," *New York Amsterdam News*, Aug. 27, 1970).
- **Derrick Bell, Nathan McCall, Henry Louis Gates,** and **Charles Johnson**, relatively recent activists and authors, have taken strong stands for women's rights.

More recent examples of men who have worked to support and advance women's rights include Alan Alda, Senator Joseph Biden (who authored the Violence Against Women Act), John Stoltenberg (anti-pornography activist and author of the book *Refusing to be a Man*, 1989), Haki Madhubuti, Michael Kimmel, Michael Kauffman (founder of the White Ribbon Campaign), Gus Kaufman (co-founder of Men Stopping Violence), Michael Awkward (author of the book *Negotiating Difference: Race, Gender and the Politics of Positionality*), Gary L. Lemons (author of the article "To be Black, Male and Feminist: Making Womanist Space for Black Men"). These are all examples of men who have accepted the initiative and worked to address an end to sexist violence.

Jon Snodgrass edited the book *For Men Against Sexism: A Book of Readings,* published in 1977. In 1980, Kalamu ya Salaam wrote *Our Women Keep Our Skies from Falling: Six Essays in Support of the Struggle to Smash Sexism/Develop Women.* Tim Beneke wrote *Men on Rape,* the first book addressing men's attitudes on rape, in 1982. Michael Kimmel edited *Men Confront Pornography,* the first book that was a speak-out of men against pornography in 1990. *Stopping Rape: A Challenge for Men*, the first book written by a man for men about stopping rape, was published in 1992 by Rus Ervin Funk. *Traps: African American Men on Gender and Sexuality* by Rudolph P. Byrd and Beverly Guy-Sheftall was published in 2001.

Men's Groups That Have Formed

Some men's groups have made strides towards relieving women of the responsibility of educating men and begun developing expertise and resources to better educate men about these issues. Men Stopping Rape (1980); Men Stopping Violence; the Oakland Men's Project; Men Overcoming Violence; Emerge (1977); the Men's Resource Center; RAVEN (Rape and Violence End Now); Montreal Men Against Sexism; Men for Change in Nova Scotia, Canada; and Men Can Stop Rape have all developed specific programming for men about issues of sexism and violence. There are examples from other countries as well, probably the best known of which is the White Ribbon Campaign from Toronto, Canada. As these programs for men have developed, they tend to focus solely on sexual assault or domestic violence, rarely both. There have been only a few examples of men's organized efforts against sexual harassment, pornography, and prostitution, and these have tended to be short-lived.

The National Organization for Changing Men (now the National Organization for Men Against Sexism) was founded in 1978 and was the first attempt by men to organize and network nationally to confront sexism and promote pro-feminism. The organizing of men's groups continues: Black Men for the Eradication of Sexism (at Morehead College) organized in 1994; Men Against Sexual Violence in Champaign, IL in 1998; and M.E.N.—**M**obilizing (men) to **E**nd viole**N**ce in Louisville, KY was founded in 2003.*

The Contributions of Other Media and Activism

Changing Men Magazine was published consistently from the late 1970s throughout the 1990s, and *XY Magazine*, based in Australia, continues to be published regularly (www.xyonline.net). The Activist Men's Caucus was founded and continued for 12 years during the late 1980s and into the 1990s as an informal national collective of male and female organizers and activists. The Activist Men's Caucus periodically published the *Activist Men's Journal.* The Caucus was an attempt by pro-feminist activist men to network and to promote pro-feminist activism, which led to the organizing of mass actions of men against men's violence in Chicago (at the Playboy headquarters), Pittsburgh, Atlanta, and Tucson.

"BrotherPeace—the international day of men taking action to end men's violence" was organized in the early 1980s as another way to promote men's activism and to encourage men to take to the streets to end men's violence and to support the work of women who worked to end domestic violence. This action was held on a specific day in October in an attempt to encourage men's activism during Domestic Violence Awareness Month. Throughout the history of BrotherPeace, men successfully organized some very dramatic actions, including dropping banners from overpasses above the highways around St. Paul and Minneapolis, and building a "woman's memorial wall" across from the Vietnam Memorial in Washington, DC.

This brief overview of the history of men's activism demonstrates the depths of some men's commitments to ending sexism and violence. In working to educate men, it is important to recognize the ways that those who are involved are part of a deep and rich history of men who support the human rights of women. For men, this awareness can be important in helping to break some of the isolation that many men feel as a result of being involved in this work. In addition, knowing that there is a history of men's involvement, activism, and leadership in addressing sexism and combating violence can encourage other men to get involved. One of the barriers to men even listening to the issues of men's violence and men's responsibilities is that they often have no models from which to learn. Knowing the history helps to identify the role models that do exist.

**This should not be considered an exhaustive list by any means nor an endorsement. Numerous other organizations are doing tremendous work. This is just a sampling.*

The Socio-Political Context of Men's Violence

The previous sections only briefly touched on the socio-political context of men's violence. The herstory and history of these movements are grounded in a socio-political analysis. This section builds on this history and develops in more detail the ways that sexism and violence occur in a broader socio-political context.

The frequency with which men's violence occurs, coupled with the fact that men's violence is relatively consistent across cultures and generations, suggests that there is more to men perpetrating violence and abuse than the individual pathology of men who decide to rape, batter, or harass. We live in what has been defined as a "rape culture" (Sanday, 1981) which can be understood as a culture that promotes and encourages the sexualized devaluation of women. It is this systematic devaluation of women that is sexism, and it is from this foundation that men's violence is perpetrated. It is a culture in which women and what is considered feminine are systematically undervalued compared with men and what is considered masculine. This systematic devaluing of women, especially when compared to the systematic overvaluing of men, creates a dynamic in which women are seen as less than human and, thus, not deserving of the extent and range of rights afforded to men. It is within this context that individual men choose to act violently towards women and other men.

The Complexity of Sexism

As described in Chapter 9, "Racism, Homophobia, Sexism, and Men's Violence," women are not all subject to sexism in the same ways. Sexism does exist, and it affects women in ways too profound to describe here. Sexism is also, however, perpetrated on and experienced differently by women based on their age, sexual orientation, class background, race or ethnicity, religion, and so on. While sexism does exist, it is not a one-size-fits-all kind of oppression. Sexism is nuanced and changing, and these differences are part of what makes challenging sexism so complicated and difficult. Whatever form of sexism and in whatever ways that sexism may combine with other forms of oppression (such as racism or homophobia), violence and abuse are directly linked to it. Part of educating effectively about sexism and violence is to understand the ways that sexism is perpetrated against different groups of women.

The Dehumanizing of Sexism

To perpetrate violence against another person, one must first see that person as "other" (i.e., different), strip the other person of a layer of her or his humanity, and deny that the behavior is violent. Thus, racist violence is perpetrated against "niggers" or "spicks" rather than human beings, and sexist violence targets "bitches" or "sluts" rather than women who are someone's sister, daughter, and friend. Perpetrating violence against this "other" becomes acceptable and is not defined as violence.

Perhaps the easiest way to conceive of this is by participating in the following exercise.

DOING YOUR WORK: *What It Means to Be a "Man"; "Woman"*

1. Write down on a sheet of paper the heading "Women" and on the other side "Men."
2. Under the heading "Women," list the traits that society says women should have.
3. Under the heading "Men," list the traits that society says men should have.
4. Cover up the headings.
5. While looking at the two lists of traits as a whole, which list of traits does society value more? It becomes clear that those traits that are associated with men are valued more highly.

When women are not valued equally with men, the use of violence directed at women and the harms that they experience are not recognized or acknowledged. This is clearly seen in practice every day. For example, U.S. laws addressing assault and battery were actually written to protect men, with separate standards put in place to justify men's use of violence or force against women. The "rule of thumb" was a part of English Common Law that was brought to the U.S. It allowed a man to beat his wife or children with a stick as long as it was not bigger around than the thickness of his thumb.

"U.S. laws addressing assault and battery were actually written to protect men, with separate standards put in place to justify men's use of violence or force against women."

These laws parallel the laws that sanctioned men's use of violence against other groups of people who were seen as "other" or "less valuable" than men. For example, white men's violence against men of color was seen as similarly justifiable (although not codified in law in the same way as men's violence against women). If men were peers, however, the use of violence was defined as assault. It is only men's violence against women or other men who were seen as "less than" (i.e., enslaved Americans, Native Americans, and so on) that has been sanctioned by law. In addition, the "rule of thumb" was seen as an improvement in the previous law. Prior to the implementation of the "rule of thumb," men could hit women or children with anything they could get their hands on. This law was an attempt to limit the means by which men could use violence against women and children.

The Role of the Definition of Manhood in Men's Violence

In addition to the systemic devaluing of women and femininity, there are other ways in which culture creates a context for men's violence. Men are taught that to really be a man, they must be in control. The better a man is at demonstrating how in control he is, the more masculine he is seen. Being in control is certainly true in relation to men's emotions and themselves, but also in control of others and situations. The mythology of manhood suggests that the more in control men are—the more they control other people, other lives, other situations—the more "manly" they are. Men are, in fact, taught to feel entitled to be in control. Consider for a moment how common it is for manhood to be attributed to one's ability to take charge. This need to be in control is particularly evident in situations in which men are talking with a woman or group of women. Men tend to interrupt women more, talk over or past women, not pay attention to women, and otherwise depict the ways that men are in control of situations with women. Men tend to feel uncomfortable when they are around women and not in control.

When that control is threatened, men are taught that they have the right to get angry and to use violence as a way of expressing this anger. (Men's feeling of entitlement to use violence as a means of expressing anger is one reason why some erroneously use anger management techniques in working with men who batter. One of the myths to be exposed is that domestic violence is just unmanaged anger.) As a result, when men are dating or married and feel their control threatened, or when men want sex and can't get it, or when men see women they feel attracted to, or for a myriad of other reasons, men feel the right, indeed feel entitled, to act in ways that demonstrate they are in control. One cannot ever control another person. The more men try to control others and the more their attempts to control others escalate, the more likely they are to become abusive or violent. Thus, violence becomes one way in which men believe they can demonstrate their control and their manhood.

The Continuum of Sexism

Acts of sexist violence are not isolated incidents. They occur in a context, both a broader socio-political context and within the context of the relationship of the two people involved (which itself exists in a broader socio-political context). This broader context is sexism. Fully understanding sexist violence requires an examination of sexism.

As Suzanne Brown, director of the Washington Coalition of Sexual Assault Programs, states,

> *Rape is a part of a larger continuum of violence that finds its roots in the innocuous... All forms of sexual violence feed and draw strength from one another. Sexual abuse can begin... with leers, comments and gestures." She goes on to say that "Language that degrades and demeans whole groups of people allows for a conception of individuals that renders them less valuable...." (2003, p. 8)*

It is these "leers, comments, and gestures," coupled with the broader cultural context in which women are seen as less valuable, that defines sexism. It is also these leers, comments, and gestures that create the social environment in which some men choose to be violent and abusive.

Although not all men perpetrate sexist violence, all men act in ways and have certain attitudes that fall somewhere along a continuum of behaviors and attitudes with sexism on one end and more extreme acts of violence on the other. All men also benefit from sexism and sexist violence even if they perpetrate only the more subtle forms of sexism. Figures 10.1 and 10.2 attempt to graphically depict this notion.

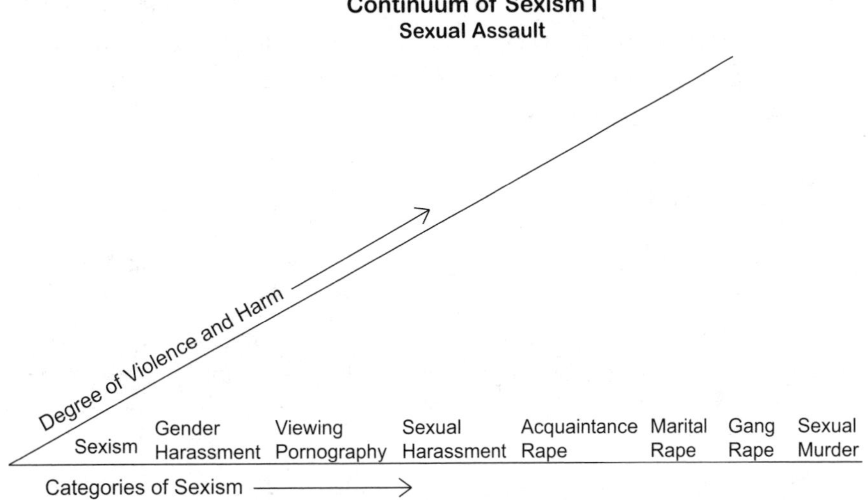

Figure 10.1

Figure 10.2

"I first sought to "control" my girlfriend through my verbal tirades and then finally through violence—the highest form of sexism." (emphasis added)

POWELL, 1992

As Kevin Powell describes above, referring to his own behavior and patterns, his use of sexism began in other ways and when those forms didn't work to get him what he felt he was entitled to ("control" in the relationship), he utilized violence. Using sexist language is connected to using sexist violence.

These continua are tools that help move a discussion of sexist violence away from blame, shame, or guilt. Because all men struggle with some expressions of sexist attitudes and behavior, all men have to work to address sexism even as they confront other men on their behavior or attitudes.

CASE STUDY

I will use myself as an example. Just because I am an anti-rape activist and educator does not mean that I am any better off than the most violent sex offenders. I'm one end of the very same continuum as are they. I too act in ways that are sexist. I too benefit from a system that grants men more privilege than women, and I still take advantage of those unearned privileges.

Effectively addressing sexism and violence, and working with men to address sexism and violence, requires moving away from false notions of "good" men and "bad" men, and it requires compassionate engagement with men about how they can partner to

- Work to make the world a better place for women
- Infuse gender justice in all areas of their lives

The continua in Figures 10.1 and 10.2 graphically demonstrate this connection.

Part of how these attitudes and behaviors are connected is exposed by the feelings reported by the people who are victimized. Regardless of the specific behavior, the people to whom the sexism is directed report almost identical responses: shame, disgust, self-doubt, self-blame, anger, hurt, fear (that it will continue or get worse), and so on. Obviously, the feelings increase with intensity as one proceeds along the continuum, but the feelings are virtually the same. This suggests that the behaviors are fundamentally the same.

These attitudes and behaviors are connected in that each of them, in their own way and in concert with the other behaviors listed, work to maintain a system in which men are valued more than women. This is done by defining women as the appropriate targets. It is acceptable and in many ways encouraged for men to look at women, make comments to and about women's appearance, approach women, and so on. It is acceptable and even promoted for men to look at pornography and other propaganda that limits women to their physical appearance and for men to take charge in their dating relationships with women by restricting women's options (who she goes out with, what she wears, how much makeup she wears, and so on). As described above, these are the broader structures of institutional sexism.

CASE STUDY

Flyers were recently discovered at rest stops promoting a new dating service for single Christian men. The title of the flyer was "Men: Are you *hunting* for a wife?" It did not say "searching" or "looking" or "longing" for a wife. "Hunting" suggests that women are targeted prizes; they are to be obtained or captured. There is a link between the mindset of hunting for someone, hunting for another human being, and using violence towards that person.

For a woman, every act of sexism or violence reminds her that the abuse could have been or could get worse. This may not be clear when talking about acts of sexism, but forms of sexist violence or abuse are not isolated acts. They are done in a larger situational context—that context is that men's violence against women is so common and women are so sensitized to understand men's violence that any form of men's abusiveness sends a message to women that the man could have chosen to escalate the abusiveness to more extreme forms of violence.

Strategies for Presenting on Sexism and Violence

The continua of sexism are important tools for helping men understand the dynamic interaction of sexism and sexist violence. The continua provide a nonjudgmental way to help men to begin critically examining some of their own behaviors and attitudes, as well as the attitudes that they allow to be expressed in their presence—attitudes that may suggest the willingness to use violence.

Explore the Impact of Various Forms of Sexism

You can use the continua to provide a means to explore the impact of various forms of sexism on women's lives. While not all women experience the more severe forms of violence, most (if not all) women experience some expressions of sexism. Helping men to understand the connection between various forms of sexism with violence and abuse helps increase men's empathy and helps them find ways to engage. While ending rape, pornography, dating abuse, or other forms of sexist violence may be beyond what a man is willing or able to do, addressing some of the attitudes or behaviors on the continua that are not violent may be seen as do-able by men.

Discuss Sexism and Men's Violence Objectively

You can use the continua to provide an effective means to have a discussion with men about sexism and violence. To avoid putting them on the defensive, describe the work that men *together* have to do. Ultimately, the continua are tools that highlight men's *abilities* to respond to sexism and violence. As discussed earlier, identifying response-ability is not blaming men but, instead, is encouraging men to identify the ways that they can be involved.

Be Prepared to Discuss Women's Violence

You can use the continua to help men better understand how to respond when the issue turns to women's violence, abuse, or harassment against men.

For example, there is a reported increase in women's harassment of men in high school hallways. Although women's harassment is still wrong, it is important for men to understand (and remind others) that when men are harassed by women, the men almost never report feeling threatened or afraid that it could get worse. Women's harassment of men also almost never results in a change in men's behavior. Although the men may report feeling annoyed, embarrassed, and humiliated by women's harassment (which deserves an appropriate response both on the individual and institutional levels), this is profoundly different than women's responses to men's harassment.

When men harass women, women often report experiencing that harassment as threatening, and it is very common for women to report changing their behaviors as a result. The continua provide a means to discuss and then explain these differences, as well as point out that sexual harassment of women occurs in a broader context of sexism, and as such, is also fundamentally different than women's harassment of men.

Simultaneously Personalize and Depersonalize Sexism and Men's Violence

You can also use the continua to help men simultaneously personalize and depersonalize sexism and violence. As discussed earlier, men often respond with feelings of guilt and blame to any presentation of sexist violence. This comes, in part, from men's over-personalizing the discussion.

To label sexist violence as men's violence is not to say that all men are personally responsible for every act of sexism and violence that occurs. Presenting these continua, and the conversation that follows, provide a means by which men can understand and own that, while they are not personally responsible for every act of sexism that occurs, they must still accept some level of personal responsibility to address these issues.

At the same time, the continua provides a means by which men can personalize the ways they have acted in sexist ways and, thus, provide a means by which men can take personal responsibility for their own behaviors and attitudes. The continua also provide a framework to begin discussing how men can take personal response-ability to become part of the solution. Accepting personal response-ability is very different from accepting blame or guilt for being men.

Resources

Web

Women's Human Rights Net. An international network of organizations and individuals working for the expansion of women's rights as human rights. www.whrnet.org

Print

Blee, K. M. (1998). *No middle ground: Women and radical protest.* New York: New York University Press.

Coover, V., Deacon, E., Esser, C., & Moore, C. (1985). *Resource manual for a living revolution: A handbook of skills & tools for social change activists.* Philadelphia, PA: New Society Publishers.

Kimmel, M. (1996). *Manhood in America: A cultural history.* New York: The Free Press.

Kimmel, M. L., & Mosmiller, T. E. (1992). *Against the tide: Profeminist men in the United States 1776–1990: A documentary history.* Boston, MA: Beacon Press.

Naples, N. A. (1998). *Community activism and feminist politics: Organizing across race, class, and gender.* New York: Routledge Press.

CHAPTER 11

Educating Men to Take Action

Educating men, especially educating men to take action, requires educators to offer specific and concrete ideas of how men can combat sexism and violence. Educated men are not necessarily any less likely to perpetrate sexist violence and abuse than under-educated men (men who have not been educated about the issues of sexism and men's violence). Educating men is only the first step in a long process of social change. One goal, as defined much earlier in this manual, of educating men is to move them towards taking action as allies for women. Additional steps (that are beyond the scope of this manual) include organizing and mobilizing men to confront men's sexist violence on both the individual and institutional levels. Educating men can be a step in mobilizing and organizing men, but the processes and specific actions needed to mobilize and organize men are somewhat different, and more involved, than educating men. It is akin to when white people work to combat racism, or heterosexuals work to combat homophobia and heterosexism. Acting as allies against oppression can have profound effects on ending the injustice.

On Being an Ally

One purpose of educating men is to be allies for women. It seems important, particularly at this point of discussing men's taking action, to more clearly define what is meant by being an ally.

The idea of an ally was briefly discussed in Chapter 2 on moving men from being bystanders to being allies. That discussion was specific to making comments and acting on the very interpersonal level when sexist acts occur around a man. In this section, the notion of an ally builds on the interpersonal dynamics and encourages men to be allies in more public forums.

"Allies are people who are not members of that group but who act to support a person or group, at times even against what may seem (on the surface) to be their own self-interests."

The concept of an ally is grounded in numerous movements for social justice. Being an ally begins with the recognition that a person or a group is being unfairly treated. Allies are people who are not members of that group but who act to support a person or group, at times even against what may seem (on the surface) to be their own self-interests. Historically, the notion of allies as used here came out of anti-racism and anti-homophobia social change, identifying European Americans and heterosexuals, respectively, who acted in support of people of color or members of GLBT communities as they fought against oppression and violence and struggled to realize their civil and human rights. The term allies, of course, is not unknown to most readers of this book. There is, however, specific meaning attached to the notion of an ally within a social change/political movement context. It is this social change context to which I am referring when I speak of allies.

For men to act as allies for women is really no different. It begins with recognizing that women, as a group, are unfairly treated and harmed. After that, it means that men join to support women as they struggle against sexism and violence and seek to realize their full human potential. This is a crucial difference. There are many people who recognize that women are unfairly treated, but an ally *takes action.*

There are several characteristics that make up an ally. Allies

- **Listen.** They seek the perspective and listen to the voices of women in leadership as they say what they need and want from men. An ally also listens to women in general to learn more about the forms and expressions of sexism and how they impact women's lives.
- **Avoid Defensiveness.** Allies remain open to concerns and criticism by feminists and women. They respond to criticism without defensiveness.
- **Accept Responsibility.** It is not women's responsibility to educate men. It is men's responsibility to educate themselves. Men should notice and respond when acts of sexism occur. Allies do not wait for women to tell them to do something. They take the initiative.
- **Own the Issue.** In accepting the responsibility to speak out, allies speak for themselves. Allies don't speak out against sexism on behalf of women but because it affects and offends them. Male allies speak out on their own behalf.

  Male allies also identify ways that they can speak up or act in ways in support of women or to challenge sexism and male entitlement overtly and directly.
- **Open Doors.** Rather than accepting opportunities for themselves, male allies strive to advance opportunities for women.

- **Take Chances.** There are few road maps for what it means to be a male ally. Much of what male allies do is learned as they go. Even though men may be afraid of doing the wrong thing or stepping out of line, it is important that they do so anyway. Sometimes allies make mistakes. It is important that they learn from those mistakes, are open about the process, and not allow mistakes to keep them from trying.
- **Seek Support.** Men cannot be effective allies on their own. They deserve and need support to continue the hard work of being an ally. That being said, it is decidedly *not* the responsibility of women to support men who are acting as allies. It is men's responsibility to seek the support they need and deserve. Seek out and create, if necessary, means to gather such support with and from other men.
- **Earn Trust.** It is men's responsibility to earn women's trust when working to address sexism and violence. Women are not obligated to trust men. It is up to men to act in ways that demonstrate to women that they are trustworthy.
- **Act Reliably.** Male allies act in a consistent manner. Acting reliably is a key way to earn trust, but it is also an important activity in its own right. Acting reliably means that men follow through and that women know that they can depend on men to do what men say they are going to do, and to do what men need to do.
- **Take the Lead (at Times).** There are times when male allies need to take the lead in attacking sexism and men's violence. Acting as an ally means knowing when to take charge and when not to be in formal leadership roles. Being an ally means knowing the difference and knowing both *when* and *how* to take the lead.
- **Check in.** Male allies have a way of checking in with the local feminist leadership to make sure that what they are doing is benefiting (or at least not running counter to) the feminist leadership's goals.

  Male allies also have a means by which they check in with others (other men as well as women) to make sure that their behaviors (personally and politically) follow their stated beliefs and attitudes.
- **Are Accountable.** Perhaps most importantly, male allies are accountable. Being accountable means doing what one promises to do. Accountability also means acting in a manner that is consistent with one's stated beliefs and attitudes. It also means recognizing when one makes mistakes and coming forward in a straightforward manner to accept responsibility for those mistakes and making amends.

There is more to being an ally than is listed here. This list is still in development, and being an ally is an ongoing learning process. This list, however, does provide some of the key characteristics for men and women to consider as they become allies. Educators need to understand these points (and develop them further as needed), as well, if they are going to train and mobilize men to become allies for women.

Men Taking Action

The number of specific actions that men can do, and increasingly are doing, to end sexist violence is vast. The ideas and actions are limited only by the bounds of creativity, courage, and determination. Any step that a man or a collective group of men takes is a step towards solutions that have not been considered before.

Actions an Individual Can Take

Following are suggestions of actions an individual can take to end sexist violence:

- Challenge men's sexism
- Stop using pornography
- Read men's anti-sexist books
- Read books written by feminists
- Start book discussion groups on the books read
- Organize men's discussion groups
- Organize a fundraiser for a local rape crisis/battered women's shelter
- Train yourself and other men to be anti-sexist facilitators
- Organize a men's pro-feminist activist group
- Write a letter to the editor
- Write a letter to a politician
- Vote for women candidates*
- Organize a concert of female performers, or female and male performers, as an anti-sexist event
- Hang up a sign denouncing sexism at sports events
- Offer to do child care so that women can attend a special event (or an everyday event)
- Ask before you touch your female lover(s), kiss her, hold her hand, touch her breast, and so on
- Leaflet a speaker who presents topics that are anti-feminist or anti-women
- Photograph men leaving a pornography establishment and create a photo essay
- Hold a men's discussion during a Take Back the Night event

**There are those that will argue with this suggestion, claiming that I am tokenizing women by suggesting that men vote for women just because they are women. The point is to think about who we're voting for and to recognize that there are more than a handful of less than mediocre male politicians. One could argue that women have just as much right to be mediocre as men.*

Actions a Group of Individuals Can Take

Following are suggestions of actions a group or groups can take to end sexist violence:

- Organize men to use their Superbowl parties (which can also be used for the Final Four, Daytona, or Indianapolis 500, The U.S. Open, or any other sporting event where men congregate) as a fundraising event for local domestic violence or rape crisis programs.
- Gather men to approach a local battered women's shelter and ask them for their wish list. Then go on a shopping excursion, buying things on the wish list.
- During October (Domestic Violence Awareness Month) or April (Sexual Assault Awareness Month), organize with other men to stand at strategic intersections with hand-signs that call for an end to sexist violence.
- Gather data on where women have been killed in the local community and, with permission of their families, go to where they were killed and draw chalk outlines with the message: "A man killed (or raped, or battered, or prostituted, or harassed…) another woman here."
- Organize men's speak-outs against sexism and violence to occur at various locations throughout your community.
- Write letters to the editor, in a collective manner, about the issues of sexist violence.

Effective Actions Men Have Taken

Some specific examples of what men and men's groups have done include the following:

- In 1989, DC Men Against Rape built a "Women's Memorial Wall" to remember the women killed by their male partners. They put the wall next to the Vietnam Memorial Wall in Washington, DC.
- In 1989, after the Montreal Massacre, men organized memorial services and speak-outs in various places throughout Canada and the United States, including the Canadian Embassy in Washington, DC. In 1999, the tenth anniversary of this horrible event, some commemorative events were organized.
- In 1999, Men for Gender Justice (Maryland) organized a special Valentine's Day event, calling for men to demonstrate their love for a woman and their love for all women by working to end all forms of men's violence.
- In Boston, men paid for a billboard that called attention to men working to end domestic violence.
- Several communities have had men's marches against men's violence.
- A men's group in Michigan has organized a Father's Day action encouraging fathers to step out and teach their sons how to respect women.

- In 2000, a men's group at the University of Alabama organized a "Give Back the Night" event. This kind of action could occur in conjunction with a women-led Take Back the Night event and could incorporate a variety of activities, including providing child care so women can attend, holding consciousness raising discussions for men, organizing fund-raising events for local rape crisis programs, and more.
- In 2004, Mobilizing to End violeNce (a men's group) in Louisville, KY, cooked and then served a Mother's Day luncheon to the women and children staying in the battered women's shelter.
- In 2005, a high school men's group (Men of Honor) in Louisville, KY organized a men's pledge campaign. They created four posters with one pledge each (such as "I will not call a woman 'B' or whore") and then invited male students to sign the posters. The posters were then laminated and posted in the school hallways. This was followed up with these same male students organizing a bake sale on their campus (the baked goods mostly supplied by male students) as a fundraiser for the local domestic violence/rape crisis center.

These are just a few ideas of what men are doing, have done, and will continue to do to combat men's violence and sexism. It is much easier to come up with creative and combative ideas when one is in a group than it is to create these ideas in isolation. So, form or join a men's anti-sexist group. There are a couple of good men's discussion lists on the Internet (listed at the end of this chapter) that are very useful as men begin getting involved to help break the isolation that they may feel.

Legislative Advocacy (Lobbying 101)

One possible target for men's activism, one population of men who are in need of education about sexism and violence, is the state and federal legislators. Because the majority of legislators in most parts of the U.S. are male, there seems to be a crucial and natural role for male allies to talk with these men about the issues of sexist violence and about ways to strengthen our laws to be more responsive to the needs of women or men who are victimized.

For most people, lobbying or legislative advocacy is seen as daunting and threatening. However, once debunked of much of the aura, it becomes clear that legislators are no different than any other group. They are as in need for education about sexism and violence as anyone else. Because of their position to enact laws that are sensitive to the needs of women or men who are victimized, they are in some ways a more urgent focus for educational efforts than the general public.

Anybody can and should lobby. The term *lobbying* may be too daunting to think about, so it may be easier to use the term "legislative education." It is important to keep in mind that legislators often know relatively little about the issues for which they write legislation. Their job is to know how to make laws. Because of this, consider a relationship with legislators to be a partnership. Advocates or educators provide the crucial information legislators need about key issues that affect their constituencies, and legislators provide the expertise about how to address those issues through law. As a partnership, lobbying becomes a much easier and more meaningful process.

Getting Started

All states in the U.S. have statewide coalitions addressing issues of sexual assault or domestic violence. In some states, these are joint coalitions, while in others these are separate (although most work closely together in many respects). There are painfully few state coalitions that address sexual harassment, pornography, or prostitution, although some state sexual assault or domestic violence coalitions include these issues in their efforts. Stalking is often considered a form of domestic violence and, as such, is often addressed by state domestic violence coalitions.

As the main state "voice" on these issues, state coalitions often accept the crucial role of legislative advocacy. One way to begin lobbying is to contact the state coalition and inquire as to the kind of legislative work they are doing and the role of lay people in that process. Some state coalitions offer training on the legislative process and how citizens can impact the legislative process. At the very least, state coalitions generally keep track of different forms of legislation and are aware of the impact on the women or men who are victimized as well as the programs that support those people. The coalitions often also have some way of keeping interested people aware of legislation and sharing how others can be a part of the process, a "legislative alert" system of some kind.

Educating Legislators

As with most members of any community, legislators are as subject to the misinformation, myths, and lack of knowledge about the issues of sexism and violence as any other part of the community. Because of their positions, legislators have a significant impact on women or men who have been victimized or the programs that work with and support people who have been victimized. Thus, male legislators should be one of the target populations for educators.

There are many ways to communicate with legislators. However, the heart of lobbying is to actually talk to and with legislators. While good work is certainly possible through letter writing, phone calls, and e-mails, the real work involves actually meeting with and talking to elected officials. By meeting with legislators directly, educators

- Have the opportunity to explain points and make arguments that are simply impossible in a letter or phone call

- Can better understand the positions of elected officials and the concerns they may have, thus being better able to address these concerns
- Have opportunities to create relationships with legislators and, therefore, create opportunities for more collaborative work in the future
- Are better positioned to hold legislators accountable for their decisions

For many nonprofit organizations (for which most educators work), there are some limits to actual lobbying.* However, the federal government guidelines on what constitutes lobbying consist of the application of pressure on an elected official to vote for or against a certain policy. This means, in effect, an educator telling a legislator to support this or that law.

Talking with a legislator in order to inform her or him about an issue or about the impact of a particular law or policy is not considered lobbying. Going to a legislator and explaining the impact of a piece of legislation (educating legislators) is different than going to a legislator and urging them to vote for or against a bill (lobbying). There are no limits for nonprofit organizations on educating legislators. Furthermore, as private citizens, everybody has the right, indeed the responsibility, to communicate with elected officials on legislative decisions. The following sections give tips for educating legislators.

Steps in Lobbying

Call for an Appointment

A first step in educating legislators is, obviously, to schedule an appointment to meet with them. Legislators tend to be quite busy, especially while the legislature is "in session" (that period of time when they are in the capital working on legislative issues). So call them and explain the reasons for the meeting.

Have *One* Goal Per Visit

Clearly describe the goal to the legislator: to talk about specific legislation (that either has been submitted or that is wanted), to address the issues and discuss possible legislative responses, or to discuss other information. It is not uncommon for educators to have several things on the agenda to talk about with legislators. It is more effective, however, to narrow the focus to one topic, or a few closely related topics, per visit. There may be times when a package of closely related bills has been submitted, in which case one can get away with talking about the package of bills. As a general rule, however, one topic per visit.

**For more information about the rights of nonprofits to lobby, contact the Alliance for Justice at www.allianceforjustice.org. This organization is the premier organization providing information, resources, and training on citizen lobbying and nonprofit advocacy efforts.*

Work with the Aide

Educators/advocates may be referred to one of the legislator's aides. Do not be surprised, offended, or put-off if this happens. Very often, the aides are the legislators' in-house experts on given topics, and advocates can often have a more thoughtful conversation with an aide than with the legislator (this is not to say that aides are necessarily more thoughtful, only that they generally are more informed).

Be Respectful

One must always be respectful. Refer to the legislators by their legislative title and use "Ma'am" and "Sir" when talking with them. Educators must not, under any circumstances, talk badly about another legislator to the one with whom they are currently talking. This behavior is very disrespectful and will destroy one's credibility.

Be Confident

While being respectful, educators need to remain confident in their message and in their expertise. Educators have every right to have their opinions heard. Educators know these issues and should feel confident about the knowledge they have to share. Legislators often act as if they are the authority. (Creating an aura of authority is one of the ways that legislators become effective. By convincing other legislators and/or the general public that they are the expert on a particular issue, they are more effective in getting legislation passed.) Do not allow them to sway you. Educators are the true expert on these issues, and it is important to approach legislators with confidence.

Provide Accurate Information

If providing information, make sure that it is accurate and resist the temptation to expound on it to emphasize a point. If there are questions that you are unclear about, take the question and reply at a later date with the answer. If a legislator or aide cites information or statistics that are different than the information or statistics that you have, discuss this difference and provide additional background information.

Send a Written Thank-You

After a visit, be sure to thank the legislator or aide for the time. It is helpful to write a letter to the legislator and specifically to the aide with whom one visited. In this letter, thank the legislator (and/or the aide) for her or his time, reminding her or him about what the discussion was and any decisions or agreements that were made.

Testifying

Another effective form of educating legislators is to testify before a legislative committee. Most legislatures have committees that address specific kinds of legislation. Issues of sexist violence often fall under the jurisdiction of committees such as Health and Human Services or Judiciary. As specific bills are presented to the legislature, they are referred to a committee for further exploration. It is within these committees that much of the work on drafting the language and the provisions of the bill is done. It is often within these committees that educators can have a great impact on the development of a bill.

Frequently, as a bill works its way through the process, a hearing is organized for that bill, or a series of related bills, during which time the committee will set aside time to formally listen to citizens, advocates, and experts on particular issues as a tool in decision-making. Testifying before a legislative committee can be one of the most frustrating and aggravating experiences for educators, but it can also be a valuable opportunity to not only educate legislators in mass, but also the general public (the media often covers these hearings and an educator's testimony can be used as part of the media coverage of the hearing).

Recognize the Purpose of the Testimony

It is important to be clear that the point of testifying is not for legislators to actually listen to the testimony. The point of testifying is to get the testimony to be part of the public record, which legislators will probably refer back to as they decide how to vote.

Be Well-Prepared

There is usually a time limit on testimony (3 to 5 minutes), so it is crucial to be well prepared. If possible, organize with other advocates who are going to offer testimony on the same legislation and try to get the various points covered by each speaker. For example, if you are testifying in favor of a bill that would allow teenagers to get protective orders, an educator could be part of a panel with each panelist developing a specific argument about why this needs to happen.

"The point of testifying is to get the testimony to be part of the public record, which legislators will probably refer back to as they decide how to vote."

Have Written Versions of the Testimony

Because of the time limit on testifying, and as a way to ensure that the legislators do, in fact, have access to the testimony, provide the committee with written versions of the verbal testimony. Those versions can also be provided to the media as a way to get attention about the issues. By providing the committee with written versions of the testimony, not only will the testimony be in the record, but one can be assured that the main points will be covered, regardless of how nervous or flustered an educator might get when actually speaking. In addition, written versions of the testimony provide an opportunity to expand on the issues beyond what the constraints of the verbal testimony process allow.

Identify the Supportive Legislators

One of the frustrating parts of testifying is that the legislators are often not very attentive. They get up and leave, they have side conversations, they read other materials, and they do other things. Many of them may not even be in the room during the hearing. Legislators are not trying to be rude, but they are busy. Educators need to know that the testimony offered is in the record, and when legislators have time, they will get to it. Within every committee, there will be legislators who are supportive. It is helpful to identify them ahead of time and direct any oral testimony to them.

Make the Testimony Compelling

When testifying, balance real life stories with facts. Legislators are human and most of them are in office because of legitimate and deeply felt convictions that this is a way for them to do what is best for their communities. They do care about people and the issues that are of concern, and they have good hearts. Speaking about personal experiences is a good strategy to use to get their attention about an issue.

Be Solution Oriented

Be careful not to rely solely on their good natures, though. Legislators also have to make hard decisions, and they need factual information to help them make those decisions. Just hearing how bad sexual assault is and how deeply it harms people is not enough to get legislators to strengthen laws regarding police training (or any other issue). They need to know how the solution being offered is going to resolve the problems.

Final Thoughts

Educating legislators is one of the most important tasks that educators can be involved in while working to address issues of sexist violence. Educators are knowledgeable about the issues and have the skills to speak to people in ways that gets their messages across. Educators know how to speak in ways that motivate and persuade. This array of skills, expertise, and knowledge about sexist violence can be a powerful tool in working with elected officials to improve laws or to keep bad laws from being passed. Legislators, like any other segment of the population, need to be informed, sensitized, and persuaded. Because most legislatures, city and county councils, boards of election, and certainly our national legislature are still mostly male, there is an added incentive for educators who want to focus on or expand their energies to reaching men.

Working with the Media

Educating men also involves working with the media. Not only are many of the people who control the media men, but the media is a powerful and effective tool to reach men in the general public. This is one area that tends to get short shrift in the general work to end sexism and violence, and certainly in men's work.

There are many reasons to work with the media:

- To raise awareness about particular issues
- To publicize an event
- To respond to a situation or a crisis
- To make a point

In addition, the media may also want to contact advocates to get their opinions about an issue or a story that they are working on. There are also a variety of options for working with the media: interviews, initiating work with the local press, press conferences, and media events, among others. This section is not meant to be a comprehensive guide to working with the media. It is, rather, an overview that offers some basic tenets. There are other resources listed at the end of this chapter that offer more thorough guides to working with the press or media.

Handling the Conflicting Goals

Working with the media is often a challenging task, and one that all educators are often called to do. The main challenge is one of time. As any educator knows, the issues of sexism and violence are complex and in order to fully convey a message, there is a need for adequate time. The media, however, is not designed nor does it have the responsibility to provide a full and complete story. The goal of the media is to provide a snapshot—to peak people's interest. At best, the media's job is to provide the parameters of a story. In general, it is not their job to cover the full depths and complexities of any issue. This is perhaps one of the most frustrating aspects of working with the media, knowing that whatever messages educators are trying to offer will be truncated.

That being said, the media is a natural partner in the work to reach men about sexism and violence. People in the media need the expertise, understanding, and sensitivity of educators and advocates as much as advocates need the media. There is no story without advocates. In the process of working with the media, educators must negotiate some things about how they and the story are covered. Educators should not give up their voice just because the media call. It is important that educators ask tough questions and ensure that the media will work for them in each situation.

Working with Radio and TV

When being interviewed for radio or TV, either live or taped, be sure to have predetermined key points and use the interview to focus on those. These are the infamous "sound bites." The actual coverage will likely be from 15 seconds to 2 minutes. Before the interview, ask the reporter how much time the "piece" will show on the air. If it is a live interview, educators must be succinct and talk in short sentences. In a taped interview, the reporter will likely engage in a longer interview, much of which will be edited out in order to fit into the segment that they are allowed, the 15 seconds to 2 minutes they have. Either way, there will be insufficient time to explain a complicated point. There is only time to *make* a point. Therefore, it is important to think and plan ahead to identify the main point and reemphasize that point in response to any questions that are asked.

There is also the occasional opportunity for a longer segment, an interview for a local morning talk show, for example. In these situations, there is some time to expand upon the points and to actually enter into a dialogue. But, even in these situations, there is not the luxury to fully develop the main points. The main points can be addressed with limited opportunity to explain them. Plan for a three- to five-minute interview.

Before agreeing to longer interviews, get a sense of the perspective of the show and the interviewer. Listen to the show a few times. Look at the show's and interviewer's Web sites and see what can be learned about them and the perspectives they provide. It is important, if possible, to know before getting in front of the camera or microphone, whether the interviewer is really interested in the issue, just neutral, or outright hostile.

Ask for the Questions in Advance

It is also important, particularly if doing a live interview, to talk with the interviewer beforehand about the kinds of questions they are likely to ask. Every interviewee has the right to ask for, read, and approve of the questions they will be asked ahead of time. (You may not get them, but you need to ask.) Even when a list of questions is provided ahead of time, one must be prepared for unexpected questions. Educators should use these unexpected questions to answer in ways that reemphasize the main points.

Plan What You Will Wear

As with anything else, packaging is important. When preparing for a television interview, consider the wardrobe that will make it more likely that the audience will hear the message. Wear clothing that is comfortable but also professional and respectful. Be aware of the jewelry—how much and what kind—and how that might distract people from what is being said. For example, if doing a show that is geared for teenagers, a suit or formal dress is probably not the kind of wardrobe that speaks to the audience. If, on the other hand, the show is targeted for a Christian audience, more formal dress may be called for.

It is important to not only consider the audience, but, also, some of the technical realities of being pictured on TV. Lines, stripes, checks, or any kind of "busy patterns" are generally a bad idea. Choose solid colors, but be aware that TV lights have a tendency to bleach colors and people out a bit.

Talk to the Camera People

It is always a good idea to talk with the interviewer and the camera person/people about how they want to "frame" the interview. In general, the interviewer will be positioned between the guest and the camera so that as the conversation proceeds and the guest engages with the interviewer, the guest is looking in the direction of the camera and, thus, appears to be looking at the audience. To make a particularly dramatic point, look directly into the camera. This has the effect of making direct eye contact with the audience.

The camera people are important allies for any TV show. They have enormous power to dictate what the audience sees on the television. The camera people's view is what is transmitted. It is extremely important to introduce oneself to the camera people and ask for opinions about where to look and how to engage the audience. By getting the camera people interested in the topic, and in the educator as a guest, there is a greater likelihood of being seen in a positive light.

When being interviewed with another person, be aware that the camera may be focused on either guest, regardless of who is speaking. When another guest is speaking, focus your eyes towards the other person's face. Look engaged and interested, regardless of who is speaking. Even when disagreeing, an interested look conveys respect.

Practice

Be aware of how body language and facial expressions expose feelings or opinions. It is helpful to practice beforehand with friends or in front of the mirror to learn how you express your reactions through your facial expressions and body movements.

Working with the Print Media

The print media (newspapers, local or regional magazines, and so on) often offer many more options and opportunities. Educators often have more opportunities to make longer and more complicated points, and can respond via a letter to the editor after the article appears in order to make a clarification. It is still important to do background work on the paper and the reporter with which one may be working. Ask some questions such as:

- What is the newspaper and/or the reporter looking to address?
- What is the "angle" are they trying to cover?
- Is the story about an individual and that individual only (as in a personal interest story)?
- Are several people being interviewed?

These kinds of questions need to be answered when working with any media, but are particularly crucial with print media.

Educators also have opportunities to write their own articles. Depending on the size of the local papers or magazines, "op ed" (opinion editorial) articles are an excellent option to explore. The benefit of either of these is that an educator can take more control of the content and the points made. Op ed pieces are particularly powerful in this regard. The editorial pages are often the most widely and consistently read pages of most newspapers, and thus educators potentially reach more people through this means than through news stories.

Planning a Media Event

Media events are any of a wide array of events that are organized in order to attract the media, or which target the media as the primary audience. These can include a press conference, a candlelight vigil, a demonstration, or any of a number of other actions. Any kind of media event needs to make sure to have someone who is responsible for greeting and speaking with the media.

A press conference is one form of media event. When planning a press conference, planners need to decide ahead of time who is going to speak to what piece of the message. Each speaker should prepare her or his comments in writing ahead of time. Then, these written statements can be combined into a press packet that can be shared with the media who are present. The press can use this information to pick quotes as well as to use for background information as they develop the story.

Having written comments and prepared texts also helps the press conference be more organized. If each speaker is prepared, and subsequent speakers make slightly different points that build on previous points, the press conference as a whole will come across as coordinated and organized. Furthermore, many more points can be made from which the press will pick a few. Planners must be sure to leave time for questions from the press as they will likely want to explore one or two points made by one of the speakers.

Establish Relationships Before You Need Them

Establish relationships with various people in the media before planning any event (most notably with the reporters themselves, but also the editors and producers) so that when making a phone call or sending a press release, the educator's name will be recognized. People tend to respond more quickly and more efficiently to people whom they know than they do to strangers, regardless of the event.

Consider the Timing

When planning a media event (such as a press conference or a vigil), it is important to know a bit about the local media outlets and which days tend to be slow in terms of news coverage. As a general rule, Mondays are not good choices for a press event. Usually, much happens over the weekend that the media needs to cover, whereas Fridays and Saturdays tend to be less busy.

It is also important to consider the time of day. It is a delicate balance to organize an event at a time when people can attend, while also being aware of the timeline of the press so that the event occurs at a time when it will be aired during a high view period. If the event is time sensitive, be sure to organize it in a manner that allows the press to cover the issue and develop the story in time for them to print or air the story. For example, when there is a vote in the city council that an educator wants to make sure that the public knows about, it is important to consider planning an event so that there will be enough time for the press to cover it and the public to respond.

Create Interesting Visual Images

When planning an event to which the media is going to be invited, it is important to keep certain ideas in mind. All media, even print media, like "visuals," things that will catch the eye of the camera (and thus the audience). For example, the Clothesline Project, enlarged pictures of battered women, enlarged versions of men's anti-violence pledges, and so on can provide a visual picture that helps to enforce the point, as well as give the media something to "look at" while covering the story. Visuals are also helpful for the audience; they provide another look at the issues.

In short, when working with the media, it is best to see them as partners in attempting to present a message. Working with the media requires taking the initiative to create a sense of a partnership coupled with a focus on the main points that an advocate wants to get across to the audience.

Resources

Web

Both of the following lists provide useful information and resources and help to break the isolation that may occur for men who are just getting involved.

menagainstviolence@yahoogroups.com. This is a Yahoo group. Those who are interested need to go to the Yahoo main page and sign up to join this group through their process. This is an open list that is a means to discuss any issue related to men working against men's violence.

mensresourcesintl@yahoogroups.com. This is also a Yahoo group. It is primarily a list for men and women who are involved in developing men's resource centers, but a wide variety of topics are discussed.

Emerge. A Boston-based program working with men who batter and working to educate men about domestic violence. www.emergedv.com

Mainly Men Against Violence and Sexism. A statewide effort mobilizing men in Maine to address sexism and violence. www.mmavs.org/

Men Against Violence Webring. www.interactivetheatre.org/mav/

Men Against Sexual Violence (MASV). A project of the Pennsylvania Coalition Against Rape. Provides resources and activities to mobilize men against sexual assault. www.menagainstsexualviolence.org

Men's Initiative of Jane Doe. A project of the Jane Doe Coalition in Massachusetts—working within the state to mobilize and organize men to address domestic violence. www.mijd.org

Men Overcoming Violence. San Francisco-based men's organization. 1385 Mission Street, Suite 300, San Francisco, CA 94103. (415) 626-6683

Men's Resource Center. Amherst, Massachusetts-based men's organization providing an array of services and activities, including publishing monthly magazine. www.mensresourcecenter.org

Men Can Stop Rape, Inc. Washington, DC-based men's organization. www.mencanstoprape.org

Men Stopping Rape. Madison, Wisconsin-based men's organization. http://www.men-stopping-rape.org/

Men Stopping Violence. Atlanta-based men's organization. www.menstoppingviolence.org

Mentors on Violence Prevention. Works with men primarily targeting athletes and college campuses, on ending violence against women. www.sportsinsociety.org

Nonviolence Alliance. Domestic violence training project focused on working with men who batter. www.endingviolence.com

White Ribbon Campaign. Toronto-based, international movement to raise awareness about men's responsibility to end men's violence. www.whiteribbon.ca

XY: men, masculinities, and gender politics. Australian-based Web site focused on men, masculinities, and gender politics. XY is a space for the exploration of issues of gender and sexuality, the daily issues of men's and women's lives, and practical discussion of personal and social change. www.xyonline.net

Print

Beneki, T. (1997). *Proving manhood. Reflections on men and sexism.* Berkeley, CA: University of California Press.

Connell, R. W. (2000). *The men and the boys.* Berkeley, CA: University of California Press.

Connell, R. W. (1995). *Masculinities.* Berkeley, CA: University of California Press.

Frosh, S., Phoenix, A., & Pattman, R. (2001). *Young masculinities: Understanding boys in contemporary society.* New York: Palgrave Publishing.

Greig, A. (Ed.). (2002). *Partners in change: Working with men to end gender-based violence.* United Nations International Research and Training Institute for the Advancement of Women. Santo Domingo, Dominican Republic. (Available from www.un-instraw.org)

Johnson, A. G. (1997). *The gender knot: Unraveling our patriarchal legacy.* Philadelphia, PA: Temple University Press.

Kimmel, M. (1995). *The politics of manhood: Profeminist men respond to the mythopoetic men's movement (and the mythopoetic leaders answer).* Philadelphia, PA: Temple University Press.

Kivel, P. (2000). *Boys will be men: Raising sons for commitment, community and compassion.* Philadelphia, PA: New Society Publishers.

Pease, B. (1997). *Men and sexual politics: Towards a profeminist practice.* Adelaide, South Australia: Dulwich Centre Publications.

Savran, D. (1998). *Taking it like a man: White masculinity, masochism and contemporary American culture.* Princeton, NJ: Princeton University Press.

Stoltenberg, J. (1993). *The end of manhood. A book for men of conscience.* New York: Dutton Books.

Stoltenberg, J. (1989). *Refusing to be a man: Essays on sex and justice.* Portland, OR: Breitenbush Books.

Whitehead, S. M., & Barrett, F. J. (Eds.). (2001). *The masculinities reader.* Cambridge, England: Polity Press.

CHAPTER 12

Sustainability

Once men have been educated about sexism and men's violence and have become engaged in addressing these issues, it is important for them to consider how they will best sustain their interest and their engagement. Educators have an additional responsibility to assist men in thinking about how to sustain their efforts.

One key part of sustaining men's engagement is accountability. Men's organizing to hold each other accountable and to support women who do this work can be some of the most powerful work for social change that can occur. By being accountable, men also find sources of support, encouragement, and ongoing critical assessment of their efforts. This chapter provides an in depth look at the issues and forms of accountability that are important for both educators and the men that educators work with.

Perhaps one of the most crucial aspects of sustainability is self- (and other) care. Nobody lasts in this work (educators nor men) without learning some significant lessons about self-care. A part of our responsibility to each other is to care for each other as well as we care for ourselves. This chapter concludes with an exploration about self- (and other) care, how they're connected, and some suggestions for how to take care of ourselves (and each other).

Accountability

Any discussion of educating men about sexism and violence requires a conversation about accountability. For the purposes of educating men, there are two kinds of accountability to keep in mind: the accountability of educators, and the accountability of men being educated.

What Is Accountability?

Every person is accountable to others. Sometimes, people choose to act accountably, while at other times they don't. Being accountable means, in part, that a person accepts responsibility for the ramifications of his or her actions. Everything people do has consequences, both intended and unintended. All are responsible for the consequences of their actions, both positive and negative, regardless of the intention of the actors.

Being accountable is a dynamic and ongoing process that is based in part on the relationships that people have with each other, with organizations, and, in this case, with representatives for people who have been harmed. The specifics of how one is accountable change as relationships grow and change, as the context within which the relationship changes, and as other dynamics come into play.

Most people know how to act in an accountable manner—doing what they say they are going to do, providing an explanation if they don't, making an apology when they need to, etc. Another example of being accountable is graciously accepting a compliment for doing something that they consider rather insignificant. They graciously accept the compliment. These are examples of being accountable. Making these kinds of behaviors conscious is the beginning of being accountable as educators, or as men working to address sexism and violence. Being accountable and being courteous have a lot of similarities.

Being accountable is more of a process than a position. It is a process in which people make an accounting of what they do. By making an accounting, I mean that people acknowledge what they did, accept responsibility for the effects of what they did (both positive and negative) explain their decision-making process, and, if there were negative consequences, strive to minimize those consequences or make amends, when possible. Accountability is not something that people do once and are finished.

For example, male allies act in an accountable manner when they put processes in place by which they inform feminist leadership in their community about the events, efforts, or plans being made and accept the responsibility to ensure that these actions are in keeping with the goals of the feminist leadership.

Levels of Accountability

There are also different levels of accountability. People act accountable in different ways depending on their position, status, relationship with the other person(s), and the context of the relationship. For example, when educators are first hired, they have one level of accountability to the supervisor, the agency as a whole, with co-workers, and to the community or communities in which they educate. As the educators become more invested and better known in the agency and in the community, the level and kinds of accountability shifts. Because educators move up to more responsible positions within the agency, the level of accountability continues to shift. Note that one is never *not* accountable. It's *how* one is accountable that shifts.

Accountability also means striving, openly, to live up to the ideals and values that one purports to have. This means, of course, that educators and men strive not to act in harmful or abusive ways. This also means that educators and men strive to not act in sexist, homophobic, or racist ways. "Striving to" does not mean achieve. It is likely that educators and men are going to fall short from time to time, and they aren't going to live as well as their ideals suggest. Being accountable means being willing to acknowledge these times as well.

The easiest way to become unaccountable and to begin having unintended negative consequences is to stop thinking carefully about being accountable. This is true for educators and for men, and is most definitely true for male educators. The point of this discussion about accountability is to enforce the importance of being accountable and to encourage educators who work with men to think carefully about how to be accountable.

Accountable to Whom?

As educators and as men, the first line of accountability is to the women or men harmed by sexism or violence. Educators are accountable to do *what is best* for those who are harmed, which is a very different starting place than being accountable to do no harm. Being accountable to do what is best means that one thinks about what would most benefit those who are harmed. This also means that educators put people who are victimized first and foremost in their thinking and planning about education. When asked to do a presentation, respond to a media inquiry, speak at a public event, and so on, the first question for anyone offering education should be, "How does this benefit the women or men who are harmed?" One way to do this is to create a process whereby women who are harmed can have input in the development of educational presentations.

Because few educators (and fewer men) have direct connection to the people who are harmed, and therefore have a more difficult time being directly accountable, they can fulfill this primary level of accountability by acting in an accountable manner to the people who work most closely with those who are harmed. This means being accountable to the domestic violence, rape crisis, and other victim-service centers, agencies, and advocates. This can be done by developing educational programs in partnership with local programs, or by developing campaigns or men's groups with open and structured guidance (i.e., an advisory group) made up of local service and advocacy organizations.

A second layer of accountability is to the movement as a whole. The second question advocates need to ask themselves (both educators and men) is "How does what is planned benefit the movement?" For example, when considering writing a manual, as well as the publishing and distribution process, the question of how the publication of the manual will benefit the impact on the movement must be foremost. The movement is far more important, long-lasting, and pressing than any educator or man. As such, the movement *has to be* one of the primary questions when one is considering what to do.

After these levels of accountability and the questions that arise from them, there are hosts of issues of accountability and additional questions that arise more particular to specific situations and contexts. These questions are related to the specific context and situation in which educators or men may work.

Educators' Accountability

It is not good enough for educators to simply go out and do the same presentation that has always been done, almost by rote, with different audiences. Educators have the responsibility, indeed the obligation, to consider each audience in context and to provide an educational program that will be meaningful for them, but that will also do good for the women or men who are harmed, assist local agencies or programs that work with people who are harmed, and benefit the movement as a whole.

To fulfill these multiple obligations, educators have to address their accountability to the following:

- The subject matter
- The women or men who are harmed
- Those who are being educated
- Themselves as educators
- The agency or organization that they represent
- The movement as a whole

In the process of being accountable, educators and men will both often find that there are challenges that they will face. Being accountable is not easy, and it requires constant attention and careful consideration. Some of the challenges faced when attempting to be accountable include the following, which will be addressed in further detail in the next sections:

- Dealing with Conflicting Agendas
- Knowing When Compromising Is Harmful
- Adapting to the Audience
- Being Accountable to One's Self

Educators who focus on reaching men have an additional and important responsibility related to accountability. Not only do they need to understand accountability as educators, but they also need to understand the accountability of men. Men, like educators, have a variety of forms of accountability related to working to address sexism and violence. When appropriate, educators need to raise the issues of accountability in conversations with men—for example, when talking with men about being allies with women.

Dealing with Conflicting Agendas

As was mentioned earlier, educators are accountable to a whole host of people and groups. There are often tensions and discrepancies amongst these different groups of people. Each group has a different idea of what they want educators to do and even what they mean by being accountable.

CASE STUDY

When doing a rape awareness presentation at a local high school, Paula is accountable to the people who have been raped, the local agencies that work with people who have been raped, the agency or organization for whom she works, the anti-rape movement, the students who are being presented to, their parents, as well as the high school. Each of these groups want and expect different things. The high school administration wants to omit content, for example, that Paula's local program thinks is crucial to include. These kinds of tensions are common, but Paula must manage them carefully.

By understanding accountability as a *process* rather than a *goal*, educators are better prepared to maneuver through these tensions while still being accountable to all the parties.

Knowing When Compromising Is Harmful

However, there are times when there is no room for flexibility or compromise. At such a time, educators need to be able to clearly state their values. These are times when an educator must act as an advocate. There are times when educators may be asked by an administration to limit so much of the content of a presentation that it will completely remove the meaning of what the educator wants and needs to provide. There will likely be times when the circumstances or limitations placed on a presentation are more harmful than positive. In these situations, an educator may have to make the difficult decision to not offer a presentation rather than to compromise the core of what they believe must be presented.

For example, when beginning to educate men, the community may (and often will) ask that educators present to an entire student body of male students on an issue of sexist violence. Educating an entire school student body of 700 students may not only not do any good, but may do harm. An educator, then, is in the position of choosing to follow through with a presentation that will have minimal effect at best and possibly do more harm, or not doing the presentation at all and risk not being invited back. If an educator believes, to his core, that he cannot in good faith provide such a presentation, then he is acting more accountably by saying no.

Adapting to the Audience

Audiences are all very different and as a conversation continues, the audience may change right in front of an educator. Being accountable to the audience means responding to the changes that each audience may experience. For example, an audience may begin the presentation by being mostly closed off to overtly hostile. If they begin to warm up to the presenter (or the topic) and become more engaged, an educator must respond in kind and shift the way that he or she is presenting.

As educators develop their efforts, strategies, and tactics to educate and mobilize men, it is crucial to engage in ongoing dialogue with the feminist leadership so that they

- Know which topics educators are presenting
- Know the educational methods the educators are using
- Understand that the educators are working for the best interests of the feminists

For educators who work for organizations that formally respond to the people who experience sexist violence, this is much simpler. Even in these situations, however, it can be very easy to fall into the trap of developing an established presentation that is then taken around to different audiences.

Educators must continue to challenge themselves (and ultimately challenge the funding sources) to do good work and to ensure that the programs that are being presented are meeting the needs of the local programs and the women and men who they serve. Educators can develop procedures, for example, to offer an opportunity for direct line staff and women or men who have been victimized to have a voice in what they want audiences to be educated about and how they will be educated. An educator could ask direct line staff (or the clients of an agency) questions such as, "What are the most important points that you think audiences (specific ages, genders, and locations) need to know?"

Being Accountable to One's Self

One part of the accountability that educators have is the professional obligation to continue to ask whether what they are doing is doing any good. It is seductively easy to believe so much in what they is doing that they don't critically evaluate whether or not what they're doing is actually doing any good. Educators need to know, and have a right to know, that what they are doing is actually having a positive impact. Educators believe that they're increasing awareness, changing attitudes, improving men's behavior, etc. But how do they know that? Part of being accountable as an educator is putting some structures in place so that an educator can know—or have a guess that is based on some kind of evidence—that they are actually achieving what they want to achieve. This relates back to the discussion much earlier in this manual about setting clear goals for each presentation with each audience. One of the reasons to set clear goals is to improve the ability to measure whether one has achieved those goals.

If an educator is working with a group of men to reduce their acceptance and support of rape myths, how does she know that the educational efforts are achieving those goals? One way is by actually testing the men in the presentation to see their degree to which their acceptance and support of rape myths have changed as a result of a presentation. This is a very different kind of evaluation than the traditional satisfaction surveys* that are so prevalent; in other words, the educator might ask participates to indicate what they learned from the presentation. In order to continue to challenge themselves and improve the effectiveness of their efforts, educators need to identify what works and what doesn't.

Strategies for Being Accountable

There are several specific behaviors that are helpful to consider when exploring the issues of accountability:

- Be honest and truthful
- Be forthcoming
- Be transparent
- Be open and sharing with what is done (i.e., what is being taught, how the education is done, and so on)
- Seek the input of the agencies or programs that work with women or men who are harmed

Strive to make sure that the educating is done with a purpose in mind. Educating for the sake of educating needs to be changed to be educating for specific purposes. Not only, then, is it important to consider the specific purposes for doing education, but knowing whether these goals have been achieved is significant.

Educators must remain passionate about the topics, the issues, and most importantly, about the women and men who are harmed. It is crucial to know the topics, which demands that educators continue to educate themselves as the body of knowledge continues to grow. It is just as important to keep abreast of the developments in education theory and practice in general, and particularly the developments in educating within the movement.

One must, it should go without saying, be caring about the men being educated, about the women and men who are being educated about, about the movement as a whole, and about the people who are doing the educating. By maintaining care and compassion in the mental framework while developing and implementing educational programs, educators increase their effectiveness. Being caring and compassionate means remembering that the people educators are talking to and about are human beings and that all people are in a process of learning and development. This does not mean that educators should edit what they have to say or not confront attitudes, behaviors, or even people when necessary. In fact, being compassionate often requires

**A satisfaction survey is a tool that asks how much someone liked a program or thought that they got something out of it. It is also the most common form of "evaluation" that is used after educational programs.*

educators to confront attitudes or behaviors that are disrespectful or mean. But being caring and compassionate also influences how educators confront when they find they need to do so.

Men's Accountability

Men working to end sexism and violence also have a particular accountability. Like educators, men who are involved in addressing sexism and violence have an accountability to those who are harmed, the movements to end sexism and violence, the local agencies and programs that work with the people who are harmed, the local communities, themselves, and each other. This list is virtually the same as the list of accountability for educators.

Recognizing the Differences Male Privilege Creates

The dynamics of sexism (and other oppressive dynamics, such as racism, homophobia, classism, and so on) create an environment that require men to pay particular attention to the issues of accountability. This is true because of the nature of privilege. Because men (in the case of sexism) haven't had to think a whole lot about how they relate to women, and as such, have inadvertently acted in sexist, abusive, or harmful ways, and because some men choose to act in sexist and abusive ways towards women, all men need to think consciously about how they're interacting with women.

For men who get involved (as individuals or as organized groups), it is particularly important to create processes and structures of accountability so that the women who are harmed and the local programs that work with women or men who are harmed all know *what* the men are doing and *how* they are doing it. It is easy for men to "forget" that they are men, even when working to end sexism and violence. Being a man changes the meaning of the work, and in some cases, changes the kind of work that is done. It is not a matter of being better or worse, just different. For example, men who educate other men about sexism and violence get responded to differently than women. Being accountable means, in part, that men continue to remember that they are men doing work against sexism and violence and to keep in mind some of what those differences are.

Checking Your Best Intentions

There are many examples, in any work for justice, of people doing things with the best of intentions and the best of analyses, but with the worst of results. It is not only crucial for men to work with each other to end sexist violence; it is just as crucial that men do this work in ways that support the efforts of the local feminist leadership. Without clear lines of communication and structures defining how to relate, people may do great things, but these efforts may not meet the local needs of the feminist leadership or the women who are harmed. They may, in fact, run counter to what these groups need and want. The best way to reduce the risk of this happening is for men to check in before initiating an action and to continue communicating on a regular basis.

CASE STUDY

Several years ago, I was approached by a male minister who wanted me to help him organize a men's march against men's violence against women. I really liked the idea. It was dramatic, it made a statement, and it was a public demonstration of men taking action. When I called the local feminist leadership, however, they were less than enthused. Because of the budget and funding crisis at the time, they felt that it was much more beneficial, necessary, and urgent to use that energy and skill to organize male fundraisers than to plan a men's march. None of the women, as I recall, were opposed to a men's march, but they clearly stated their priorities as being different than that of a men's march.

Being accountable means deferring to the women who are in the forefront, who work most closely with the women, children, and men who are impacted and victimized by men's violence. It means listening to what women need and want from men, and using that information to guide men's decision and actions.

To be allies with women to end sexist violence, *men* must do the work to be accountable: the thinking, the strategizing, the planning, and the creating of structures and processes of accountability. It is not women's responsibility to make sure that men are accountable. It is men's responsibility to make sure that they are accountable to the women and the local communities. This begins with creating relationships with the women who are in the local leadership positions (both formal and informal).

A final question often arises: "To which feminists are men accountable?" As with any other movement, feminism does not have one definition, and feminists hold more than one view on any topic. There are feminists who argue that the anti-violence movement has gone too far and that Rape Crisis Centers and Domestic Violence programs are manipulating the system for their own benefit. There are feminists on every angle in the debate about pornography and prostitution, and there are feminists who argue that men should be integrally involved, just as there are feminists who believe that men should not be involved at all. Being accountable is never easy.

To help with this question, it is important for men to focus on being accountable to those women (ideally, self-defined feminists) who speak for, to, and on behalf of women, children, and men who have been harmed. There are women who have taken a position on issues of sexism and violence that is contrary to the position taken by women who work directly with women in the battered women shelters, rape crisis centers, and on the streets with women who have been prostituted or used in pornography. For men working on these issues, it is to the feminists who are on the streets, who work in the shelters and at the rape crisis centers, that accountability is due.

This is not to say that all feminists who work at domestic violence shelters agree, or that men will necessarily agree with what the feminist leadership determines. One model of accountability is to offer the feminist leadership in the local communities "veto power," (that is, men propose an idea of what they want to do, and the feminist leadership has the right to veto that action) but this is only one model. For men working to address sexism and violence, it is important to develop a model that makes the most sense to the women's leadership, to the men themselves, and to the community or communities in which they work. Being accountable does not mean, necessarily, doing what women think men should do. This is often one form of accountability, but there are ways that men can act accountably and still disagree with women, including feminists. As long as men who do this work create a transparent, open process in which the local women's leadership has a voice and input, a voice that is listened to and input that is acknowledged, then men will have come a long way in creating accountability.

Taking Care of One's Self and Others

"Never forget to take care of yourself as well as you take care of the world."

Anonymous

Educating, mobilizing, and organizing men around sexism and men's violence is extremely difficult, tiring, and challenging. Not only are educators faced with the difficult task of talking about topics that are tremendously painful, but they also have to find ways to keep the conversations meaningful (in other words, maintain a level of honestly and truthfulness with real stories and true experiences) while not overwhelming audiences. This requires that educators not only be in touch with their own truth while educating, but also to remain vigilantly in touch with the audience, constantly watching the audience to gauge the emotional states of participants. Because educating about sexism and violence requires that educators connect with strong emotions, they have the obligation to assist participants in being able to make sure that the emotions don't overwhelm them. Good educators do not leave this crucial task to the participants of the educational program. In addition to this, educators who work with men are also placed in positions of educating groups of people for whom these are new topics, who may be disinterested, or who may be outright hostile. All of these tasks, in addition to the hard work of teaching, means that educators are subject to high rates of burn out.

In order to educate about sexism and violence, to do it effectively, and to do it longer than a month or two, educators need and deserve to consider how to best take care of themselves while working with men. In addition to taking care of themselves in order to last through the long haul, educators *deserve* being cared for, simply by virtue of being human beings.

Self-Care

Self-care is different than burnout prevention. Self-care is proactive whereas burnout prevention is reactive; self-care is nurturing whereas burnout prevention is averting. Self-care can happen in the moment, while offering educational programs or talking with a person who is disclosing that they have been victimized. Burnout prevention happens afterwards. By doing active self-care, educators are, in fact, reducing the chance that they will burn out, but they are also doing so much more. They are caring for themselves in an ongoing and active manner.

Recognize What Already Works

A first step that educators can take towards improving their self-care is to notice and be conscious of what they already do to take care of themselves. By nature, people are designed to do what is best for themselves. Human beings inherently know what they need and often figure out how to get those needs met. Unfortunately, most people, particularly those who work around issues of sexism and violence, have learned to ignore or disregard what their bodies tell them until their bodies start screaming (stress-related symptoms, burnout, sleeplessness or constant fatigue, and so on). A way to begin thinking about self-care is for educators to begin noticing how they are already taking care of themselves. By bringing this to consciousness, educators become better aware of the processes that they already have in place, and then they can begin to make more concrete decisions about *how* they want to care for themselves in the future.

DOING YOUR WORK: *Consider Your Self-Care Techniques*

Some parts of this manual have undoubtedly been difficult to read. Think back to those parts, or some other time when you experienced stress, and list the kinds of self-care techniques you automatically used. Did you curl your toes in your shoes, hunch your shoulders, breathe more shallowly, or become very thirsty?

List other self-care techniques you can develop. For example, a reader may take a break from the manual to watch some TV, eat something, or get some exercise while reading difficult passages.

All these are ways that bodies respond to stress and begin working at self-care. As educators begin noticing their innate patterns of self-care, they can make decisions to either continue to use these patterns or to respond in different kinds of ways.

Recognize Negative Responses

A second step in self-care is for educators to notice what is difficult or hard for them about educating men. There are likely certain groups of men who are harder for some educators to talk to than others (male prisoners, male judges, high school men, religious men, and so on). There may also be certain times when educating men is particularly challenging (in the morning, on Fridays, after a high-profile assault). There may be some topics that educators find particularly challenging. The educators need to recognize the negative responses their bodies give in those situations.

CASE STUDY

When I do something that makes me uncomfortable, my hands may begin to sweat, my heart may begin to beat more quickly, my stomach may tighten up, and I may crave chocolate.

Educators need to know themselves well enough to know what is difficult and to examine what they do to address these difficulties. Some educators avoid these kinds of situations or topics altogether, or drink lots of water, eat chocolate, smoke, go out for lunch afterwards, go for a drive, and so on. All of these are, in part, legitimate self-care strategies.

Have Fun

Fun is an important self-care strategy. This may seem like a contradiction or impossibility when discussing rape, domestic violence, pornography, and so on, but educators can and should have fun even in the midst of doing this work, even while taking the topics and the people who are harmed by these behaviors very seriously. This is not to say that all the work will, or should, be fun. But if educators are unable to have fun with it, then it may not be worth doing. There can be laughter even in the midst of this work.

"There can be laughter even in the midst of this work."

It is also important that educators take time away from this work. Going biking, hiking, taking long walks, reading a good book (that has nothing do to with violence or abuse), watching a movie, buying a new music CD, taking a class to learn Spanish, eating good food, spending time with friends, going dancing, spending time on a beach, gardening, having a glass of really good wine, drinking tea, playing an instrument, or just having fun: do things that are replenishing.

The bottom line of self-care is that every person who does this work deserves to be thought about as attentively as the work itself. There has been a great deal of space in this manual devoted to the topics, the audiences, and the needs of the people educators speak about. Most educators take very seriously the role educator and work tremendously hard to try to create educational programs that fit their audiences. The people who do this work, the educators themselves, are no less deserving of that same kind and amount of attention than are the work, the audiences, and the people.

Care of Others

In the midst of this discussion of self-care, there is a danger that some people, especially men, may focus on themselves and forget (or ignore) that they are doing this work with other people. This work is consistently referred to as a *movement* throughout this manual for a reason. Educators do this work alongside other people, even if those others aren't visible. There are people in every corner of this country and in most other countries who educate men about sexism and violence, and/or who work with the people who are victimized or the people who perpetrate this violence. All those people are allies and part of the global movement for racial, sexual, and gender justice.

Because educators are part of a broader movement, part of something that is bigger than their individual efforts, they also have a responsibility to others who do this kind of work. This means that educators have an obligation to reach out and care for and about the others who do this work as well. If the core of the work educators do truly is to create a world that is more than not-violent—that is based on the principles of justice, care, and compassion, then getting to or creating this world begins by the way educators and advocates relate to and treat each other. There is no such thing as being too kind.

As educators learn better what is difficult for them about doing this work and how their bodies take care of themselves, it is also important to notice the other people. Notice what is hard for them, and how their bodies take care of them too. As educators get better at self-care, they can begin to look out for their colleagues and help them take care of themselves, too. One can support colleagues by asking the same questions asked in this chapter and by working together to create caring work environments from which the work to create justice stems. We are all in this together. We might as well act like it.

In Conclusion

Educating men is a crucial step in the efforts to end all forms of sexism and violence. Creating gender justice requires that men be intimately involved in the efforts, and the first step for men getting involved in this struggle is that they be educated about gender injustice. With well-conceived, organized, and implemented efforts, men can become part of the movement, as is demonstrated by the men who have already become involved. They all had to be educated at some point.

The very nature of sexism and violence is both personal and political. Therefore, the work with men requires efforts and education on both fronts: namely, how men can take this issue personally and how men can be involved politically. Ending sexism and violence is not solely about individual men treating women with more respect and care, nor is it solely about men working en masse to expose and undermine the institutions of sexism. Educating men about sexist violence means educating men about both the personal and the political. In this manual, I hope to have provided a brief overview of the ways that this work can be offered and accomplished.

Working with men to end sexism and violence is a relatively new practice and is a very new movement. The opportunities are still endless, we still know far less than we need to know, and there are still lots and lots of ways to learn better what is involved in educating men, how to best educate men, and how to use education to mobilize and organize men to take action. This manual offers a few ideas that I hope will help and motivate educators to educate men, to be creative, and to try new things. There are a few other manuals available. Each has its own strengths, and none is the end all and be all. Educators are encouraged to take what they like from each of these manuals and use whatever they take to their advantage and the advantage of their educational programs.

On a personal note, I appreciate your taking the time to read this manual, and I am more grateful than words can express for the work you do. Thank you, from the bottom of my heart, for what you do.

APPENDIX A

Sample Outlines

This appendix contains several sample outlines on different topics related to talking with men. These outlines are developed with both male-only and mixed-gender groups in mind and identify which group they are geared for. They are examples that educators can use.

These outlines are not copyrighted, so feel to duplicate them. Use them as they are, change them as you need to, or develop them further. You do not need to check with the author or JIST Publishing, nor do you need to give credit for using them (although it would be appreciated if you did). The outlines are

- Rape 101
- Domestic Violence
- Responding to Loved Ones Who Are Victimized
- What Is Sexual Harassment?
- Stopping Rape Is Men's Work
- Rape Trauma Syndrome

Rape 101

(CREATED FOR A MALE-ONLY AUDIENCE, BUT COULD BE USED IN A MIXED-GENDER SETTING)

I. Introduction

Hi, I'm ______________ and I am from the ______________ organization and I'm here to talk with you a bit about sexual assault.

II. Definitions

A. Legal definitions (based on the laws of the state)

B. Feminist-centered definitions (any forced or unwanted sexual contact as defined by the person touched)

III. Overview

A. 1 in 4 women are sexually assaulted in their lifetimes

B. 1 in 7 men are sexually assaulted in their lifetimes

C. Over 60% of men say that they would commit a sexual assault if they knew they would get away with it

IV. Dynamics

A. Most sexual assault is perpetrated by someone the person knows (for male-only audiences, get specific and ask questions about the women that men know and love, making a reference to the statistics via these women)

B. Most often it is perpetrated using manipulation and coercion rather than violence or force

V. Impact

A. Impact of rape on women or men who experience it

B. Impact of the threat of rape (how women limit their lives because of the threat)

C. (For male-only audiences) How the presence of rape impacts men (See the "Guided Imagery" exercise in Appendix B)

(For mixed-gender audiences) Examine the impact for all women (See "The Fishbowl" exercise or the "Introductory Questions" exercise in Appendix B)

VI. Men's Response

A. Responding to friends who are victimized

B. Own the issue and become part of the solution

VII. Local Resources

Domestic Violence

(FOR USE WITH EITHER MALE-ONLY OR MIXED-GENDER AUDIENCES)

I. Introduction

Hi, I'm ______________ and I am from the ______________ organization and I'm here to talk with you a bit about domestic violence.

II. Overview

Domestic violence is the leading cause of injury to women, resulting in more ER visits by women than rapes, muggings, and car accidents combined

III. Dynamics

A. Ask:

What you think of when you hear the words "domestic violence?

B. Write what they say on a chalkboard or paper. These are some of the common tactics used by men who batter.

C. Say:

The tactics you identified are usually the ones that occur last. Men who batter use violence and other forms of abuse to maintain power and control in the relationships. The tactics they use are designed to maintain their dominance in the relationship.

D. Introduce the Power and Control Wheel by saying,

The Power and Control Wheel describes how these tactics are used by an abusive partner in concert to maintain their dominance in a relationship. As you examine the Power and Control Wheel, which of these tactics are illegal? (Then pause).

Sometimes threats can be illegal, but generally not. We all know how to threaten someone (a look, a gesture, etc.) without making an overt threat. And sometimes sexual assault can be illegal. But there are forms of sexual assault that are not illegal.

Now if we were to be honest, in this room, we'd probably all acknowledge that each of us has done at least two or three of the tactics described on the Power and Control Wheel. All of us have some area of power and control that we struggle with. Not all of us are batterers. It is the pattern of behaviors, in concert (i.e. using more than one or two of these strategically) that makes up domestic violence.

E. Complete the "What Would You Do?" exercise.

(continued)

(continued)

i. Men who batter need one main thing in order to have power and control in a relationship—a person to be in a relationship with. In order to ensure they have a relationship, they are going to use other tactics to get the relationship going before relying on violence and abuse. Often these tactics begin with isolation and name calling.

ii. Domestic violence always begins with subtle behaviors

IV. Impact

A. Ask:

What do you think the impact of living with someone has on women or men who are being abused?

B. Say:

I'm going to offer a brief description of the impact of domestic violence.

i. Why does she stay/why does he hit?

ii. What you can do about it.

V. Local Resources

Responding to Loved Ones Who Are Victimized

(FOR MALE-ONLY AUDIENCES)

I. Introduction

Hi, I'm ______________ and I am from the ______________ organization and I'm here to talk with you about responding to a friend or loved one who has been victimized by rape (domestic violence or any other form of victimization).

Most men know at least one person who has been through this kind of dreadful experience. Even if you don't know someone yet, you likely will. Rape is so common that all men know and love someone who has been raped even if men don't know that about their loved ones.

II. Definitions

A. Legal definitions (based on the laws of the state)

B. Feminist-centered definitions (any forced or unwanted sexual contact as defined by the person touched)

III. Overview

IV. Dynamics

A. Most sexual assault is perpetrated by someone the person knows

B. It is most often perpetrated using manipulation and coercion rather than violence or force

V. Impact of rape on women or men who experience it

VI. Men's Responses

A. Complete the "Act Like a Man" exercise in Appendix B.

B. Say:

Given what we're taught about how to "be a man" how do most men respond if their mother, sister, daughter, or girlfriend is raped?

While these behaviors are perfectly understandable and normal, they are not going to be experienced by a friend or loved one who was raped as supportive.

C. Describe responses that *are* supportive.

D. Talk about men's need to attend to their own feelings (anger, rage, shock, blame, and so on).

VII. Local Resources

What Is Sexual Harassment?

(FOR MALE-ONLY OR MIXED-GENDER AUDIENCES)

I. Introduction

Hi, I'm _______________ and I am from the _______________ organization and I'm here to talk with you a bit about sexual harassment.

II. Definitions

A. Legal definitions

i. Quid pro quo

ii. Hostile environment

B. Feminist-centered definitions

III. Overview

A. Statistics

IV. Dynamics

A. Most often it is women who are harassed by men

B. Men are also harassed by other men

C. Rarely do women harass men

D. Impact and intent

Context of sexual harassment (even though the behaviors are the same, the impact is very different)

V. Impact

A. Impact of being harassed

B. Impact of the threat of rape (how women limit their lives because of the threat)

VI. Men's Responses

A. Responding to friends who are victimized

B. Own the issue and become part of the solution

VII. Local Resources

Stopping Rape Is Men's Work

(CREATED FOR MALE-ONLY, BUT CAN BE USED FOR MIXED-GENDER AUDIENCES)

I. Introduction

Hi, I'm ______________ and I am from the ______________ organization and I'm here to talk with you a bit how men can work to stop rape (domestic violence, sexual harassment, pornography/prostitution, stalking, sexism...)

II. Rape Is a Men's Issue

- A. Men do it
- B. Men are victimized too
- C. Men know and love women and men who are raped
- D. Men know and love men who rape
- E. The threat of rape means all men are looked at with suspicion (refer to the "Guided Imagery" exercise in Appendix B)

III. Men's Responses

- A. What gets in the way of men taking action
- B. What men can do

IV. Local Resources

Rape Trauma Syndrome

(FOR BOTH MALE-ONLY AND MIXED-GENDER AUDIENCES)

The ***Acute Stage*** is the stage immediately following the assault and is characterized by:

- Shock
- Denial
- "Acute distress" (physical and emotional symptoms)

During the Acute Stage, people who are victimized need:

- To feel safe
- To be accepted, believed, and understood
- To make decisions about
  - seeking medical attention (injury, STD/HIV testing, pregnancy)
  - evidence collection
  - reporting to the police
  - whom to tell and how
- To regain a feeling of control over their lives
- To act on their decisions

The next stage is the ***Disorientation Stage***. During this stage, people who are raped often:

- Try to suppress the symptoms and feelings
- Deny what happened and that anything is wrong
- Claim they are "over it"
- Isolate themselves

They may (and often do) experience their friends and family as expecting them to be "over it" by now. During this stage, they may quit dating altogether or date a great deal. They may move to a new location (which may mean to a new home or apartment, or to a new town). This is the time when students (both high school and college) are more likely to drop out of school.

During this stage, people who are victimized need:

- To be allowed time and space to cope with their experience
- To be given permission to not deal with it anymore, but also the support to if that's what they need
- To be listened to when they are ready to talk

The final stage of RTS is the ***Reorientation Stage***. During this stage, people who are raped often experience:

- Depression
- Anger at the perpetrator(s)
- An inability to continue to deny that the rape impacts on their life
- More constructive ways of dealing with what happened

What they need is to:

- Talk about what happened
- Discover and express what they have been suppressing (the feelings, thoughts, images, and so on)
- Resolve negative self-feelings
- See self as normal
- Reexamine relationships with friends, family, partner, and others
- Reestablish independence

It is during this final stage that people who are raped begin to reclaim control of their memories and experience of being raped, rather than have the experience control them through flashbacks, nightmares, "day-mares," fears, and so on. The Reorientation Stage can be the most difficult and trying for loved ones as this is the period in which people who are raped begin to come to a new understanding of themselves not as "victims" of the experience, but as "survivors." This shift in self-definition/self-understanding can have a profound impact on how they identify and relate to others and to the broader world. For example, as women proceed through the healing process and enter the Reorientation Stage, they may come to redefine themselves and stop doing some of the things that they used to enjoy. As they come to accept a new understanding of their personal power, they may choose to accept that power in ways that those around them are unused to.

APPENDIX B

Exercises

This appendix contains several exercises or activities on different topics related to sexism and violence. They are not copyrighted, so feel free to use them as they seem appropriate for your audiences. Use them as they are, change them if you need to, or develop them further. You do not need to check with the author or JIST Life for permission to use them, nor do are you required to give credit for using them (although it would be appreciated if you did). The exercises are

- Introductory Questions
- Act Like a Man
- Men's Stand-Ups
- Influence Continuum
- Is This Consent?
- Disclosure
- The Fishbowl
- "Gender-Neutral" Speech
- "Typical" Man/"Typical" Woman
- Continuum—"Make Your Case"
- Why Is Sexual Assault So Devastating?
- Guided Imagery
- What Would You Do?
- Why Men Rape or Batter

INTRODUCTORY QUESTIONS

These questions are good conversation starters and are helpful to get men to begin thinking on a deeper level about the issues of sexist violence and men's responsibilities. You can use any form of sexist violence in the question, but be as specific as you can when you ask the question so that they can begin to see the connections. This set of questions is also a great lead-in to a discussion about the theoretical foundations of doing this work and the connection of different forms of oppression.

1. How does rape (domestic violence, sexual assault, stalking, pornography, dating abuse, prostitution) affect women?

   Even the fairly uninitiated will likely come up with a long list of ways that they are able to see how women are affected by men's violence. List them so that everyone can see the answers and you can discuss them.

2. How does rape (domestic violence, sexual assault, stalking, pornography, dating abuse, prostitution) affect men?

   This question will likely be much harder for men to answer initially. They will likely begin with answering in terms of men who are close to women who are victimized (i.e., "You feel helpless," "It makes you angry but you don't know what to do with it," and so on.) They may begin to explore being labeled as potential perpetrators, which is important to help them identify. Finally, men may make statements reflecting that they don't feel like it is their issue and they don't know what to do about it (hopelessness). As these different levels of awareness come up, it is important to label them, acknowledge them, and help the men to understand them in a broader context.

3. How is violence against women similar to gay bashing?

4. How is violence against women similar to violence against people of color?

   For this last question, it may be helpful to specify a specific form of violence against people of color—for example, police brutality.

   As the men answer these questions, you can talk with them about how this discussion is the beginning of men accepting responsibility for men's violence. By noticing that men are affected (a fact that by and large goes unnoticed by men), they begin to have a personal stake in the issues.

There is little need to facilitate beyond these suggestions. If possible, leave this exercise for the end of the training or program and allow the men to reflect as they leave.

ACT LIKE A MAN

This exercise is adapted from Paul Kivel's Men's Work *and from work done by the Oakland Men's Project (and used with the permission of the author). The purpose of the exercise is to engage men in dialogue about where and how they developed their ideas of masculinity and to identify the links that exist between stereotypical masculinity and violence, sexism, domination, power and control, and homophobia.*

1. Draw a circle on the board large enough to write a few words inside.
2. Ask the group this question:

   What are some feelings typically not acceptable for men to feel?
3. Write the responses inside the circle. (Responses such as "sad," "scared," "hurt," and "weak" are typical.)
4. Continue the discussion with the following:

   In response to a boy or man having these feelings, someone might say, "Act like a man!"

   What are they telling you that you are supposed to do or be like when they say this?
5. Draw a large box around the circle and write the responses inside the box but outside the circle. ("Be tough or strong," "don't cry," "don't show emotion," and "keep it in" are typical responses.)
6. Continue the discussion with the following:

   This is an "Act-Like-a-Man" box. It shows how stereotypical masculinity traps or hides who we are inside. What potentially happens when we hold this inside for a long period of time? We explode, either by actively or inactively damaging ourselves or by hurting someone else.

   What names do boys and men get called when they do show the feelings you see here?
7. Write the names outside the box on the right. (Typical responses include "girl," "faggot," "gay," "homo," "weak," "mama's boy," "sissy," and "pussy.")
8. Ask these questions:

   What effect do these names have? What happens to boys and men physically when they do not act like men "should"?
9. Write the effects on the left side of the box. (Typical responses include "beaten up," "hit," "kicked," "attacked," "slapped," and "abused.")
10. Continue the discussion with the following:

    A kind of physical mistreatment males experience that doesn't get much attention is sexual abuse. A study by David Finkelhor in 1992 found that one of six males was sexually abused by the age of 18. Most of these boys are sexually abused by a man who is not gay, and, like most perpetrators of sexual assault, he appears "normal."

(continued)

(continued)

As you can imagine, the ways boys and men are mistreated and boxed in make it extremely difficult to talk about being abused or to seek help. When we combine all these variables, we can see how males are being trained to walk around like a time bomb. It's very possible that this has much to do with the rate of violence committed by males.

Additional Discussion Questions

1. What times in your life have you felt "boxed in"?
2. How does this pressure affect your relationships with other men? What about with women?
3. What can you do or what have you done to resist the pressure or to "re-write" what is expected of men?
4. Identify three qualities from the "Act-Like-a-Man" Box that you are still trying to unlearn.
5. What were some of the names used in your youth to keep guys in the box? Are there any new ones? Are there any that you find yourself using on other people?

MEN'S STAND-UPS

This exercise is used by permission of Allan Creighton and the Oakland Men's Project. These Men's Stand-Ups are meant to provide a final real-life example for men of how their masculinity was constructed in a way that limits them and that inhibits them from being fully human.

1. Say the following to the audience:

   I am going to read a number of statements. It is important that this exercise be done in silence. If you decide the statement is true for you, please stand up. Each of you decide for yourself whether you want to stand. If you decide to stand up, do so silently, look around the room to see who is standing with you, and sit back down. Notice what you are feeling and thinking as each statement is read.

   Stand up if you have ever:

   Worn blue jeans

   Worried you were not tough enough

   Exercised to make yourself tougher

   Been disrespected by an adult

   Been called a wimp, queer, or a fag

   Been told to act like a man

   Been hit by an older man

   Been forced to fight

   Been in a fight because you felt you had to prove you were a man

   Been deliberately physically injured by another person

   Been injured on a job

   Been physically injured and hid the pain

   Been sexually abused or touched in a way that you did not like by another person

   Stopped yourself from showing affection, hugging, or touching another man because of how it might look

   Got so mad while driving you drove fast or lost control of the car

   Drank or taken drugs to cover your feelings or hide pain

   Felt like blowing yourself away

   Hurt another person physically or sexually

(continued)

(continued)

2. Give the men a minute or so to collect their thoughts. Depending on the size of the group, ask the following questions all together or break into small groups and give each group a piece of paper containing the additional questions.

Additional Discussion Questions

1. What feelings or thoughts did you have while going through the list of statements?
2. Which of these experiences are most alive in your memory? Which of these experiences have been the most painful?
3. Do you have any "fighting words" that make you feel attacked and make you want to defend yourself? Why are they so powerful for you?
4. What are you doing to take care of yourself and to unlearn these things?

INFLUENCE CONTINUUM

This exercise is taken from Adjudicating Cases of Alleged Sexual Assault: A Judicial Training Manual *by Vicki Mistr, Steven M. Janosik, Anne C. Schroer-Lamont, Lawrence A. Tucker, and Rebecca Weybright, 1993, State Council of Higher Education for Virginia, and is used with their permission.*

This is a good exercise for examining the issues of consent. These scenarios are designed so that there will be general agreement on both extremes and lots of disagreement in the middle.

As you go over each of the following statements, simply pause for brief period and allow the statement to sink it. Then engage in a conversation with the group about whether or not this scene describes consent. As you proceed, you will find increasing disagreement amongst the audience. Be careful of shutting down the discussion/disagreement too early. Allow plenty of time for them to struggle with the topic.

Verbal Request or Invitation

Michael and Kathy have been dating for two months. One night, Kathy asks Michael, "Would you like to have sex tonight?" He says, "Yes," and they have intercourse.

Nonverbal Request

Dave and Amy are in his room lying on the bed. They are kissing, and Dave begins to remove Amy's blouse. Amy removes Dave's shirt, and they take off each other's pants. They have intercourse.

Bargaining with Positive Consequences

Steve wants Sarah to have sex with him, but she tells him that she is unsure if she is ready. He tells her, "If we have sex, we'll be so much closer." She agrees, and they have intercourse.

Quid Pro Quo Bargaining

Jason and Annie meet at a party. Afterwards, they go back to his room. They are kissing on his bed. When Jason pushes Annie's skirt up, she pulls it back down. Jason says, "I know you want this by the way that you've been leading me on all night." Annie agrees that she has been flirting with him. They have intercourse.

Bargaining with Negative Consequences

James and Tina have been dating for one month, though she has been interested in him for several months. He wants to have sex with her, but she argues that it is too soon for her. James tells Tina, "If you won't have sex with me, I'll go out with Robin. She'll give me anything I want." Tina and James have intercourse.

Bargaining with Fraudulent Claims

Tom has a history of STDs. He wants to have sex with Mary and thinks that she wants to have sex with him as well. Mary has heard that he has STDs and asks him directly. He does not tell her about his past. They have intercourse.

(continued)

(continued)

Emotional Threats

Jack and Deb are high school sweethearts and have been dating for a couple of years. After listening to her wishes to wait until after marriage to have sex, Jack tells Deb, "If you don't have sex with me, I will never speak to again. We're through!" They have intercourse.

Emotional Intimidation

Pam and Tim meet at a dance and decide to see one another the next night. Tim realizes they are alone in her apartment and demands to have sex. He says, "I've heard all about you and I know you're a whore. If you don't have sex with me, I'm going to tell all the guys that we did anyway." They have intercourse.

Role Intimidation

Jenny stays after class to ask her T.A., Sam, a question about her assignment. Sam leads Jenny into his office, closes and locks the door, and tells her that if she wants to pass the class, she has to have sex with him. They have intercourse.

Physical Intimidation

Bob walks into Jamie's room, closes the door behind him, and locks it. He blocks the door and demands sex from Jamie, who is sitting on the bed. They have intercourse.

Use of Physical Force to Dominate or Compel

Tony and Kim are making out and are into heavy petting. As Tony begins to remove Kim's shirt, she pulls it back down. He then grabs both her hands and holds them above her head. They have intercourse.

Use of Physical Force to Cause Additional Injury

Chris and Brian leave a party to go to Chris's room. After they kiss for a while, Chris asks Brian to leave. Brian refuses and takes off his pants. Chris continues to protest and pushes Brian towards the door. Brian throws himself on the bed on top of Chris and grabs Chris by the throat. They have intercourse.

Use of a Weapon

Connie and Jim are working together on a project. Jim pulls out a knife, pushes Connie against the wall, and holds the knife to her neck. He tells her to take off her clothes and lie on the floor. They have intercourse.

Wrap up

At the completion of this exercise, call the audiences attention to the dynamics of what happened. The first and last few scenarios probably had lots of agreement, whereas those in the middle had lots of discussion. From outside of the situation, we can have our opinions, but consent doesn't happen outside of the situation. There is no hard and fast line in the sand about where consent is or is not. We can't know for sure—the best we can do is take for granted the voice of the person who was in the situation, and in particular, the voice of the person who claims that they were harmed.

IS THIS CONSENT?

This exercise is a good discussion starter to address the question of consent. This exercise is also good for both male-only and mixed-gender groups.

1. Ask the audience these questions:

   What is your definition of sexual assault?

   What are the key elements of a sexual assault?

2. Write on the board (or paper) the key words that they offer. (With some assistance, they will probably get to something like "forced or unwanted sexual contact." This is a good basic definition, but ask them if it means anything to them.

3. Present the following scenario:

   A heterosexual couple is making out. As they get increasingly into it (you know, some bumping and grinding, moaning and groaning), he touches her breast. She pushes his hand away and says, "I really don't want to do that, but I'm really liking this..." and they continue to kiss. A bit later, they're into it again and he touches her breast again.

4. Ask the following question:

   Is this a sexual assault?

5. Allow the audience time to respond and then remind them of their definition.

   His touching her breast is a sexual contact, which meets one of the elements of sexual assault on our list. It was unwanted in that she said she didn't want it and pushed his hand away, meeting the second element.

   Furthermore, one could argue that force can mean overcoming resistance. Her saying no and pushing his hand away was a form of resistance, so this could be seen as a forced touch, meeting the third element.

   It seems to me that this is a forced and *unwanted sexual contact. Thus, this is a form of sexual assault.*

6. Now the discussion will likely get very heated as folks disagree and argue. Allow discussion to continue for some time and then ask the following:

   Okay. This is clearly an ambiguous situation, but what if it was not the second time he touched her breast after she said no—it was the fifth? Or what if it wasn't over her clothes, but under her clothes? Or what if it was her vagina instead of her breast and it was the third time she said no? Or what if it wasn't his finger, but his penis that he was touching her with?

(continued)

(continued)

The point of this conversation is not to get agreement. Rather it is to emphasize that it is important for men to really listen to our partners when we're engaging in sexual behaviors. In addition, it is to suggest how common it is for men to disrespect women (and men) when we're engaged sexually, thus leading to a conversation about the normative nature of sexual assault.

Cautionary Note: *It is tempting for participants to get sidetracked by her behavior—"What is she still doing there?" "She should have left," "She should have slapped him," and so on. This not only begins to slide into victim-blaming, but is also not the point of the conversation. The purpose is to look at his behavior, not hers. When sidetracking occurs, note it, define it as victim-blaming, and redirect folks to look at his behaviors, not hers.*

DISCLOSURE

This exercise can be used in either same-sex or mixed-gender settings. It is a powerful tool to help participants truly understand the serious challenges and difficulties people have when faced with the decision to disclose and report their histories of being sexually assaulted. It is a great tool to use when the discussion devolves into questions about the false-reporting rate for rape/sexual assault. A good way to close out this exercise is to highlight the incredible courage and bravery demonstrated by women or men who have been sexually assaulted, who do report to the police.

1. Ask the group to break into groups of two or three and say:

   Decide who is going to talk, who is going to listen, and, if there is a third person, who is going to just notice the process.

2. Allow time for the participants to get into dyads or triads. (They will ask some questions about what they're going to talk about; just say that you'll tell them in a minute).
3. Say the following:

   Okay, have you chosen your partners? Are you ready? I want the person who is going to talk to share your best sexual experience.

4. Allow one to two minutes to consider sharing. Be careful not to interrupt this too soon. Allow time for the discomfort, nervousness, and anxiety to rise. They will first look at you to see whether you're serious. For a moment or two, pretend that you are. Take the position that you absolutely expect them to follow through with the exercise.
5. After a moment or two, interrupt them by saying:

   I didn't really mean it!

6. There will likely be a lot of laughter and discussion going on, so you will probably have to try several times to get their attention again. Initially, allow the conversation to stay light and fun, and then say:

   For those of you who were going to share, what was it like for me to ask you to share your best sexual experience?

7. Allow the men time to answer. Do not answer for them.
8. Repeat some of the answers that people share with you and then say:

   I heard lots of laughter, which suggests some levels of discomfort and maybe embarrassment. Were some of you nervous about sharing with this person? After all, you don't know that person all that well. Were any of you upset or even angry at me for daring to ask such a thing?

   Hold on to whatever feelings you may be having for a moment.

(continued)

(continued)

Imagine that you aren't being asked to share your best sexual experience, but your worst. And the person listening isn't a colleague or a friend but a police officer with a gun, a badge, and a walkie-talkie. And this person, as professionally and gently as he or she can, is asking for the gruesome details of your worst sexual experience.

And you know that tomorrow you are going to have to talk with another police officer (this one a detective) and tell him or her your worst sexual experience, and this person too will ask you all the gruesome details.

And a week or so from now, you will have to talk with the prosecuting attorney and share all the details of your worst sexual experience, and if you are really lucky, in a year or so, you'll get to sit in front of a room full of strangers and share your worst sexual experience with a lawyer who is not so gentle and who will ask for all the gruesome details, and this time the perpetrator is sitting right there.

9. Point to a chair just out of arm's reach from you, pause, and then say, raising your own hand as you speak:

   Now, give me a show of hands. How many of you are willing to share your story?

   The same reasons that you are uncomfortable about sharing your best sexual experience, magnified, are the reasons that women and men are hesitant to disclose a sexual assault.

   Those who do demonstrate remarkable courage and bravery.

THE FISHBOWL

This is a great exercise for mixed-gender groups or any groups that you can set up as two distinct categories (i.e., men of color and European American men, fraternity men and non-frat men, and so on). You can come up with questions to ask the people you put in the "fishbowl." The point is to provide a means for the people who are on the outside of the fishbowl looking in to get a deeper sense of what their lives (vis-à-vis men's violence) is like. If doing a mixed-gender discussion, asking women specifically about issues they face related to sexual assault or dating abuse can be very eye-opening for men.

1. Arrange the chairs in the room into two circles, one inside the other, both facing inward.
2. Explain that you are going to ask for volunteers who will sit in the middle and will be asked a couple of questions about the topic. The folks in the outer circle will be asked to silently bear witness (listen carefully) to what the people in the fishbowl discuss.
3. Ask for volunteers (usually 4–8) and allow them to get comfortable. Make sure that you have volunteers of the group that you want in the middle (i.e. all women, all men, all African American men, etc.). For example, "Can I get 4–8 women who'd be willing to be in the middle of the fishbowl to begin?"
4. Ask a question about the issues. If you have a mixed-gender group, ask:

   Describe a time when you felt threatened, or

   What kinds of things do you routinely do to reduce your risk of being victimized?

   If you have all males, ask:

   What would you do if a man abused you (or your sister, mother, or friend)?
5. Allow the group to continue talking for 15–30 minutes and then ask them to wrap up and return to the larger circle.
6. Ask those who were bearing witness to describe what they heard and the impact it had on them.

"GENDER-NEUTRAL" SPEECH

This exercise is good to provide as "homework" and to get men and women to think about the impact of sexism on women's daily lives. It may seem like a stretch to relate this to violence issues at first.

1. Ask the participants to spend a day using the generic *she* pronoun rather than the generic *he* pronoun. For example, rather than referring to congressman/men, fireman/men, or chairman/men when they do not know the gender, they should use congresswoman/women, firewoman/women, or chairwoman/women. (If you are feeing particularly brave, you can use as an example the Christian trilogy of the Father, Son, and Holy Ghost or the Mother, Daughter, and Holy Ghostess).
2. Ask them to note their own reaction and the reaction of those around them as they do this exercise. For example:

   What did they feel?

   What did others say?
3. Ask them to imagine what that must be like for women to do (often unconsciously) all the time.

"What do you think it's like for women to have to edit themselves into conversations all the time?"

"What do you think it's like for women to have to figure out whether or not the conversation really does include them—is this the gender-neutral use of "man" or is this a gender-specific example?"

4. Discuss what it means for us as a society to take the pain of women seriously when they are not even present in our language.

"TYPICAL" MAN/"TYPICAL" WOMAN

This is a good way to begin generating discussion about the issue of sexism in general and how it relates to sexist violence.

1. Using a chalkboard, dry-erase board, or flip chart, create two columns.
2. Write "man" at the top of one column and "woman" at the top of the other.
3. Ask the participants to brainstorm and list the words that they use or have heard to describe the "typical" man and the "typical" woman. (To get things started, sometimes it helps to ask them to refer to a stereotypical man and stereotypical woman.)
4. Allow this brainstorming to go on for several minutes.
5. When you have a list, erase or cover the "man" or "woman" at the top of the page and ask two questions:

   Of these two lists of characteristics, which would you rather be? Why?

   Which of these two lists of characteristics, in general, does our society value more?

CONTINUUM—"MAKE YOUR CASE"

This exercise is a good one for male-only or mixed-gender audiences. It is particularly good because it requires that the audience members physically move around. Getting them to physically move increases the likelihood of their engaging in the verbal aspects. And encouraging them to dialogue with each other is a good way to get at the misconceptions or myths that the audience members may hold.

1. Draw an imaginary continuum across the room. On one side is "agree," on the other is "disagree," and in the middle is "neutral."
2. Ask the participants to position themselves along the continuum based on the way they respond to the statements you are about to make. Let them know that you are going to ask them to make their case as to why they are standing where they're standing.
3. Make each of the following statements (or write some of your own) and use the discussion after each to explore and debunk the myths that emerge.

Sometimes women really mean yes when they say no.

A woman who goes to a fraternity party, gets drunk, and goes up to a brother's room should know what to expect.

There are times when a man gets so excited he "needs it."

Women often lie about rape to get a man in trouble or because they realize afterwards that they should not have had sex.

Some women are "just asking for it."

Women are as abusive as men.

Dating abuse is a relationship problem; both are at fault.

Most sexual assaults are committed by someone the woman knows.

Women who stay in a relationship with someone who is abusive are sick or they secretly like it.

WHY IS SEXUAL ASSAULT SO DEVASTATING?

Many men believe that rape and sexual assault is a devastating act, but have rarely thought of why. This exercise helps men to better understand why it is so devastating, which, in turn, helps to build men's empathy.

1. Using an easel (or chalkboard or dry-erase board), ask the participants why they think sexual assault is so devastating.
2. Record the answers they come up with as a way to make visible what they are saying. If they get stuck, you can begin a brief discussion comparing sexual assault to physical assault and get consensus to the notion that sexual assault is more devastating than physical assault. (This is generally a fairly easy consensus to reach.)
3. Repeat the question about whether sexual assault is more devastating than physical assault and why.
4. As you write down what participants say, begin to identify themes that you see emerging and facilitate a conversation about those themes.

Facilitator Note: *To bring the point home, ask the participants to consider themselves as sexual beings. As they think about who they are sexually, encourage them to think beyond who they are attracted to or the kinds of sexual behavior they find most satisfying to include their gender identity and the ways they express their gender as well as sexual orientation. Urge them to consider that who we are sexually is one of the (if not the) most sacred and personal parts of who we are.*

GUIDED IMAGERY

This is an excellent exercise to use with men to help them recognize the ways that they are affected by the presence of sexist violence. Most men experience times when women are afraid of them for no other reason than they are a man and in order to be safe, women have to be somewhat afraid—or at least wary. Most men experience this as an affront to how they view themselves, which is, not a threat. This exercise helps men to get to that emotional memory—which can then be used to engage men in working to address sexism and violence.

1. Begin the meeting by saying:

   I am going to take you on a guided imagery. Now, guided imagery does not work for everyone, so if this does not work for you, don't worry about it.

   Get yourself comfortable. Close your eyes if you are comfortable with that, uncross your legs, sit back in the chair, and take a couple of deep breaths.

2. Take a couple of deep breaths particularly loudly for the group as a whole to set the tone, and then say:

   As you continue to breathe deeply, I want you to notice the sound of my voice. Notice the temperature in the room and your butt on the chair.

3. Soften your own voice and begin talking more quietly and slowly. Also, notice what else is going on in the room and point that out. For example, the temperature, noises in the room or outside that are leaking into the room, and so on. Doing so will help the participants get increasingly comfortable.

4. Resume the guided imagery.

   As you continue to breathe, you are going to notice that you are starting to feel less solid in the chair. You begin to feel yourself floating up off the chair and towards the ceiling. You find yourself now looking down at the tops of our heads. Continue breathing and feel yourself float through the ceiling and into the sky.

5. Bring in what is going on outside: For example, day or night, clouds or sun, birds singing, wind blowing, and so on. Make it as concrete and real as you can.

6. Resume the guided imagery.

   You continue to float up and then begin to float back down towards a restaurant.

7. Add some local descriptors here, such as the name of a popular area restaurant, a busy and well-known street name, and so on, and then resume the imagery.

   It's a comfortable spring evening. You float into the restaurant through the ceiling and you notice the top of your own head and begin floating towards yourself. Notice the sound in the room, the clinking of glasses and dishes, the roar of conversation, laughter, and so on.

You find yourself sitting at a table with several of your friends. You have just finished dinner and are paying the bill. Someone has just told a funny story and you are all laughing. You feel really good here.

You all get up to leave the restaurant and head outside. Because you all came separately, you spend a couple of minutes in front of the restaurant continuing to chat and then say goodbye.

You turn off the busy street onto a side street towards your car. You're still a little "buzzed" from the dinner and fun time you had with your friends and are thinking about them. You notice, up ahead about a half-block ahead of you, a woman walking towards you. But your mind is on the evening and you don't pay her a lot of attention.

You continue walking, thinking about your dinner, and you notice her again and notice something strange, but you don't pay much attention. As you continue walking towards her, you notice that she is looking anxious. She seems to be avoiding your eyes and is holding more tightly onto her purse. You try to catch her eye to reassure her, but she avoids your eyes.

You are pretty close to her now and you think that she has quickened her pace. You pass her and get to your car. You turn to look at her as you unlock the door and notice that she seems less anxious but glances over her shoulder at you.

As you get into your car, you begin to become more aware of my voice again. It slowly becomes stronger and louder and you notice that you are beginning to float gently out of your car and back into the night sky. You notice your breathing and begin to float back down.

8. Refer to what the outside in "real time" actually is like—sunny, windy, cloudy, and so on—and then resume the imagery.

   You float back into this building and into the room. You notice the tops of our heads and are very aware of my voice again. You float back into your chair and are again aware of the temperature in the room.

9. Be specific as you can about the surroundings as you bring them back and then end with this:

   Take a couple of deep breaths and, as you get comfortable, open your eyes.

10. After the guided imagery, lead them into a discussion about the experience, asking these questions:

    What was that like for you?

    What did you notice?

    What was it like to notice that woman afraid of you?

    What did you want to do or say?

    It might be tempting to blame the woman for being afraid of you, but women, in order to be safe, need to be somewhat afraid of us as men. Doesn't it make more sense for men to work to remove men as a threat to women than to blame women for doing what they need to do to be safe?

WHAT WOULD YOU DO?

In this exercise, you describe a rape or dating abuse scenario and ask the participants to describe how they would respond, who they think is responsible, and what they feel they should do. Then you continue to retell the scenario. At each telling, the relationship between the participants and the characters in the scenario becomes increasingly closer until the characters in the last scenario are a best male friend who rapes or abuses a sister.

1. Give the following instructions to the men:

   I am going to describe a typical rape (date abuse) scenario and I want you to respond. I'm going to stop at different points along the story and ask for your responses.

2. Take a deep breath and begin the exercise with

   You hear through the grapevine that one of the women on your campus has been raped (abused by her boyfriend).

   What is your reaction? Who do you see as responsible?

   As you learn more, you discover that she lives in your dorm.

   How does this change your reaction?

   You come to find out that the accused man is in one of your classes.

   How does this change your reaction?

   Your sister's best friend comes to tell you that she needs to talk to you, and she tells you that your sister is the one who was raped. As you finish that conversation, one of your best friends comes to you and says that he's been accused of rape.

   How does this change your reaction?

3. Use this scenario to explore how their reactions might change, why, and what they would want to do now that they realize a friend of theirs has raped their sister.

WHY MEN RAPE OR BATTER

This good, if somewhat shocking, exercise helps people normalize and better understand why men batter or rape. It is best to let the exercise end without any kind of discussion. Allow the impact to take hold of the participants.

1. Divide a paper into three columns. Label the columns "Crimes I Would Commit," "Why," and "Crimes I Would Not Commit."
2. Ask the participants to list all the crimes that they would commit. Write them in the first column.
3. Ask the participants to list the crimes that they would not commit. Write them in the third column.
4. Facilitate a conversation about the difference.
5. Ask the participants why they would commit the crimes that they would commit. Write their reasons in the second column.
6. After they have finished, replace "Why" with "Men Rape/Batter." The reasons that we would commit the crimes that we commit are the reasons/justifications that men use to commit rape or domestic violence.

The table below depicts some of the more common reactions that men have to this exercise, and it demonstrates what the work area will look like once you've completed it with men.

Crimes I Would Commit	***Why***	***Crimes I Would Not Commit***
	(Men Rape/Batter)	
Speeding	Doesn't hurt anyone	Murder
Wear seat belt	Entitlement/libertarian	Child crimes
Sodomy	Make a point	Assault
Petty theft	Feels good	Battery
Under-aged drinking	"Victimless"	Armed robbery
Drug use	Won't get caught	Arson
Prostitution	Minor	
Loitering	Few consequences	

APPENDIX C

Additional Writings

These additional writings are by Rus Funk. The article offers a model of how to address men about these topics in writing (which is one form of educating men) and examine additional issues. The poems are examples of ways to use one form of art to engage men and offer another way to convey the messages of men's response-abilities to sexism and violence.

Pornography: What's the Harm?*

Rus Ervin Funk

This is a conversation about pornography. Specifically, I plan to address heterosexual and gay male pornography. I am not, nor have I ever been a lesbian; neither have I ever consumed lesbian pornography. As such, I think it incumbent upon myself to steer away from critiquing too directly a medium that I do not know and don't have a context of using. In addition, given the sheer amount of male pornography use as compared to female pornography use, any behavior on my part to point fingers at another group seems more than a bit contradictory. This being said, there are aspects of my critique of pornography that will relate to lesbian pornography.

As a bisexual, I have used both heterosexual and gay male pornography—and have since become critical of both. I grew up in a sexual liberal household (my parents were, for a time, sexuality educators in our community and at the local college). As such, I had open access to heterosexual pornography. It was available under the guise of encouraging us as kids to be open about sex and sexuality. The pornography I had access to was presented as no different from the first issue of *Our Bodies Ourselves* which my parents got as soon as it was published.

As I came to terms with my bisexuality, I used gay male pornography to explore my sexual interests and what gayness and bi-ness might mean. Growing up in South Texas (including my college years) in the 1970s and 80s, I did not have access to GLBT youth groups or ANY GLBT that I knew of. My parents raised me to be open and accepting. I remember vividly my parents inviting local gay male and lesbian activists home for dinner. No one has ever been expected to be closeted in our home! Even still, as I came to terms with my own bisexuality, in college, there were no gay clubs, hotlines, or meeting spaces for me to meet other gay or bisexual men and find out what I was finding out about me. What there was, was gay male pornography.

I, like many women in heterosexual relationships, had other men use pornography to "turn me on" or provide me with examples of what they'd like to do with (to?) me. I want to be clear! I am not saying, nor do I feel, that any of the men I've been with ever victimized, exploited, or coerced me in any way. I also know that for many of us, in whatever context, we often learn our boundaries by crossing over and realizing that our boundaries were passed over. This is to say that pornography is often used as a tool to get people to do, or at least consider doing, what they may not be initially comfortable with. This is a hint into one of the harms of pornography.

So pornography has been a large part of a lot of my life. My critiques of pornography come from a human rights and social justice perspective. I am a sex positive activist who lives and fights for social justice across the spectrums, including GLBT people. I am an active supporter of women's reproductive rights, I support positive sexual expressions (including sexual explicit expressions) and I am highly critical of pornography.

Defining Pornography

For the purposes of our discussion, I'm going to offer a definition of pornography. The definition I offer is asking for a paradigm shift on your part. The definition I'm offering is *not* based on the obscenity standard that is the basis of U.S. definitions of pornography and the frame from which most folks consider and discuss pornography. I'll come back to this issue momentarily.

The definition I offer is based on the work of Diana Russell: *material that combines sex and/or the exposure of genitals with abuse or degradation in a manner that appears to endorse, condone, or encourage such behavior.* As such, sexually explicit material in and of itself is not my concern. Similarly, there is material that is not necessarily sexually explicit that I would find as pornographic. The *Sports Illustrated* Swimsuit Issue is a prime example of such. It is the combination of sexually explicit with abuse or degradation that is problematic—that is pornographic.

From this perspective, it is important to not only examine the explicit *presence* of abuse or degradation, but also the context of the material to identify if abuse or degradation that may be a part of the material. For example, the Swimsuit Issue. In and of itself, it isn't necessarily problematic. Placed in the context of *Sports Illustrated*, and one can more easily identify the abuse and degradation that makes this material pornographic. That context includes a lack of meaningful coverage of women at any other time during the subscription cycle, the lack of women athletes who are chosen to grace the cover of *SI*, who the readership is, and the lack of any Swimsuit Issue for men. Given the context of *SI* and the presence of the Swimsuit Issue, it leads to a half-facetious question of what "sport" *SI* is promoting with this issue? What the Swimsuit Issue (especially in context) exposes is the degree to which women's strength is defined by their "beauty" (using very narrow terms) and their sexual availability to men.

Addressing Obscenity

Any current understanding of pornography in the U.S. is influenced primarily by the obscenity standard. The way pornography is currently defined is the degree to which that material is "obscene." This definition falls far short on any measure of justice, fairness, dignity, or human rights. Using the obscenity standard places the "harm" on "community standards." This has not only proven to be an extremely elusive standard by which to identify and assess harm, but it also masks and silences the real harm and the real voices of those who are harmed. By this definition, some of the people who are harmed in the production and distribution of pornography—the women, children, and some men (in the case of gay male pornography) are defined as part of the problem. Their harms are not addressed and as such, they are provided with no recourse for the harm they experience. Thus, the obscenity standard empowers the state, not the people who are victimized. Not only does this label some of the victims of pornography as part of the problem, but it also strengthens the dynamics that are set up to systematically silence those women, children, and some men who would speak out against pornography by strengthening the state rather than empowering the people who are victimized.

Ultimately, what the obscenity standard does is moves the debate about pornography to the conceptual level. Rather than assessing the harm and exploring ways to address the harms that are caused, the general public is stuck in an endless debate about whether a picture is or is not obscene. The ways that the women, children, and some men are treated in the taking of the pictures escapes any scrutiny whatsoever.

Lack of a Definition (as is true in most cases, e.g., rape)

One issue that is not addressed by the definition that I offer, like that which is not addressed by the obscenity perspective, is the lack of **a** clear and concise definition of what is or what isn't pornography. This is because much of what makes material pornographic is the context of that material and the environment in which the material is presented. While there certainly are some standards that make this clear, much of the time it is determined by the context in which the material is displayed, how the material is displayed, what else may be going on around the material, and the person's experience relative to the material. In this way, it is not terribly different than a lot of things that we defined as problematic, social injustice, human wrongs, and so on. For example, if I were to ask, I suspect that each one of us would have some very distinct differences in our definitions of what rape is and what it isn't. And together we likely collectively have a definition that is very different than Kentucky state law, which is, in turn, very different than the state laws in Indiana, Tennessee, Missouri, and Ohio. This is similarly true with any issue—particularly any social justice issue—that we address: racism, homophobia, violence in general, and so on.

Just because there isn't **a** definition of rape that we all agree on with all the nuances does not mean that rape is not harmful. Yet with pornography, that fact that we don't have **a** definition is often used to discount the critiques of pornography, discount the definition we offer, and discount that there is ever any harm. I would further submit that the definition I offer above is much clearer and much closer to being a concise definition than anything available from an obscenity perspective.

Defining the Harm

What is pornography, really? It is a multibillion dollars-a-year industry, substantially larger than the music and movie industries combined. Best current estimates indicate that there are more than 1,000 hard core pornographic movies made **every week** in the U.S. Pornographic magazines (such as *Playboy*, *Penthouse,* and *Hustler*) now make up a minority of the market as increasing numbers of men (and some women) find access to pornography through video, DVDs, and over the Internet. Similarly, what has historically been defined as "soft-core" pornography (that is, pornography that does not show a man's erection or actual penetration) also makes an increasingly shrinking share of the market. Pornography has become increasingly violent, and has pushed the enveloped between the viewer and the person(s) being depicted.

Although it was never really true, it has become increasingly so that the line between pornography and prostitution is really nonexistent. Prostitution can be understood as buying someone for sex—and isn't that exactly what pornography is? Buying a (man-made) image of a woman (or man in the case of gay male pornography) that is also an actual human being for sexual pleasure? Similarly, the line between pornography, prostitution, and trafficking is also increasingly blurry. There is fairly widespread technology, for example, that allows a viewer sitting in his living room in Louisville to type his desires onto the computer and "order" the woman on the other side (who may be in Great Britain, Chicago, or Bangkok) to "perform" in the way that he wants to. He pays for these services (on credit card along a secured link, of course). So what is this? Is this pornography, prostitution, or trafficking?

Pornography is the depiction of women (and sometimes men in the case of gay male pornography) in sexually suggestive positions, almost always smiling (unless their look of displeasure, disgust, fear, sadness, embarrassment, or anger is part of the eroticization of the portrayal). Regardless of what is going on or what is being done to her, she is smiling, or at least looking enticing (there are some eroticized positions that include looking serious, studious, or pouting, but inherent within the context and content is that she is enjoying it).

The Harm of Production

Some of the women and men are forced to participate and/or are "participating" without their knowledge or input. What is not seen from the view as consumers is what else may be going on just outside of camera range. We don't see the threats that may be made, we don't see the abuse that the woman or man was subject to the night before the camera shoot, or the night after, we don't know what is going on behind the scenes. What we *do* know from survivors is that this is not unheard of. For multiple reasons, we don't know how common it is.

With the growth of technology, we've also seen an advance of women's (there hasn't been any of men posted that we know of...yet) pictures being taken and posted without their knowledge and certainly without their consent. The phenomenon of "upskirts" photos, the "wild girls" videos, the use of camera phones to take and share pictures of women who strip, or girlfriends taking a shower... There is a huge market for these kind of pictures in the pornography industry. None of these women submitted to having their pictures taken or distributed but increasingly what we're finding is that once these pictures are made available, it is exceedingly difficult for women to get their distribution stopped.

During the production of pornography, there is little concern for the wellbeing of the "actors"—their comfort, their wellbeing, or their health. Joey Stefano, perhaps THE gay male pornography star of the late 80s and early 90s, reported towards the end of his life of the contempt that he faced by the producers, videographers, and directors. He also candidly detailed the pressure he felt to have unprotected sex during the filming. Based on Mr. Stefano's report, this was not an unusual practice. At a time when the AIDS crisis was at its height, this utter disregard for the health of those who participate in pornography should be criminal. Given the recent outbreak of HIV and the scare within heterosexual pornography recently, it appears that this practice is not exclusive to gay male pornography.

Even after the pictures are taken and a woman has escaped the pornography industry, it does not mean that the pictures are no longer in distribution. People who are photographed in pornography have no rights to their pictures or how they are used or distributed. It is also not uncommon for women who may have volunteered to have pictures taken of them to move on in their lives and find these pictures continue to resurface. For example, we're already hearing of reports of women who participate in the "wild girls" videos graduating from college, securing a job in some kind of professional setting, and then finding pictures of themselves taped to their door, or stuffed in their mailbox, or distributed throughout the office during their first week of their new job.

The Harm of Consumption

The Message to Women of Hetero Pornography

What's the message that heterosexual pornography sends to women? What's the message that adolescent and pre-adolescent girls are getting by looking at pornography? What does pornography say about women—who women are, how women relate to men, women's strength, women's empowerment, women's sexuality? The message inherent in pornography is that women are subordinate to men, and women's sexual pleasure is subordinate and secondary to men's. Heterosexual pornography is boringly predictable. There are three main forms of heterosexual pornography:

- Pics or displays of women posed solo or with one or two other women.
- Pics or displays of women being penetrated by one or more men with some weak attempt at a story line.
- "Gonzo," which are movies that are just displays of women being penetrated by a man or men in multiple different ways. There is no attempt at a story line in these productions.

Regardless of the format, the message of heterosexual pornography is that women are accessible to men for sexual penetration. Their desires, wishes, or sexual expression is only relevant vis-à-vis men's enjoyment. The message of heterosexual pornography to women is that women's sexual pleasure is based on men's sexual fulfillment.

The Message to Men About Women in Hetero Pornography

What is the message that men get about women when they look at pornography? What do men get as the message about how to look at women in general? What messages do men get about their own power, their own sexuality, and their power and sexuality in relation to women? The main messages for men include the following:

- Sex is all (or primarily) physical sensation with little or no emotional engagement.
- Men's sexual release and pleasure is primary.
- If women have an orgasm or sexual pleasure, it is only secondary to men's.
- If women receive sexual pleasure, it is often as a result of men's sexual pleasure.
- Women are always ready and willing to have any kind of sex with any kind of man—all they need is a penis.
- Women find sexual pleasure in being humiliated (called names, having their hair pulled, being "manhandled" into the proper position…)
- Women may say no initially, but are quickly persuaded that they really like it.

The Pornographer's Gaze

Men who look at pornography do not stop the pornographer's gaze simply because they stop looking at pornography. The way that men look at women in heterosexual pornography or at other men in gay male pornography is transmitted to the way they look at women or men in general. Pornography creates a way of men looking at women or other men. When men who look at pornography start looking at women or other men, they look at them with the same gaze they use to look at the women or men who are portrayed in pornography. The pornographer's gaze is objectifying, predatory (masked as erotic), controlling, and judgmental. Through the pornographers' gaze, women and other men are stripped of their humanity and seen as potential receptacles of men's sexual attention.

In addition, they often look at women or men in general and judge them compared to the women or men they've looked at in pornography—"she looks like the kind of girl who would..." "he looks like he'd like to..."

The gaze (which is objectifying and dehumanizing and problematic in its own right) far too often transmits into behavior. Women report increased incidents of street harassment outside of "adult" bookstores.

Re-enforcing Male Entitlement

Perhaps one of the most problematic aspects of pornography is the way that it reinforces male entitlement. There is already way too much support of men's sense of entitlement: to sex, to women's attention, to being heard, and so on. Pornography reinforces these messages. The messages rampant throughout pornography is that once turned on, men are entitled to have sexual release. Not that any woman ever would, but they really aren't presented as having any voice in determining what kind of sexual activity occurs. It is all male-driven. This is further reinforced by men's sexual release. If one learns a particular lesson and then has an orgasm connected to that lesson, the lesson becomes *strongly* reinforced for that person. This is what pornography does.

Coercion of Sexual Partners

The evidence is also quite clear that many men, after viewing pornography, attempt to get their sexual partners to do what they saw done in pornography. Men watch pornography, and then ask, or plead, or coerce, or sometimes just try to do to their sexual partners what they saw the men in pornography do to the women or men in pornography. For example, battered women report that their husbands who used pornography would frequently try to get them to do what they saw done in pornography (Websdale, 1998). Obviously, in the context of domestic violence, a battered woman's ability to say no or negotiate is extremely limited and unlikely.

What's to Be Done

I know there are First Amendment concerns that arise with any critique of pornography. We can discuss this further if the question arises here, but let me say briefly that it is painfully obvious to me given my experience in talking with women and men who have survived pornography, that it is pornography itself that is the threat to freedom of speech. I would contend, moreover, that rather than threatening the First Amendment, critiquing pornography is in fact using freedom of speech to expand freedom of speech.

There are many actions that can be done. First and foremost, of course, is for men to pledge to stop using pornography and to challenge other men to do the same. If men stopped using pornography, then these lessons would have no place to go (although it is certainly true that these lessons are available through plenty of other venues).

In addition to this, men along with women, can work to confront pornography—especially from a sex-positive position. Writing letters to the editors of local newspapers, organizing speak-outs, holding debates, picketing shops that sell pornography, boycotting businesses that sell pornography and "girlcotting" (strategically shopping at those stores that do the right thing) businesses that do not sell pornography. There are multitudes of things that people can do to combat and confront pornography.

The point is that we do something. It is time to act! It is time to recognize the link between pornography and other forms of racism, sexism, homophobia, and violence. It is time to recognize pornography as a form of racist, sexist, and homophobic abuse.

References

Check, J. (1995). Teenage training: The effects of pornography on adolescent males. In L. Lederer and R. Delgado (Eds.), *The price we pay: The case against racist speech, hate propaganda, and pornography*. New York: Hill and Wang Press.

Funk, R. E. (2005). What pornography says about me(n): How I became an anti-pornography activist. In C. Stark and R. Whisnant (Eds.), *Not for sale: Feminists resisting prostitution and pornography*. Victoria, Australia: Spinifex Press.

Kendall, C. & Funk, R. E. (2003). Gay male pornography's "actors": When "fantasy" isn't." In M. Farley (Ed.), *Prostitution, trafficking, and traumatic stress*. Binghamton, NY: Haworth Press.

Websdale, N. (1998). *Rural woman battering and the justice system*. Thousand Oaks, CA: Sage Publications.

Zillman, D. & Bryant, J. (1989). *Pornography: Research advances and policy considerations*. Hillsdale, NJ: Erlbaum Press.

Spittin' Nails

I'm so angry
I could just spit nails

That's what Momma used to say
I never quite understood what she meant til today
and now I realize there really is no other way
for me to say
To say how angry I am

I'm so angry
I could just spit nails

I want to see him hurt
I want to hurt him
to hear him cry out in pain
to see the fear and pain in his eyes
to see…and feel his blood on my hands
I want him to pay
I WANT HIM TO PAY!

I'm so angry
I could just spit nails
But I'm here with you right now
here with you, my sister, wife, girlfriend, boyfriend, daughter, mother, son, friend, aunt, roommate, study pal, neighbor, my child's baby sitter…
how is my being angry at him
supporting you?
how is my focusing on him
helping you out?

I'm so sorry and sad and scared and frustrated and disappointed and ashamed and confused and…

I'm so angry
I could just spit nails
I'm mad at you for not telling me when it happened
I'm mad at me for not being the kind of man who you thought you could tell when it happened

Folks say "a man is supposed to protect 'his woman'"
did I fail you?
am I failing you now?

I want to hold you
        but don't know how
        and don't know if you want me to

I want to take your pain away
        but don't know how
        and don't know if I can handle it
I want to make it right
        but don't know how
        and couldn't if I did
I want to make you safe
        but don't know how
        and aren't sure that I should
I want to understand
        but don't know how
        and anyway, there ain't no understanding this

Face it!
    I don't know how to do much of anything right now
        except be mad
        except to love you
        except to try
            and stay right here
                        right now
                            and be with you

I'm so angry
        I could just spit nails

© 2005 by Rus Ervin Funk

By candle light

These candles we do light
to show our commitment to continue the fight
to ensure you will always have the right
to be free from the fear of men's violence.

It was on a night just as this
a gunshot shattered your marital bliss
killed by the man who shared your first kiss
yet another victim of men's violence.

There are others too whose lives ended thus
men who they loved who shattered their trust
they lost their dominion so their love was a bust
one more perp of men's violence.

Another death another shedding of tears
remembering the killings all through the years
we stare our promise through the cheers and the jeers
to put a stop to men's violence.

Women and children and men are all killed
the promise of life not allowed to be filled
a travesty of justice that must be revealed
all different forms of men's violence.

So together we stand to shoulder our trust
ending men's violence is nothing less than a must
from the breaking of dawn to the last rays of dust
we ***WILL*** put an end to men's violence.

© 1998 by Rus Ervin Funk

APPENDIX D

Bibliography

Adams, D. C. (1984). Stages of anti-sexist awareness and change for men who batter. Paper presented at the annual meeting of the American Psychological Association. Toronto, Canada.

Alliance Against Sexual Coercion. (1979). *Fighting sexual harassment.* Boston, MA: Allyson Publications Inc.

Altman, D. (2001). *Global sex.* Chicago, IL: University of Chicago Press.

American Association of University Women (AAUW). (2001). *Hostile hallways: Bullying, teasing, and sexual harassment in school.* AAUW, Washington, DC. (Available from www.aauw.org)

Awkward, M. (1995). *Negotiating difference: Race, gender, and the politics of positionality.* Chicago: University of Chicago Press.

Baker, G. (1999). Boom in the sex sites on the Internet. In *Age* (Melbourne, Australia). Nov. 6, 1999.

Barry, K. (1984). *Female sexual slavery.* New York: New York University Press.

Barry, K. (1995). *The prostitution of sexuality: The global exploitation of women.* New York: New York University Press.

Beneke, T. (1982). *Men on rape: What they have to say about sexual violence.* New York: St Martin's Press. (No longer in print.)

Berkowitz, A. D. (2001-a). Are Foubert's claims about "the men's program" overstated? Unpublished paper available from the author at http://myweb.fltg.net.users.alan.

Berkowitz, A. D. (2001-b). Critical elements of sexual-assault prevention and risk-reduction programs for men and women. In C. Kilmartin, *Sexual assault in context: Teaching college men about gender.* Holmes Beach, FL: Learning Publications.

Bernard, E. (1990). Black women and the backwash of harassment. *Washington Post, Aug. 12 at C8.*

Bowman, C. G. (1993). Street harassment and the informal ghettoization of women. *Harvard Law Review, 106 (517), January 1993,* 516–580.

Brown, S. (2003). Feminist history of rape. In *Connections—the journal of the Washington Coalition of Sexual Assault Programs, 14(2),* 6–9.

Brownmiller, S. (1975). *Against our will: Men, woman and rape.* New York: The Ballantine Publishing Group.

Byrd, R. P., & Guy-Sheftall, B. (Eds.). (2001). *Traps: African American men on gender and sexuality.* Bloomington, IN: Indiana University Press.

Carter, V. (2004). Prostitution and the new slavery. In C. Stark and R. Whisnant, *Not for sale: Feminists resisting prostitution and pornography (pp. 85–88).* Sidney, Australia: Spinifex Press.

Connell, N., & Wilson, C. (Eds.). (1974). *Rape: The first sourcebook for women.* New York: Plume Books. (No longer in print.)

Davis, A. (1983). *Women, race and class.* New York: Random House Publishing.

DeKeseredy, W. S. (1990). Male peer support and women abuse: The current state of knowledge. *Sociological Focus, 23,* 129–139.

DeKeseredy, W. S., Joseph, C., & Edgar, J. (2003). Understanding separation/divorce sexual assault in rural communities: The contributions of an exploratory Ohio study. Presented at the 2003 National Institute of Justice Conference on Criminal Justice Research and Evaluation, Washington, DC.

di Leonardo, M. (1981). Political economy of street harassment. *Aegis, Summer,* 51–52.

Dines, G., Jenson, B., & Russo, A. (1998). *Pornography: The production and consumption of inequality.* New York: Routledge Press.

Dobash, R. E., & Dobash, R. P. (1972). *Women, violence, and social change.* New York: Routledge Press.

Dworkin, A. (1979). *Pornography: Men possessing women.* New York: Perigree Books.

Dworkin, A. (1988). I want a twenty-four-hour truce in which there is no rape. In A. Dworkin, *Letters from a War Zone.* New York: Dutton Books.

Dworkin, A., & MacKinnon, C. A. (1988). *Pornography and civil rights: A new day for women's equality.* New York: Dworkin and MacKinnon.

Epstein, D., & Johnson, R. (1998). *Schooling sexualities.* Buckingham: Open University Press.

Farley, M. (2003). Prostitution and the invisibility of harm. *Women and Therapy, 26,* 1–4. (Special Issue on Women and Invisible Disabilities, M. Banks and R. Ackerman, Eds.)

Farley, M., Cotton, A., Lynne, J., Zumbeck, S., Spiwak, F., Reyes, M. E., et al. (2003). Prostitution and trafficking in nine countries: An update on violence and posttraumatic stress disorder. In M. Farley (Ed.), *Prostitution, trafficking, and traumatic stress* (pp. 33–74). Binghamton, NY: Haworth Press.

Foubert, J. D., & Marriott, J. A. (1997). Effects of a sexual assault peer education program on men's beliefs in rape myths. *Sex Roles, 36 (3–4),* 259–268.

Freire, P. (1970). *Pedagogy of the oppressed.* New York: Continuum Books.

Freire, P. (1973). *Education for critical consciousness.* New York: Continuum Books.

Funk, R. E. (1992). *Stopping rape: A challenge for men.* Philadelphia, PA: New Society Publishers.

Funk, R. E. (2004). What does pornography say about me(n)?: How I became an anti-pornography activist. In C. Stark & R. Whisnant (Eds.), *Not For sale: Feminists resisting prostitution and pornography* (pp. 331-351). Melbourne, Australia: Spinifex Press.

Funk, R. E. (2006). Queer men and sexual assault: What being raped says about being a man. In W. Martino & C. Kendall (Eds.), *Gendered outcasts and sexual outlaws: Sexual oppression and hierarchies in queer men's lives.* Binghamton, NY: Haworth Press.

Gager, N., & Schurr, C. (1976). *Sexual assault: Confronting rape in America.* New York: Grosset and Dunlap books. (No longer in print.)

Giroux, H. A. (1997). *Pedagogy and the politics of hope: Theory culture and schooling.* New York: Westview Press.

Gordon, M. T., & Riger, S. (1989). *The female fear.* New York: The Free Press.

Gruber, J. E., & Smith, M. (1995). Women's responses to sexual harassment: A multivariate approach. *Basic and Applied Social Psychology, 17,* 543–562.

Gutek, B. (1985). *Sex and the workplace.* San Francisco, CA: Jossey-Bass Publishers.

Heppner, M. J., Neville, H. A., Smith, K., Kivlighan, D. M., Jr., & Gershuny, B. S. (1999). Examining immediate and long-term efficacy of rape prevention programming with racially diverse college men. *Journal of Counseling Psychology, 46(1),* 16–26.

Hernton, C. (2001). Breaking silences. In R. P. Byrd, & B. Guy-Sheftall (Eds.), *Traps: African American men on gender and sexuality (pp. 153–157).* Bloomington, IN: Indiana University Press.

Holsopple, K. (1998). Stripclubs according to strippers: Exposing workplace violence. Available at www.uri.edu/artsci/wms/hughes/stripc3.htm

hooks, b. (1981). *Ain't I a woman: Black women and feminism.* Boston, MA: South End Press.

hooks, b. (1994). *Teaching to transgress: Education as the practice of freedom.* New York: Routledge Press.

Hughes, D. M. (2000). Men create the demand: Women are the supply. Lectures presented at the Queen Sofia Center, Valencia, Spain, November.

Jaimes, M. A. (1992). *The state of native America: Genocide, colonization and resistance.* Boston, MA: South End Press.

Kelly, L. (1989). *Surviving sexual violence.* Minneapolis, MN: University of Minnesota Press.

Kendall, C. (2004). *Gay Male Pornography: An Issue of Sex Discrimination.* University of British Columbia Press. Vancouver, Canada.

Kendall, C., & Funk, R. E. (2003). Gay male pornography's "actors": When "fantasy" isn't. In M. Farley (Ed.), *Prostitution, trafficking, and traumatic stress* (pp. 93-114). Binghamton, NY: Haworth Press.

Kennedy-Bergen, R. (1999). *Marital rape.* Paper available on line from VAWnet. www.vawnet.org.

Kimmel, M. (Ed.). (1990). *Men confront pornography*. New York: Crown Publishers.

Kimmel, M. (1996). *Manhood in America: A cultural history*. New York: The Free Press.

Kimmel, M. (Ed.). (2002). "Gender Symmetry" in domestic violence: A substantive and methodical research review. *Violence against women, 8 (11),* 1332-1363.

King, V. (1992). *Manhandled: Black females breaking the bondage and reclaiming our lives.* Nashville, TN: Winston-Derek Publishing.

Kopels, S., & Dupper, D. R. (1999). School-based peer sexual harassment. *Child Welfare, 78(4),* 435–460.

Koss, M. P., Gidycz, C. A., & Wisniewski, N. (1987). The scope of rape: Incidence and prevalence of sexual aggression and victimization in a national sample of higher education students. *Journal of Consulting and Clinical Psychology, 55,* p. 162–170.

LaViolette, A. D., & Barnett, O. W. (2000). *It could happen to anyone: Why battered women stay.* Thousand Oaks, CA: Sage Press.

Lerderer, L. (Ed.). (1980). *Take back the night: Women on pornography*. New York: William Morrow and Company.

Lerner, G. (Ed.). (1972). *Black women in white America: A documentary history*. New York: Pantheon Books.

Lewis, J. (1998). Lap dancing: Personal and legal implications for exotic dancers. In J. A. Elias, V. L. Bullough, V. Elias, & G. Brewer (Eds.), *Prostitution: On whores, hustlers, and johns*. Amherst, NY: Prometheus Books.

Linz, D., & Bryant, J. (1984). Effects of massive exposure to pornography. In N. Malamuth & E. Donnerstein (Eds.), *Pornography and sexual aggression*. New York: Academic Press.

Lonsway, K. A. (1996). Ending acquaintance rape through education: What do we know? *Psychology of Women Quarterly, 20,* 229–265.

Mac an Ghaill, M. (1994). *The making of men: Masculinities, sexualities and schooling*. Buckingham. Open University Press.

MacKinnon, C. A. (1979). *The sexual harassment of working women.* New Haven, CT: Yale University Press.

MacKinnon, C. A., & Dworkin, A. (1997). *In harm's way: The pornography civil rights hearing.* Cambridge: Harvard University Press.

Malamuth, N., & Donnerstein, D. (1984). *Pornography and sexual aggression*. New York: Academic Press.

Marchiano, L. (1980). *Ordeal.* Necaucaus, NJ: Citadel Press.

Martin, D. (1976). *Battered wives.* Volcano, CA: Volcano Press.

Martino, W. (1999). "Cool boys," "party animals," "squids," and "poofters": Interrogating the dynamics and politics of adolescent masculinities in school. *British Journal of Sociology of Education, 20(2),* 239–263.

Mattingly, C. (1998). *Well-tempered women: Nineteenth-century temperance rhetoric.* Carbondale, IL: Southern Illinois University Press.

Medea, A., & Thompson, K. (1974). *Against rape: A survival manual for women: How to avoid entrapment and how to cope with rape physically and emotionally.* New York: Farrar, Straus and Giroux.

Myers, D. A. (1995). Eliminating the battering of women by men: Some considerations for behavioral analysis. *Journal of Applied Behavioral Analysis, 28,* 493–507.

Nayak, A., & Kehily, M. (1996). Playing it straight: Masculinities, homophobias and schooling. *Journal of Gender Studies, 5(2),* 211–230.

Paludi, M. A. (Ed.). (1990). *Ivory power: Sexual harassment on campus.* Albany, NY: State University of New York Press.

Pathe, M., & Mullen, P.E. (1997). The impact of stalkers on their victims. *The British Journal of Psychiatry, 170 (January),* 12–17.

Pharr, S. (1988). *Homophobia: A weapon of sexism.* Inverness, CA: Charon Press.

Phoenix, A., Frosh, S., & Pattman, R. (2003). Producing contradictory masculine subject positions: Producing narratives of threat, homophobia and bullying in 11–14 year-old boys. *Journal of Social Issues, 59(1),* 179–195.

Powell, K. (1992). The sexist in me—a man fights his own sexist attitudes. *Essence, Aug. 1992.*

Price, E. L., & Byers, E. S. (1999). Risk factors for boys psychologically abusive behaviors in dating relationships. Paper presented at the 6th International Family Violence Conference. Durham, NH. July.

Rich, F. (1998). What's the point of this story? Sex! So quit pontificating. *International Herald Tribune,* February 5.

Ross, C. A., Farley, M., & Schwartz, H. L. (2003). Dissociation among women in prostitution. In M. Farley (Ed.), *Prostitution, trafficking, and traumatic stress.* Binghamton, NY: Haworth Press.

Russell, D. E. H. (1993-a). *Against pornography: The evidence of harm.* Berkley, CA: Russell Publications.

Russell, D. E. H. (1993-b). *Making violence sexy: Feminist views on pornography.* New York: Teachers College Press.

Sampson, R. (undated). *Acquaintance rape of college students.* Washington, DC: U.S. Department of Justice. Available from www.cops.usdoj.gov.

Sanday, P. R. (1981). *Female power and male dominance: On the origins of sexual inequality.* New York: Press Syndicate.

Schewe, P., & O'Donohue, W. (1996). Rape prevention with high risk males: Short-term outcome of two interventions. *Archives of Sexual Behavior, 25(5),* 455–471.

Sheridan, L., Blaauw, E., & Davies, G. M. (2003). Stalking: Knowns and unknowns. *Trauma, Violence & Abuse: A Review Journal, 4,* 148–162.

Silbert, M. H., & Pines, A. M. (1981). Sexual child abuse as an antecedent to prostitution. *Child abuse and neglect, 5,* 407–411.

Silbert, M. H., & Pines, A. M. (1982). Victimization of street prostitutes. *Victimology, 7,* 122–133.

Silverman, J. G., Raj, A., Mucci, L. A., & Hathaway, J. E. (2001). Dating violence against adolescent girls and associated substance abuse, unhealthy weight control, sexual risk behavior, pregnancy, and suicidality. *Journal of the American Medical Association, 286(5),* 572–579.

Silverman, J. G., & Williamson, G. W. (1997). Social ecology and entitlement in battering by heterosexual males: *Contribution of family and peers. Violence and victims, 12,* 147–164.

Silverstein, L. B. (1996). Fathering is a feminist issue. *Psychology of Women Quarterly, 20,* 3–37.

Tjaden, P., & Thoennes, N. (1998). Stalking in America: Findings from the National Violence Against Women Survey. *Research in Brief.* National Institute of Justice, Centers for Disease and Control Prevention. Available from the Department of Justice, National Institute of Justice–NCJ 169592.

Wantland, R. Coordinator of Sexual Assault Education at the University of Illinois, Champaign-Urbana. Contact him at wantland@ad.uiuc.edu.

Warshaw, R. (1994). *I never called it rape.* New York: HarperCollins Publishing.

Websdale, N. (1998). *Rural woman battering and the justice system.* Thousand Oaks. CA: Sage Publications.

Welsh, S. (2000). The multidimensional nature of sexual harassment: An empirical analysis of women's sexual harassment complaints. *Violence Against Women, 6(2),* 118–141.

West, R. L. (1987). The difference in women's hedonic lives: A phenomenological critique of feminist legal theory. *Wisconsin Women's Law Journal, 81,* 83–85.

West, R. L. (1997). *Caring for justice.* New York: New York University Press.

Whisnant, R. (2003). Confronting pornography: Some conceptual basics. In C. Stark and R. Whisnant, *Not for sale: Feminists resisting prostitution and pornography (pp. 15-27).* Sidney, Australia: Spinifex Press.

Whisnant, R. & Stark, C. (2004). *Not for sale: Feminists resisting prostitution and pornography.* Sidney, Australia: Spinifex Press.

Women's Legal Education and Action Fund. (1992). Factum in *R. v. Butler,* before the Canadian Supreme Court.

Ya Salaam, K. (2001). Women's rights are human rights. In R. Byrd & B. Guy-Sheftall (Eds.), *Traps: African American men on gender and sexuality (*pp. 113-118). Bloomington, IN: Indiana University Press.

Zillman, D., & Bryant, J. (1989). *Pornography: Research advances and policy considerations.* Hillsdale, NJ: Erlbaum Press.

About the Author

Rus Ervin Funk, MSW, is an activist and therapist who is currently Research and Prevention Specialist at the Center for Women and Families (an agency addressing rape/sexual assault, domestic violence, and economic hardship). He is also a professor at the Kent School of Social Work at the University of Louisville, and a professor at the Spalding University School of Social Work (also in Louisville). Since 1983, he has worked with people of all ages who have been victimized as well as with men who batter and adolescents and adults who sexually offend.

Rus is a community organizer who has helped launch numerous men's groups and has worked with several state coalitions and local programs to develop programs to work with men. He is the co-founder of DC Men Against Rape (now Men Can Stop Rape, Inc.), the Baltimore Alliance Against Child Sexual Abuse, the Washington Area Clinic Defense Task Force, the People's Coalition for Justice, and most recently, the Louisville Peace Action Community, M.E.N. (Mobilizing to End violeNce), the Louisville Teen Dating Abuse Task Force, and the listserv Feminists Against Pornography and Prostitution.

Rus has written extensively, including:

- *Willy, Clarence, Mike and Me: A Training for Men.* (1992). One of the first training manuals for men to talk with other men about sexual violence. Self-published.
- *Stopping Rape: A Challenge for Men.* (1993). The first and still the only book by a man for men about stopping rape. New Society Publishers.
- *Leaving no child behind: Baltimore City's response to child sexual victimization.* (1997). Family and Children's Services of Central Maryland.
- Men who are raped: A profeminist perspective. (1997). In *Male on male rape: The hidden toll of stigma and shame.* Insight Books.
- *What to do with men: A manual for rape crisis centers.* (1999). Self-published.
- *A beginning of a beginning: Multicultural competence for sexual assault workers.* (1999). Self-published.

- A coordinated community approach to address and combat teen dating abuse. In A. Grieg (Ed.), *Partners in change: Working with men to end gender-based violence.*(2002). Published by the United Nations, available from www.un-instraw.org.
- Gay male pornography's "actors": When "fantasy" isn't. (Co-written with Christopher Kendall.) In M. Farley (Ed.), *Prostitution, trafficking, and traumatic stress.* (2004). Haworth Press.
- What pornography says about me(n): How I became an anti-pornography activist. In C. Stark and R. Whisnant (Eds.), *Not for sale: Feminists resisting prostitution and pornography.* (2005). Spinifex Press.
- Queer men and sexual assault: What being raped says about being a man. In W. Martino and C. Kendall (Eds.), *Gendered outcasts and sexual outlaws: Sexual oppression and hierarchies in queer men's lives.* (2005). Haworth Press.

Rus currently serves on the boards of directors of the National Center on Domestic and Sexual Violence, and the Indiana Coalition Against Domestic Violence, is on the Coordinating Council for the Fairness Campaign (in Louisville, KY), and chairs the Pornography Task Force for the Jefferson County (KY) Chapter of NOW.

He lives in Louisville, KY with his partner and their cat.

APPENDIX F

About the Indiana Coalition Against Domestic Violence

The mission of the Indiana Coalition Against Domestic Violence, Inc. (ICADV) is to eliminate domestic violence throughout the state of Indiana. A not-for-profit corporation located in Indianapolis, ICADV was incorporated in 1980. We are a coalition comprised of 47 residential and non-residential domestic violence programs and more than 200 members statewide.

Our primary focus is to provide public awareness and education, advocate for systemic and societal change, and influence public policy and the allocation of resources. In addition to promoting statewide comprehensive domestic violence services, ICADV offers technical assistance and training to coalition members, houses an extensive resource library, operates a statewide 24-hour toll-free crisis line, and provides legal assistance to low-income victims of domestic violence. To achieve our mission, ICADV collaborates with numerous state and local agencies, Indiana domestic violence programs, and with other community partners who share our vision.

ICADV has an extensive resource library with over 1,500 books, manuals, videos, and other materials related to domestic violence. These materials are available for loan free of charge. Contact ICADV directly to find out more.

ICADV believes that violence is endemic to our society. We believe patriarchal values and attitudes support and perpetuate violence, and we seek to confront the roots of that violence within ourselves and within larger economic, social, and political systems.

- We believe that no human being deserves to be beaten or violated by another. We believe in the right of all persons to live without fear, oppression, or sexual, emotional, or physical abuse.
- We believe domestic violence is the use of force or threat to achieve and maintain control over others in personal relationships.
- We believe batterers should be held accountable for their actions.

- We believe in inclusiveness and respect for diversity.
- Our goal is to empower individuals to achieve self-determination.
- We are committed to the ideas and practices of a supportive, non-competitive atmosphere in ICADV, which fosters open communication, respect, and cooperation among all members of the coalition.
- We believe the elimination of domestic violence is best achieved by utilizing a multi-faceted approach.
- We believe that while the majority of victims of domestic violence are women and children, everyone is affected by it and the solution involves everyone.

The Indiana Coalition Against Domestic Violence

www.violenceresource.org

(800) 538-3393

Index

C

D

E

F

G

Q

R

S

X–Z